In/Justice

Ethics and Policies, Volume 3

Artur Victoria

Published by Artur Victoria, 2025.

AF722056

While every precaution has been taken in the preparation of this book, the publisher assumes no responsibility for errors or omissions, or for damages resulting from the use of the information contained herein.

IN/JUSTICE

First edition. May 2, 2025.

Copyright © 2025 Artur Victoria.

ISBN: 979-8231650255

Written by Artur Victoria.

To my wife Karen, sons Nicole, José Miguel, Filipe and Alexandre and grand sons Pedro, Filipe, Tomás, Rodrigo e José Maria

Copyright © 2025

All rights reserved. No part of this publication may be reproduced, distributed, or transmitted in any form or by any means, including photocopying, recording, or other electronic or mechanical methods, without the prior written permission of the publisher, except in the case of brief quotations embodied in critical reviews and certain other non-commercial uses permitted by copyright law.

Front cover image by Auhor

Book design by Author

Table of Contents

The Common Good

Notion of the Common Good

Governance and the Rule of Law

Social Justice

Ethical Considerations

Public Goods

Education

Healthcare

Infrastructure

Representation

Social Inclusion

Sustainability

Solidarity

Civic Engagement

The Judiciary

Case Study Bibliography

Preface

By IVES GANDRA DA SILVA MARTINS *

Once again, my dear friend and great humanist, Artur Victoria, has surprised me with a book addressing one of the most important issues in human history and one that continues, despite advances in civilisation, to challenge social coexistence: that of injustice between men.

In the 19th century, Bastiat wrote a short book entitled 'The Law', in which he said that the law should, rather than promoting formal justice, not allow injustice.

In his 'theory of the four causes' (material, formal, efficient and final), Aristotle tried to schematise the types of motives that allow us to better understand anything we want.

In the legal field, my son Ives - a senior minister of the Superior Labour Court in Brazil, of which he was once president - recalls that the material cause would be the Law, the 'suum jus' of each person, the formal cause would be 'tribuere', giving what is rightfully yours, in the Ulpinian definition, with the abstract efficient cause being legislative production, the concrete efficient cause being the judicial decision and the final cause being social peace, as Isaias said (Opus Justitiae Pax).

We, the jusnaturalists, understand that justice begins with respect for legislative production and for those who apply it to the small bundle of natural rights inherent to every human being, which it is not up to the state to produce, but only to respect.

There is therefore no conflict between positive law and natural law, and it is up to the authorities to respect the immensity of the norms produced by the State.

It should be remembered that the Universal Declaration of Human Rights of 10 December 1946 is a charter of Natural Law, whose main author was a Thomist naturalist, René Cassin, also inspired by the lessons and writings of Jacques Maritain.

Master Artur Victoria tackles these issues in his book with insight and depth, in an irreproachable way, from those that occur in social, family and community life, but especially among those in power when they seek to remove their adversaries, punish their enemies and control those they judge, something that occurs not only in dictatorial governments, but also, unfortunately, in democracies.

Artur Victoria analyses this injustice, which thinkers of all ages have tried to condemn and correct, with no success other than to improve legislative production, which is almost never fully respected by those in power. He looks at its various forms of manifestation in the economy, at work, in the family, in access to justice and health and in politics in search of the common good, based on a thought by Saint Joseph Mary Escriva who said: 'Don't you think that equality, as they understand it, is synonymous with injustice?'.

The book, after a long introduction in which he formulates the basis of his reasoning, focuses first on the common good and then tackles injustice in the light of the judicial functions which, strictly speaking, are its greatest efficient ca

Personally, as an originalist when it comes to constitutional interpretation, I have opposed doctrinal currents such as constitutional jurisdiction, consequentialism or neo-consequentialism, which attribute to the Judiciary the competence to adapt the supreme law to current realities according to its personal exegesis, replacing the Derived Constituent Power, which is the Legislative elected by the people. In this vision of adapting the law to its image and likeness, it becomes a permanent source of injustice, as it transfigures itself into a political power, which it is not, ceasing to be, in these matters, the technical power it should be.

This reality of the Federal Supreme Court - without any judgement on the intellectual level and suitability of the Brazilian magistrates appointed by a single man (who is the President of the Republic) - is the drama that is being played out in my country, which according to polling agencies on popular opinion about it, has led to a marked loss of credibility with the population.

Doctrinally, they have incorporated theories from parliamentarian or semi-parliamentarian regimes, where the separation of powers is not as clear-cut as in presidentialism, and have started to pass judgement according to their political preferences and opinions, abandoning the origins of the political system.

With the respect I have always had for all the Justices, in my 90 years and 61 years as a university professor I allow myself to differ, understanding that these doctrinal currents were not those established by the Constituents in the 20 months of debates on the Supreme Law, which I followed, not only being heard in public hearings by the original legislators, and through permanent contact with the Constituent Assembly's rapporteur Bernardo Cabral and the president of the National Constituent Assembly Ulysses Guimarães, which allowed me, together with the late Professor Celso Bastos, to comment on the Brazilian Constitution in 15 volumes and approximately 10,000 pages for Editora Saraiva.

Artur Victoria's book is a splendid contribution to the discussion of the main core of law, which, more than doing justice, is not doing injustice.

Congratulations to my friend and teacher, and I look forward to a brilliant publishing career for his work.

Welcome Artur

* Professor Emeritus of Mackenzie, UNIP, UNIFIEO, UNIFMU Universities, CIEE/O ESTADO DE SÃO PAULO, the Army Command and Staff Schools - ECEME, Superior War College - ESG and the Magistracy of the Federal Regional Court - 1st Region; Honorary Professor at Austral University (Argentina), San Martin de Porres University (Peru) and Vasili Goldis University (Romania); Doctor Honoris Causa of the Universities of Craiova (Romania) and PUCs-Paraná and RS, and Professor at the University of Minho (Portugal); President of the Higher Law Council of FECOMERCIO - SP; former President of the Paulista Academy of Letters-APL and of the São Paulo Lawyers Institute-ASP.

Introduction

Injustice: A word that resonates with a profound sense of wrong, a violation of fairness, a betrayal of fundamental human rights. It is a concept that transcends geographical boundaries, cultural differences, and temporal contexts. This book examines injustice not as a singular event, but as a complex, interwoven web of systemic inequalities, institutional biases, and interpersonal prejudices. We explore the myriad forms that injustice takes, from the overt acts of violence and discrimination to the insidious, subtle ways in which inequality is perpetuated. We examine the mechanics of injustice, dissecting the power dynamics, social structures, and historical legacies that maintain and reinforce unfair systems. We will delve into the experiences of those who have borne the brunt of injustice, offering their voices as powerful testaments to the human cost of oppression. This book is a journey through the landscape of unfairness, from the personal to the global. Our exploration will extend to the legal and political realms, examining wrongful convictions, biased judicial processes, the suppression of human rights, and the desperate need for reform.

The pursuit of justice has been a central preoccupation of humanity throughout history. From the ancient philosophers who grappled with the nature of the good life to modern legal scholars who meticulously analyze the intricacies of legal systems, the question of how to achieve a just society has remained a persistent challenge.

This book delves into the multifaceted nature of this pursuit, exploring the complex interplay between justice, law, and morality. It examines how these seemingly distinct domains intersect and, at times, clash, shaping both individual behavior and the broader structures of our societies. The historical evolution of justice is traced, from its origins in religious and philosophical traditions to the development of modern secular legal systems. The work critically evaluates the limitations of purely formal logic in achieving justice, highlighting the crucial role of moral judgment and the unavoidable subjective elements involved. The tension between the boundless nature of morality and the often-constrained framework of law is a recurring theme, exploring the inherent challenges of unifying these two disparate realms. A central focus is on the tensions between the abstract ideals of social justice and the concrete realities of contemporary political and economic systems.

The pursuit of justice demands a judiciary that is both independent and accountable. This seemingly simple statement encapsulates a complex and enduring tension at the heart of many legal systems globally. Judicial independence, the freedom of judges to make decisions based on law and conscience without fear of political reprisal or undue influence, is a fundamental pillar of a fair and just society. Without it, the rule of law becomes a hollow promise, and individual rights are left vulnerable. However, this independence is not absolute. Judges, like all public officials, are entrusted with significant power, and mechanisms must exist to ensure they exercise that power responsibly and ethically. The need for judicial accountability stems from the inherent risk of abuse, bias, corruption, or simple error. Accountability mechanisms aim to maintain public trust in the judiciary, to deter misconduct, and to provide remedies when wrongdoing occurs. The challenge lies in creating a system of accountability that is effective in addressing misconduct without undermining the very independence that is crucial for a fair and impartial judicial system. This book delves into the complexities of this challenge, examining diverse approaches to judicial accountability across various legal traditions– common law, civil law, and others. We analyze the strengths and weaknesses of different mechanisms, such as appeals, legislative oversight, public scrutiny, internal disciplinary processes, and international standards.

We explore the critical role of due process and fair procedures in ensuring that accountability measures are both effective and just, protecting judges from unfair or politically motivated attacks while ensuring that serious misconduct is addressed appropriately. The analysis presented in this book is designed not just to describe existing systems, but to offer insights into how these systems can be improved, to foster a deeper understanding of the crucial balance between independence and accountability, essential for a just and stable society.

The ultimate aim of this book is not simply to illuminate the dark corners of injustice, but to empower readers to become active agents of change. We hope to equip readers with the knowledge, tools, and inspiration to confront injustice in their own lives and communities, advocating for a world where fairness and equity become the guiding principles of our interactions and institutions. The fight for justice is a continuous process, and this book is but one step in that ongoing journey.

Defining Injustice

A Multifaceted Concept

Defining injustice is a complex undertaking, a task that has preoccupied philosophers, legal scholars, and social activists for centuries. There is no single, universally accepted definition, as the concept itself is deeply intertwined with cultural values, historical context, and individual experiences. What one society deems just, another may perceive as profoundly unjust. This inherent subjectivity doesn't diminish the importance of grappling with the concept; rather, it underscores the need for a nuanced and multifaceted understanding.

One approach to defining injustice involves examining its objective and subjective elements. Objectively, injustice can be understood as a violation of established laws, norms, or principles of fairness. This might involve acts of discrimination, denial of rights, or unequal distribution of resources that can be measured and documented.

However, injustice is not solely confined to measurable disparities. Subjectively, it encompasses the feelings of unfairness, oppression, and violation of dignity experienced by individuals and groups. These subjective experiences, while harder to quantify, are equally crucial in understanding the full impact of injustice. The emotional toll of systemic racism, for instance, cannot be fully captured by statistics alone. It encompasses the everyday micro aggressions, the constant awareness of prejudice, and the pervasive feeling of being marginalized, all of which contribute to a lived experience of injustice. Similarly, the subjective experience of gender inequality extends far beyond the pay gap to include societal expectations, limitations on opportunities, and the constant pressure to conform to gender stereotypes, all creating a pervasive sense of injustice.

Different philosophical perspectives offer varying frameworks for understanding injustice. Utilitarianism, for example, focuses on maximizing overall well-being, suggesting that an action is unjust if it results in a net decrease in happiness or well-being for the majority. This approach emphasizes the consequences of actions, prioritizing outcomes over intentions. However, critics argue that a purely utilitarian approach can justify injustices against minorities if it benefits the majority.

Deontology, in contrast, emphasizes moral duties and principles, arguing that certain actions are inherently right or wrong, regardless of their consequences. A deontological perspective on injustice might focus on the violation of fundamental human rights, such as the right to life, liberty, and equality, regardless of whether such violations maximize overall well-being.

Virtue ethics, another prominent philosophical approach, centers on the moral character of the agent. It suggests that an act is unjust if it stems from a lack of virtuous character traits, such as fairness, compassion, and integrity. From this perspective, injustice is not just about the act itself but also about the moral failings of those who perpetuate it. This framework highlights the importance of cultivating virtuous character traits in individuals and within institutions to prevent the occurrence of injustice.

These philosophical frameworks are not mutually exclusive, and their application often overlaps in real-world scenarios. The gender pay gap, for example, can be analyzed through all three lenses: utilitarian's might argue it reduces overall societal well-being due to lost economic productivity and social unrest, deontologists might highlight the violation of the principle of equal pay for equal work, and virtue ethicists might point to the lack of fairness and integrity in those perpetuating the disparity.

The understanding of injustice is further shaped by cultural contexts. What constitutes fairness and equity varies significantly across different societies. Certain practices may be considered acceptable in one culture but unjust in another. Understanding these cultural nuances is vital for developing effective strategies to combat injustice in a globalized world.

Historical context is also vital in understanding injustice. Past events and systems of oppression often leave a lasting legacy of inequality that continues to manifest in contemporary society. The transatlantic slave trade, for example, had a profound and enduring impact on racial inequalities in many parts of the world, shaping social, economic, and political structures that continue to disadvantage marginalized communities. Similarly, the historical oppression of women and the legacy of patriarchal structures profoundly shape the understanding of gender inequality.

The concept of injustice encompasses a broad spectrum of experiences and actions. It extends beyond isolated acts of cruelty or discrimination to include systemic, institutional, and interpersonal levels of oppression. Systemic injustice refers to the ways in which social structures, policies, and institutions create and perpetuate inequalities, often unintentionally. Institutional injustice involves the biased or discriminatory actions of specific institutions, such as the police, courts, or schools. Interpersonal injustice occurs in relationships between individuals, such as acts of bullying, harassment, or domestic abuse. These levels are deeply interconnected, with individual acts often reflecting broader systemic and institutional patterns of oppression.

The mechanisms that perpetuate injustice are often multifaceted and interconnected. Bias, both conscious and unconscious, plays a significant role. Implicit biases, for example, can lead to discriminatory decisions even when individuals consciously believe themselves to be unbiased. Power imbalances also contribute to injustice, as those with more power are often able to exploit and marginalize those with less. Systemic inequalities built into laws, policies, or social norms further entrench injustice across generations. Redlining in housing, for instance, created a legacy of segregation that persists to this day. Similarly, discriminatory lending practices have disproportionately impacted minority communities, perpetuating cycles of poverty and inequality. Media representations play a significant role as well; stereotypical portrayals of marginalized groups in media can reinforce harmful prejudices and stereotypes.

To understand injustice fully requires examining not just its contemporary manifestations but also its historical roots. Injustice is not a sudden phenomenon but a product of historical processes, deeply embedded in the fabric of societies across the globe. Slavery and colonialism, for example, left behind systems of oppression that continue to impact present-day inequalities. The legacy of these historical injustices can be seen in ongoing economic disparities, political marginalization, and enduring social stigma.

Measuring injustice is a significant challenge, requiring both quantitative and qualitative approaches. Quantitative data, such as income inequality statistics, incarceration rates, and health disparities, can provide valuable insights into the scale and scope of injustice. However, such data alone often fail to capture the nuances and complexities of lived experience. Qualitative methods, such as interviews, focus groups, and ethnographic studies, are needed to complement quantitative data, providing deeper insights into the subjective experiences and perspectives of those impacted by injustice. This combination of approaches, focusing on both the measurable and the subjective realities of injustice, can create a more comprehensive picture of its multifaceted nature.

Furthermore, developing methods to measure intersectional injustice, where different forms of discrimination overlap, is crucial for understanding the cumulative impacts of various forms of oppression experienced by many individuals. The challenges lie in developing robust methodologies capable of capturing the intricate interplay of various social factors contributing to injustice.

Developing standardized metrics for measuring injustice across different contexts and communities remains an ongoing endeavor, requiring rigorous research and interdisciplinary collaboration

Forms of Injustice - A Typology

Understanding the multifaceted nature of injustice requires a typology that moves beyond simple categorization. While all forms of injustice stem from a fundamental unfairness, they manifest differently depending on their scale and the mechanisms through which they operate. A useful framework for analyzing injustice recognizes three interconnected levels: systemic, institutional, and interpersonal. These levels are not mutually exclusive; they often reinforce and exacerbate one another, creating a complex web of oppression.

Systemic injustice refers to the ways in which societal structures, policies, and norms create and perpetuate inequalities. These aren't necessarily the result of deliberate malice; rather, they are often embedded within the very fabric of society, operating through seemingly neutral processes that nonetheless disproportionately impact marginalized groups. Consider the insidious effects of redlining, a historical practice in which banks and insurance companies systematically denied services to residents of certain neighbourhoods, predominantly those with large minority populations. This practice, while ostensibly about risk assessment, effectively created and maintained racially segregated housing patterns, leading to profound and lasting economic disparities. Generations later, the legacy of redlining continues to manifest in stark differences in wealth, homeownership rates, and access to quality education and resources between predominantly white and predominantly minority communities. This isn't simply a matter of individual prejudice; it's a systemic issue deeply rooted in historical policies and practices that continue to shape present-day inequalities.

Further illustrating systemic injustice is the persistent gender pay gap. While laws in many countries mandate equal pay for equal work, a significant gap remains, reflecting a complex interplay of factors including occupational segregation, implicit bias in hiring and promotion processes, and societal expectations surrounding gender roles. Women are often concentrated in lower-paying sectors, facing a "motherhood penalty" that disadvantages them in career progression. This isn't merely a series of isolated incidents of unfair compensation; it's a systemic problem deeply entrenched in workplace norms, societal expectations, and broader economic structures. The persistence of this gap, despite legal protections, highlights the enduring power of systemic biases that operate beyond individual actions.

The Impact of Systemic Injustice Extends Beyond the Economy

Environmental racism, a particularly stark example, demonstrates how systemic factors contribute to disproportionate environmental burdens for marginalized communities. The placement of polluting industries, toxic waste dumps, and other environmentally hazardous facilities in low-income, predominantly minority neighbourhoods is not accidental. These decisions often reflect a pattern of systemic disregard for the well-being of these communities, perpetuating cycles of environmental injustice and health disparities. The long-term consequences of this environmental racism, including higher rates of respiratory illness, cancer, and other health problems, highlight the devastating impact of systemic inequalities on the lives of vulnerable populations. This exemplifies how systemic injustice is not merely about unfair distribution of resources; it fundamentally shapes access to basic necessities like clean air and water.

Institutional injustice operates at the level of specific institutions—government agencies, corporations, educational systems, and other organizations. This form of injustice involves biased or discriminatory practices embedded within the structure and operations of these institutions. The criminal justice system provides a glaring example. Studies consistently reveal racial disparities in arrest rates, sentencing, and incarceration, indicating systemic bias within law enforcement, prosecution, and judicial processes. The disproportionate incarceration of indigenous individuals compared to Caucasian individuals for similar offenses is not a random occurrence; it reflects a pattern of racial profiling, implicit bias in policing and sentencing, and systemic inequalities that lead to unequal treatment under the law. These disparities are not merely the result of individual officers or judges acting with prejudice; they are rooted in institutional practices and policies that perpetuate racial inequalities.

Another compelling example lies within the healthcare system. Disparities in access to quality healthcare, based on race, ethnicity, socioeconomic status, and geographic location, reveal deep-seated institutional failings. Minority communities often face significant barriers to accessing healthcare services, including limited availability of providers, lack of insurance coverage, and implicit bias among healthcare professionals. This translates to poorer health outcomes, higher rates of chronic diseases, and lower life expectancy for marginalized groups. These institutional failures don't stem from an absence of individual acts of care, but rather from systemic flaws in the structure and provision of healthcare services that perpetuate health inequalities.

Interpersonal injustice manifests in relationships between individuals. This encompasses a wide range of acts, from bullying and harassment to domestic violence and hate crimes. While seemingly distinct from systemic and institutional injustice, interpersonal forms are often interconnected with and reflective of larger societal patterns of oppression. Gender-based violence, for example, is rooted in deep-seated patriarchal norms that normalize and perpetuate violence against women. These acts of violence are not isolated events but are symptomatic of a broader cultural climate that tolerates or even condones such behaviour. Similarly, hate crimes, driven by prejudice and discrimination against individuals based on their race, religion, sexual orientation, or other characteristics, reflect and reinforce systemic and institutional biases that create hostile environments.

Even within family structures, interpersonal injustice can manifest in many insidious forms. Economic inequality within a family, where one member bears a disproportionate burden of financial responsibility, often reveals power imbalances that undermine fairness and equality. For instance, in many cultures, women bear the primary responsibility for unpaid household labor and childcare, diminishing their economic opportunities and perpetuating economic dependence. The lack of equal distribution of resources and responsibilities in the household constitutes a form of interpersonal injustice which, over time, can have profound and enduring effects on the individuals involved.

The historical roots of injustice are critical to understanding its contemporary manifestations. The legacy of colonialism, slavery, and other forms of oppression continues to shape social, economic, and political structures, perpetuating inequalities across generations. Understanding these historical legacies is essential for developing effective strategies to address present-day injustices.

Addressing these multifaceted forms of injustice requires a multi-pronged approach that tackles systemic structures, institutional practices, and interpersonal behaviours. It necessitates challenging deeply ingrained biases, promoting equitable policies, and fostering inclusive social norms. Only through a combination of structural reforms, institutional accountability, and individual responsibility can we begin to create a fairer and more just world. The task is complex and necessitates sustained commitment, but the imperative for change is undeniable.

The insidious nature of injustice lies not just in its overt manifestations, but in the intricate mechanisms that subtly yet powerfully perpetuate it across generations. Understanding these mechanisms is vital to dismantling the systems that uphold inequality. Bias, in its various forms, serves as a cornerstone of injustice. Implicit bias, the unconscious attribution of stereotypes and prejudices, pervades decision-making processes across numerous sectors, from hiring practices to judicial sentencing. Studies consistently demonstrate that individuals, even those who consciously reject prejudice, can harbour unconscious biases that influence their actions. This can lead to seemingly neutral decisions having disparate impacts on marginalized groups..

Beyond implicit bias, explicit bias—the conscious and intentional discrimination against particular groups—remains a disturbing reality. While overt expressions of racism, sexism, homophobia, and other forms of prejudice are often condemned, they continue to manifest in various forms. The rise of hate speech online and offline demonstrates the persistence of explicit biases, fostering hostile environments and inciting acts of violence against marginalized communities. Combating these explicit biases requires not just legal mechanisms but also sustained efforts to challenge discriminatory attitudes and behaviours through education and social movements.

Power imbalances are deeply intertwined with the perpetuation of injustice. These imbalances aren't solely about formal authority; they encompass a range of factors, including economic disparities, social status, and access to resources. Economic inequality, a pervasive feature of many societies, creates a structural foundation for injustice. Those with greater economic resources tend to hold greater influence in shaping policies, accessing opportunities, and navigating social systems. This translates into a disproportionate concentration of power in the hands of the wealthy, leaving vulnerable populations with less influence and limited recourse against systemic inequalities. Consider the impact of predatory lending practices, targeting low-income communities with high-interest loans, effectively trapping them in a cycle of debt. This is not a matter of individual financial mismanagement but rather a systemic exploitation that perpetuates economic dependence and reinforces social stratification.

The influence of power dynamics extends beyond the economic realm. In many societies, historical power structures continue to shape contemporary inequalities. The enduring legacies of colonialism, apartheid, and other forms of oppression have left deep imprints on social structures, resource allocation, and political representation. Understanding the historical roots of power imbalances is central to addressing contemporary inequalities and ensuring equitable distribution of power and resources.

Systemic inequalities are the insidious mechanisms through which biases and power imbalances translate into widespread injustices. These inequalities are embedded within social institutions and societal structures, operating through seemingly neutral processes that nonetheless disproportionate impact marginalized groups.

Redlining, a discriminatory practice in the housing market that denied services to particular neighbourhoods based on race and ethnicity, had lasting repercussions on generational wealth and opportunity. The consequences continue to resonate today, manifesting in substantial differences in homeownership rates, access to quality education, and overall economic well-being between communities. These differences are not merely the result of individual choices; they are the product of systemic inequalities built over decades and perpetuated through complex interactions of policies, institutions, and social norms.

Discriminatory lending practices further demonstrate how systemic inequalities operate. Financial institutions have historically engaged in discriminatory lending practices, disproportionately denying loans to individuals from marginalized communities. This has resulted in restricted access to homeownership, business development, and other crucial economic opportunities. The cumulative impact of these discriminatory practices has significantly contributed to the wealth gap between different racial and ethnic groups. Moreover, these practices are not confined to historical contexts; contemporary evidence shows that subtle forms of discrimination remain embedded in lending algorithms and decision-making processes. The challenge of dismantling systemic inequalities requires addressing these embedded biases and challenging the structural forces that perpetuate them.

The role of media representation in perpetuating injustice cannot be overlooked. Media narratives, whether consciously or unconsciously, can reinforce harmful stereotypes and prejudices. The overrepresentation of particular groups in negative or criminalized contexts can contribute to the perpetuation of societal biases and discrimination. Conversely, underrepresentation or stereotypical portrayal of marginalized groups can limit positive representation and restrict opportunities for social mobility and empowerment. Therefore, analyzing the way media portrays diverse groups, challenging harmful stereotypes, and promoting inclusive representation is essential to promoting social justice.

Social Institutions Play an Important Role in Strengthening Inequalities

Educational institutions, for example, can perpetuate inequalities through tracking systems, biased disciplinary practices, and unequal access to resources. The criminal justice system, too, has been implicated in perpetuating systemic biases, with disparities in arrest rates, sentencing, and incarceration rates highlighting the ingrained inequalities within the system. Healthcare systems can also contribute to injustice through unequal access to quality care based on socioeconomic status, race, and ethnicity, leading to significant health disparities. Reform of these institutions is essential to dismantling the systems that contribute to injustice. This requires not only policy changes but also addressing the underlying biases and power imbalances that shape their operations. It necessitates fostering diverse leadership, implementing mechanisms for accountability and transparency, and challenging institutional norms that perpetuate inequalities.

Addressing the mechanisms of injustice requires a multi-pronged approach. It necessitates challenging deeply ingrained biases at both the individual and institutional levels, creating systems that ensure equitable distribution of power and resources, and enacting policies and practices that promote social justice. This involves reforming discriminatory practices, dismantling systemic inequalities, and promoting institutional accountability. Ultimately, creating a fairer and more equitable society demands a collective effort, combining the commitment of individuals, institutions, and policymakers. The journey toward justice is a long and complex one, but understanding the mechanisms of injustice is the essential first step in forging a path toward a more just and equitable world.

The fight for justice is not merely about achieving individual victories; it is about creating a society where the fundamental principles of fairness and equality are not just ideals, but lived realities for everyone. This requires a sustained commitment, a continuous striving for improved understanding, and a dedication to challenging existing power structures and dismantling the systems that perpetuate inequality. Only through sustained effort and collective action can we hope to build a world free from injustice.

Historical Roots of Injustice - A Legacy of Inequality

The legacy of injustice stretches far beyond contemporary events; it's deeply woven into the fabric of history, its threads extending through centuries of oppression and inequality. Understanding the historical roots of injustice is vital to dismantling its contemporary manifestations. The transatlantic slave trade, a horrific chapter in human history, serves as a stark example. For centuries, millions of Africans were forcibly removed from their homes, subjected to brutal conditions during the Middle Passage, and enslaved in the Americas. This systematic dehumanization and exploitation left an indelible scar on global society, creating lasting disparities in wealth, power, and opportunity that continue to reverberate today. The economic prosperity of many nations was built on the backs of enslaved people, a foundation of unimaginable cruelty that continues to impact social and economic structures.

The lingering effects of slavery are not merely symbolic; they manifest in systemic inequalities in education, healthcare, housing, and the justice system. The wealth accumulated through slavery fuelled the growth of many Western economies, creating a stark imbalance that persists to this day. Generations of descendants of enslaved people have faced significant barriers to accumulating wealth and upward mobility, often facing discriminatory practices that limited their access to education, land ownership, and fair employment opportunities. The historical legacy of slavery manifests in the persistent racial wealth gap, demonstrating the ongoing consequences of this profound historical injustice. This gap is not simply a matter of individual choices but a product of systemic disadvantages passed down through generations, highlighting the enduring impact of historical oppression.

Furthermore, the economic and social disparities resulting from slavery continue to fuel racial tensions and social unrest. The legacy of systemic racism deeply impacts communities, shaping the lived experiences of individuals and perpetuating cycles of poverty and marginalization. Addressing the ongoing impact of slavery requires confronting not just the historical atrocities but also the present-day manifestations of systemic racism. This necessitates both restorative justice initiatives to address the lasting harms of slavery and systemic changes to dismantle the structures that perpetuate racial inequality.

Colonialism, another potent force in shaping global injustices, left a similarly devastating legacy. Across continents, indigenous populations were subjugated, their lands seized, their cultures suppressed, and their resources exploited for the benefit of colonial powers. The devastating consequences of colonialism are evident in many post-colonial nations, where persistent poverty, political instability, and social unrest are often direct results of colonial policies and practices. The arbitrary borders drawn by colonial powers often ignored existing ethnic and cultural divisions, creating internal conflicts and hindering national unity. The extraction of resources by colonial powers without adequate compensation or investment in local infrastructure left many former colonies with depleted resources and underdeveloped economies.

The legacy of colonialism also manifests in the enduring power imbalances between former colonial powers and their former colonies. These imbalances continue to influence international relations, trade, and development assistance, often perpetuating dependence and reinforcing neo-colonial structures. Many former colonies continue to struggle with issues of political corruption, weak governance, and lack of access to basic services, direct consequences of the systemic exploitation that characterized colonial rule. The lasting psychological and cultural trauma inflicted by colonialism also has a significant impact, hindering social progress and hindering the development of resilient and self-reliant societies. Addressing the legacy of colonialism requires not only economic reparations but also cultural restoration and initiatives that empower communities to reclaim their heritage and build their own future free from the constraints of colonial legacies.

Beyond slavery and colonialism, other historical events have contributed significantly to the perpetuation of injustice. The apartheid regime in South Africa, for instance, imposed a system of racial segregation and oppression that had devastating social and economic consequences. The institutionalized discrimination against the Black African majority denied them access to basic rights, opportunities, and resources. The dismantling of apartheid, while a significant step towards justice, did not erase its legacy. The lingering effects of apartheid are evident in the ongoing inequalities in wealth, education, housing, and healthcare that continue to affect Black South Africans. Addressing these deep-seated inequalities requires sustained efforts to dismantle systemic biases, promote social inclusion, and invest in initiatives that promote economic empowerment and social justice.

The Holocaust, a state-sponsored genocide that systematically exterminated six million Jews, stands as a chilling example of the extreme consequences of hate and prejudice. The Holocaust not only resulted in unimaginable suffering and loss of life but also demonstrated the dangers of unchecked prejudice and the devastating consequences of dehumanization. Understanding the historical context of the Holocaust, including the role of propaganda, anti-Semitism, and political opportunism, is fundamental to preventing future atrocities. The lessons learned from the Holocaust must serve as a constant reminder of the importance of combating hate speech, fostering tolerance, and upholding human rights. Commemorating the victims of the

Holocaust and educating future generations about this horrific event are essential to ensuring that such atrocities are never repeated.

The Armenian Genocide, a systematic campaign to exterminate the Armenian population within the Ottoman Empire, stands as another brutal example of state-sponsored violence and oppression. The systematic massacres, deportations, and forced conversions resulted in the loss of hundreds of thousands of lives and the destruction of Armenian cultural heritage. The Armenian Genocide stands as a chilling reminder of the consequences of unchecked nationalistic fervor and ethnic hatred. The acknowledgment of the Armenian Genocide and the pursuit of justice for the victims are essential to ensuring that such atrocities are never repeated.

These historical examples underscore the enduring impact of past injustices on contemporary societies. The seemingly insurmountable challenges of tackling present-day inequality require a comprehensive understanding of the complex and interwoven historical factors that have shaped current realities. Ignoring or minimizing these historical contexts prevents a full grasp of the pervasive nature of injustice and undermines effective strategies for change. Addressing injustice demands acknowledging and confronting the historical roots of inequality, understanding how past oppression continues to shape the present, and working toward systemic change that creates a fairer and more equitable world for all. The pursuit of justice is not merely about addressing present-day wrongs; it is about healing the wounds of the past and creating a future free from the burden of historical injustice. This requires a collective commitment to truth, reconciliation, and lasting change, acknowledging the lasting impact of historical events and creating lasting solutions for future generations.

Inequalities

Measuring injustice requires moving beyond anecdotal evidence and subjective perceptions to employ rigorous methodologies capable of quantifying and analyzing the extent and impact of unfairness. This necessitates a multifaceted approach, combining quantitative and qualitative data collection techniques to paint a comprehensive picture of injustice's diverse manifestations. While no single metric can fully capture the complexities of injustice, a strategic combination of indicators can provide valuable insights into its pervasiveness and consequences.

One decisive area for measurement is economic inequality, a cornerstone of societal injustice. Income disparity, measured through the Gini coefficient, provides a quantifiable assessment of wealth distribution within a population. A high Gini coefficient indicates a large gap between the rich and the poor, highlighting significant inequality. However, the Gini coefficient alone is insufficient; it doesn't reveal the underlying mechanisms driving inequality, such as discriminatory employment practices, unequal access to education and healthcare, or historical injustices like slavery and colonialism. Therefore, supplementing the Gini coefficient with data on wealth distribution, access to resources, and intergenerational mobility provides a more nuanced understanding of economic injustice. Analyzing data disaggregated by race, ethnicity, gender, and geographic location further illuminates how economic disparities disproportionately affect marginalized communities.

The criminal justice system often serves as a potent instrument of injustice. High incarceration rates, especially when disproportionately affecting certain racial or ethnic groups, signify systemic bias and inequity. Examining incarceration rates alone, however, is insufficient. A thorough analysis requires investigating arrest rates, conviction rates, sentencing disparities, and access to legal representation. Healthcare disparities represent another critical area of focus.

Access to quality healthcare varies significantly across socioeconomic groups and racial and ethnic lines, exposing deep inequalities within the healthcare system. Quantitative indicators, such as life expectancy, infant mortality rates, and rates of chronic diseases, reveal health disparities between different communities.

Environmental injustice manifests itself in the disproportionate exposure of marginalized communities to environmental hazards.

Quantitative data on air and water pollution levels, proximity to hazardous waste sites, and exposure to toxins reveals the unequal distribution of environmental risks. For instance, comparing pollution levels in predominantly minority neighbourhoods to those in predominantly white neighbourhoods within the same metropolitan area highlights environmental racism. Similarly, analyzing the frequency and intensity of environmental disasters and their impact on vulnerable populations reveals how these communities disproportionately bear the burden of ecological degradation.

Qualitative data, including community surveys, focus groups, and interviews with residents, provide valuable insights into the lived experiences of those affected by environmental injustice, highlighting the social, economic, and health consequences of environmental hazards. Furthermore, studying the implementation of environmental regulations and the enforcement of environmental laws can help pinpoint systemic failures that perpetuate environmental inequality. Analyzing government data regarding permit approvals for polluting industries and the location of these industries in relation to marginalized communities reveals a pattern of environmental racism and exposes the inequalities in environmental protection.

Beyond these specific areas, other quantitative and qualitative indicators can shed light on various aspects of injustice. Data on gender inequality, including the gender pay gap, representation in leadership positions, and rates of gender-based violence, offer valuable insights into systemic sexism. Similarly, data on educational disparities, such as standardized test scores, graduation rates, and access to quality education, reveal inequalities in educational opportunities. Analyzing data on housing discrimination and segregation demonstrates the impact of biased practices on access to safe and affordable housing. The suppression of human rights can be measured through various indicators, including the number of political prisoners, reports of torture, and freedom of speech violations. Each of these areas demands careful quantitative and qualitative analysis to reveal the subtle and overt ways in which injustice operates.

The collection and analysis of this multifaceted data must adhere to rigorous methodological standards to ensure accuracy, validity, and reliability. Data must be collected using consistent methodologies, and careful consideration must be given to sampling techniques to ensure representativeness. Bias in data collection and analysis must be actively addressed to avoid perpetuating the very inequalities being studied. Transparency in data collection, analysis, and reporting is crucial to maintain public trust and accountability. The interpretation of data must account for contextual factors and avoid oversimplification, recognizing the complexities of injustice and its multiple intersections. Critically, data should be used not merely to document injustice but to inform policy recommendations and advocate for meaningful change. The ultimate goal is not only to measure injustice but to leverage this understanding to dismantle its systemic roots and build a more just and equitable society.

Family Dynamics and Injustice

The seemingly private sphere of the family often becomes a breeding ground for injustice, mirroring and sometimes exacerbating the larger societal inequalities we've already examined. While the family is ideally a haven of support and love, it can also be a site of profound power imbalances, where resources, labour, and decision-making power are unevenly distributed, leading to lasting emotional and material harm. This injustice manifests in diverse ways, shaped by cultural norms, socioeconomic circumstances, and individual dynamics.

One prevalent form of family injustice is the unequal division of labour. In many families, regardless of socioeconomic status, women disproportionately bear the burden of household chores, childcare, and eldercare, even when they also hold full-time jobs outside the home. This "second shift," as Arlie Hochschild famously termed it, results in significant time constraints, increased stress, and reduced opportunities for personal and professional development for women. The consequences extend beyond individual well-being, contributing to the gender pay gap and limiting women's advancement in the workplace. The normalization of this unequal division of labour often masks its inherent injustice, perpetuated by societal expectations and ingrained gender roles. Even in families where both partners work equally outside the home, the expectation that women will still shoulder the majority of the domestic responsibilities remains a significant source of tension and inequality. This unequal burden not only impacts women's well-being but also contributes to relationship strain and can ultimately affect family stability.

Another important aspect of family injustice is the unequal distribution of resources. This can range from financial resources to educational opportunities and healthcare access. In many families, particularly those facing financial hardship, the allocation of resources often prioritizes the needs of certain family members over others.

Children, especially girls in some cultures, may be denied educational opportunities, while older family members might face neglect or financial exploitation. This unequal access to essential resources can have devastating long-term consequences, perpetuating cycles of poverty and disadvantage across generations. Children denied educational opportunities are less likely to secure well-paying jobs, leading to decreased economic mobility and increased reliance on social welfare programs. Similarly, the lack of access to adequate healthcare can lead to preventable illnesses and premature death. Such disparities within families expose the deep-seated inequalities that exist within the broader societal structures.

The dynamics of power within families are also a significant factor in determining who experiences injustice. In patriarchal families, men often hold the dominant position, controlling financial resources, making major decisions, and dictating family rules.

Women and children may be subjected to verbal, emotional, or physical abuse, with limited recourse for protection or redress. This power imbalance is further exacerbated by cultural norms and societal structures that reinforce male dominance and subordinate women and children. Even in families that outwardly appear egalitarian, subtle forms of power dynamics can still lead to injustice. Family injustice often intersects with other forms of societal inequality. Racial and ethnic minorities frequently experience greater challenges within their families, facing systemic disadvantages that translate into unequal access to resources and opportunities. For example, families from marginalized communities may face discriminatory practices in housing, education, and employment, limiting their ability to achieve economic stability and provide for their children's needs. Similarly, families headed by single mothers often face greater financial burdens and societal stigmatization, leading to increased vulnerability to poverty and inequality. These challenges highlight the complex interplay of family dynamics and broader societal forces that contribute to injustice.

The consequences of family injustice are far-reaching and profound. Children who grow up in families characterized by unequal treatment, abuse, or neglect are at a higher risk of developing emotional and behavioural problems, struggling in school, and experiencing difficulties in their adult relationships. The effects of family injustice are often intergenerational, perpetuating cycles of poverty, violence, and disadvantage across generations. Adult survivors of family injustice may experience mental health challenges, strained relationships, and difficulties in forming healthy attachments. The emotional scars of injustice within the family can last a lifetime, influencing self-esteem, sense of self-worth, and capacity for healthy relationships.

Addressing family injustice requires a multifaceted approach, combining individual interventions, systemic reforms, and societal shifts in attitudes. Individual interventions such as therapy and counselling can help individuals and families address the root causes of inequality and violence within the family unit. Systemic reforms, such as stronger laws protecting vulnerable family members, increased funding for social services, and improved access to legal aid, are crucial in tackling the structural inequalities that perpetuate injustice. Moreover, societal changes in attitudes towards gender roles, family structures, and the distribution of labour are necessary to create a more equitable and just society. Educating the public about the harmful effects of family injustice, promoting healthy family dynamics, and fostering empathy and understanding are essential steps toward creating a world where all family members are treated with dignity, respect, and equality.

Furthermore, legal frameworks play a crucial role in mitigating family injustice. While legal systems vary significantly across countries, laws regarding domestic violence, child abuse, and elder abuse represent important tools for protecting vulnerable family members. However, the effectiveness of these laws depends on their enforcement and accessibility. Access to legal representation, particularly for those from low-income backgrounds, is vital to ensure that victims of family injustice can obtain legal redress and protection. In addition, legal reforms that address issues such as unequal division of assets in divorce proceedings and discriminatory inheritance laws can help to create a more equitable distribution of resources within families. Judicial systems need to be sensitive to the nuances of family dynamics and ensure fair and impartial outcomes for all parties involved in family disputes.

Beyond the legal framework, addressing family injustice also requires a deeper understanding of cultural and societal norms that perpetuate inequality. In many cultures, traditional gender roles and expectations continue to contribute to the unequal distribution of labour and resources within families. Challenging these norms and promoting gender equality are crucial steps in creating a more just society. Education and awareness campaigns can play a significant role in shifting societal attitudes and promoting healthier family dynamics. By fostering open conversations about family injustice, challenging harmful stereotypes, and promoting respect for diversity, we can contribute to creating a more equitable and inclusive society where all family members can thrive. This multifaceted approach, encompassing individual, systemic, and societal changes, is essential to effectively combat family injustice and build a more just and compassionate world. This requires a continuous effort to understand the complex web of societal and personal factors contributing to the problem and to develop comprehensive, sustained, and equitable solutions.

Workplace Discrimination and Harassment

The insidious tendrils of injustice extend far beyond the confines of the home, reaching into the very fabric of our professional lives.

The workplace, ideally a space of collaboration and productivity, can become a battleground of inequality, where subtle biases and overt discrimination erode the dignity and opportunities of countless individuals. This injustice manifests in myriad forms, from the pervasive gender pay gap to the chilling effects of workplace harassment, all fuelled by systemic prejudices and a lack of accountability.

Workplace discrimination is often insidious and difficult to prove, manifests in numerous ways. Racial discrimination, a persistent scourge in many workplaces, can take the form of overt exclusion from opportunities, subtle micro aggressions, or the creation of a hostile work environment. For instance, individuals from minority racial groups may find their qualifications overlooked in favour of less-qualified colleagues, be subjected to offensive jokes or stereotypes, or be systematically excluded from informal networks that are crucial for career advancement. Such experiences not only inflict emotional harm but also systematically disadvantage individuals, limiting their career prospects and perpetuating economic inequality. The impact extends beyond the individual, undermining workplace productivity and fostering a climate of distrust and resentment.

Gender discrimination remains a deeply entrenched problem, despite significant strides in gender equality. The persistent gender pay gap, where women earn significantly less than men for comparable work, is a stark indicator of this inequality. This disparity is rarely a result of individual merit; rather, it is often rooted in deeply ingrained societal biases that undervalue women's work and contributions. Moreover, women frequently face barriers to promotion and leadership positions, often encountering a "glass ceiling" that prevents their advancement regardless of their qualifications and performance. The underrepresentation of women in senior management roles is a clear demonstration of this systematic bias, hindering not only individual career progression but also limiting diverse perspectives and potentially harming organizational effectiveness.

Religious discrimination, often overlooked, can profoundly affect individuals' workplace experiences. Employees may face prejudice based on their faith, be subjected to discriminatory practices in hiring, promotion, or assignment of tasks, or be excluded from religious observances or accommodations. For example, individuals who wear religious garments might face criticism or pressure to conform to workplace norms that disregard their religious practices.

Similarly, employees who request time off for religious holidays may experience resistance or disapproval, hindering their ability to practice their faith. Such actions can create a hostile work environment, damaging morale and negatively impacting the well-being of affected employees.

Discrimination based on sexual orientation and gender identity is another deeply troubling aspect of workplace injustice. LGBTQ+ individuals frequently encounter hostility, prejudice, and exclusion in the workplace, ranging from subtle micro aggressions to outright harassment and discrimination. They may be denied opportunities, subjected to derogatory remarks, or face pressure to conceal their identities to avoid discrimination. This can result in a climate of fear and isolation, impacting their job satisfaction, mental health, and overall well-being. Furthermore, the lack of legal protections and societal acceptance often leaves LGBTQ+ individuals vulnerable to discriminatory practices with little recourse for redress.

Beyond discrimination, workplace harassment is a severe form of injustice, creating a hostile and intimidating environment that undermines the dignity and safety of employees. Sexual harassment, encompassing unwanted sexual advances, requests for sexual favours, and other verbal or physical conduct of a sexual nature, is particularly pernicious. It can significantly impact victims' mental health, causing anxiety, depression, and post-traumatic stress disorder. Moreover, victims may experience difficulty concentrating on their work, reduced productivity, and even forced resignation.

The prevalence of sexual harassment underscores the systemic failure to effectively address this grave issue. Beyond sexual harassment, other forms of harassment, including bullying, intimidation, and verbal abuse, can create toxic workplaces. Such harassment can stem from various sources, including supervisors, co-workers, or even clients. The persistent targeting of an employee, through verbal abuse, public humiliation, or exclusion, can inflict significant emotional distress, leading to decreased morale, lost productivity, and even physical health problems. Often, victims are reluctant to report such harassment due to fear of retaliation or a lack of confidence in their employer's ability or willingness to take appropriate action. The lack of effective reporting mechanisms and a culture of silence contribute to the perpetuation of this pervasive form of workplace injustice.

Addressing workplace discrimination and harassment requires a multifaceted approach. Strong legal frameworks are central, providing clear definitions of discrimination and harassment, establishing robust reporting mechanisms, and ensuring effective enforcement and remedies for victims. Anti-discrimination laws should cover a wide range of protected characteristics, including race, gender, religion, sexual orientation, and disability, and should be enforced rigorously. Legislation should provide for both punitive measures against perpetrators and compensation for victims.

However, legal frameworks alone are insufficient; a proactive and inclusive organizational culture is equally vital. Employers have a responsibility to create a workplace where all employees feel safe, respected, and valued. This requires comprehensive training programs for all staff on discrimination and harassment, fostering an understanding of these issues and equipping employees with the knowledge and skills to identify and address them effectively. Clear and accessible reporting mechanisms must be established, ensuring that victims feel confident in reporting incidents without fear of retaliation. Investigations into complaints should be conducted promptly, fairly, and impartially, with appropriate disciplinary actions taken against perpetrators.

Furthermore, employers should actively promote diversity and inclusion, ensuring that all employees have equal opportunities for advancement and participation. This includes implementing policies that address pay equity, promote diverse hiring practices, and create inclusive work environments.

Beyond individual workplaces, societal change is crucial. Addressing the deep-seated societal biases that fuel workplace discrimination and harassment requires a long-term commitment to education, awareness-raising, and cultural change. Challenging stereotypes, promoting diversity, and fostering empathy and understanding are essential steps towards creating a more just and equitable society. Public education campaigns can play a significant role in raising awareness of the pervasiveness of workplace discrimination and harassment, educating individuals about their rights, and challenging discriminatory attitudes. Moreover, promoting diverse representation in leadership roles serves as a powerful symbol of societal progress and inspires future generations.

Beyond Individual Workplaces, Social Change Is Key

The fight against workplace injustice is a continuous struggle, demanding constant vigilance and sustained action. It requires the collective efforts of individuals, organizations, and governments to create a world where all workers can thrive, free from discrimination, harassment, and the insidious inequalities that undermine their dignity and opportunities. The pursuit of workplace justice is not merely a matter of legal compliance; it is a moral imperative, reflecting our commitment to creating a fair and just society for all. Only through sustained efforts can we hope to build workplaces where every individual feels valued, respected, and empowered to reach their full potential, free from the shadow of injustice.

The insidious nature of injustice doesn't confine itself to formal settings like the workplace. It seeps into the seemingly informal spaces of friendship and social circles, subtly shaping interactions and profoundly impacting individuals' well-being. Here, the battleground isn't always overt discrimination; it's often a series of micro aggressions, subtle biases, and patterns of exclusion that, cumulatively, inflict significant emotional and psychological harm.

These seemingly minor acts, often dismissed as insignificant or unintentional, contribute to a wider pattern of inequality, perpetuating societal biases and undermining individuals' sense of belonging.

Similarly, individuals from lower socioeconomic backgrounds can feel excluded from social circles dominated by individuals with higher incomes. The inability to participate in expensive activities, such as fine dining, travel, or concerts, can lead to feelings of social isolation and the perception of being less valued. This isn't simply about financial limitations; it's about the ways in which social structures reinforce inequalities, making certain social circles inaccessible to those who lack the necessary financial resources.

The unspoken rules of social participation often favour those with higher socioeconomic standing, unintentionally creating an environment where those from less privileged backgrounds feel excluded and marginalized.

The exclusion isn't always intentional; it can stem from unconscious biases and ingrained social norms. For instance, a group of friends might consistently plan activities that cater to the interests of the majority, inadvertently excluding individuals with different hobbies or preferences. This seemingly innocent behaviour can reinforce feelings of isolation and exclusion, especially for individuals who already feel marginalized due to other aspects of their identity. The lack of awareness regarding these subtle forms of exclusion highlights the need for greater sensitivity and mindful consideration of the impact of seemingly innocuous choices on the well-being of others.

Moreover, bias can manifest in more insidious ways within friendships, impacting the dynamics of the relationships themselves.

The impact of subtle forms of injustice within friendship circles extends beyond individual experiences; it contributes to the perpetuation of larger societal inequalities. The normalization of exclusion and bias in informal settings reinforces societal prejudices, making it more difficult to challenge and overcome wider patterns of discrimination. When individuals constantly experience subtle forms of injustice within their closest relationships, it becomes increasingly difficult to believe in the possibility of genuine equality and belonging.

Addressing injustice within friendships and social circles requires a conscious effort to cultivate empathy, self-awareness, and a commitment to inclusivity. This involves acknowledging the existence of unconscious biases, actively challenging discriminatory behaviour, and creating spaces where all members feel valued, respected, and heard. Friendships should be spaces of mutual support and understanding, not breeding grounds for subtle forms of injustice. Developing a greater awareness of the impact of micro aggressions and implicit biases is crucial. Educating ourselves about the ways in which prejudice manifests in everyday interactions is a vital step towards creating more equitable and inclusive social circles.

Open and honest communication is essential in addressing these issues. Friends need to feel safe enough to discuss their experiences of exclusion and bias without fear of judgment or dismissal. This requires a commitment to active listening, a willingness to acknowledge one's own biases, and a dedication to creating a space where everyone's perspective is valued. Furthermore, actively challenging discriminatory jokes, comments, or behaviour is central in fostering a more inclusive environment. By consistently calling out prejudice, we contribute to the creation of a social norm that prioritizes respect, understanding, and equality.

Beyond individual actions, fostering genuine inclusivity requires a collective effort to challenge the broader societal structures that perpetuate inequalities. This includes advocating for policies that address systemic biases, promoting diversity and inclusion in education and employment, and creating spaces where individuals from marginalized communities feel empowered to share their experiences and advocate for their rights. The struggle for justice is not confined to formal legal battles or political campaigns; it also involves the ongoing effort to create more equitable and inclusive relationships within our personal lives.

The creation of truly inclusive social circles requires conscious and consistent effort. It requires confronting our own biases, actively listening to the experiences of others, and fostering a sense of mutual respect and understanding. The seemingly insignificant acts of exclusion and bias within friendships and social circles, though often overlooked, contribute to a larger pattern of injustice, perpetuating societal inequalities and undermining individuals' sense of belonging. Addressing this injustice requires a commitment to self-reflection, empathy, and a willingness to create spaces where everyone feels valued, respected, and empowered.

Only through collective effort can we transform these informal spaces from potential sources of harm into supportive communities that promote equality and belonging for all. The work is ongoing and requires continuous vigilance, self-reflection, and a commitment to building a more just and equitable world, one friendship at a time. This requires us to not only examine our own behaviours but to also actively work to dismantle the systemic inequalities that permeate our society and create the conditions that allow for these micro-injustices to thrive. The fight for justice is a continuous and multifaceted endeavour, and the battleground is not confined to institutions and systems; it extends to the intimate spaces of our friendships and social circles.

The insidious nature of systemic racism extends far beyond individual prejudices; it manifests as deeply entrenched inequalities woven into the fabric of our societal structures and institutions. Its tendrils reach into every aspect of life, shaping opportunities and outcomes in ways that disproportionately disadvantage communities of colour. Understanding this systemic nature is crucial to dismantling it, for addressing individual acts of racism without tackling the underlying structures is akin to treating a symptom while ignoring the disease.

Corruption and Governance

The insidious tendrils of corruption, woven deeply into the fabric of many political systems, represent a profound form of injustice. This abuse of power, often shielded by a lack of accountability, undermines the very foundations of democratic governance and disproportionately harms vulnerable populations. Corruption manifests in myriad ways, from petty bribery to grand larceny, each instance eroding public trust and hindering societal progress. The consequences are far-reaching, extending beyond mere financial losses to encompass the erosion of human rights, the distortion of justice, and the perpetuation of inequality.

One prevalent manifestation of corrupt governance is the misappropriation of public funds. This can take numerous forms, including embezzlement, fraud, and the diversion of resources intended for public services. Such actions deprive communities of essential resources, such as healthcare, education, and infrastructure, exacerbating existing inequalities and hindering development. For instance, in many developing countries, funds allocated for essential public services, like clean water and sanitation projects, are often diverted to the pockets of corrupt officials, leaving the most vulnerable segments of the population to suffer the consequences. This lack of basic services can have devastating effects on health, education, and overall well-being, perpetuating a cycle of poverty and marginalization.

Beyond the direct financial implications, corruption distorts the decision-making processes within government. When decisions are influenced by bribery, favouritism, or personal gain rather than the public interest, the result is often policies that benefit a select few at the expense of the broader population. This can manifest in the awarding of lucrative contracts to cronies, the deregulation of industries for personal enrichment, and the manipulation of legislation to serve narrow interests. These actions not only undermine the integrity of government but also impede economic development and sustainable growth, creating a climate of uncertainty and hindering investment.

Moreover, corruption severely undermines the rule of law. When individuals in positions of power are above the law, it erodes public trust in institutions, making it more difficult to hold those responsible for wrongdoing accountable. This impunity creates a vicious cycle, emboldening further corrupt practices and discouraging citizens from reporting abuses. The lack of effective mechanisms for investigating and prosecuting corruption allows such offenses to flourish, creating a culture of permissiveness that undermines the very principles of justice and fairness.

The impact of corruption extends far beyond the political arena. It has far-reaching consequences for social and economic development. It undermines investor confidence, discourages foreign investment, and impedes economic growth. Businesses operating in corrupt environments often face extra costs associated with bribery and kickbacks, which reduces their competitiveness and limits job creation. Furthermore, corruption can exacerbate existing social inequalities, as marginalized communities are often more vulnerable to its effects, lacking the resources to navigate the complexities of a corrupt system.

Specific case studies illuminate the devastating consequences of corrupt governance. The ongoing crisis in several African nations, marked by systematic looting of state resources and widespread impunity for corrupt officials, is a stark reminder of the destructive nature of unchecked corruption. Millions of people have been denied access to basic services and opportunities due to the misappropriation of funds intended for development. Similar situations can be seen in numerous countries across the globe, highlighting the universality of this problem and its devastating effects on human development.

Combating corruption requires a multifaceted approach. One essential element is strengthening institutions responsible for governance and oversight. Independent anti-corruption agencies, with adequate resources and authority to investigate and prosecute corrupt officials, are critical. These agencies need to be shielded from political interference and empowered to operate effectively, ensuring impartiality and accountability.

Furthermore, promoting transparency and accountability within government is essential. Public access to government information, including budget allocations, procurement processes, and financial records, can expose corrupt practices and deter future wrongdoing. The implementation of robust regulatory frameworks, including effective mechanisms for conflict of interest management and asset declaration requirements, can help prevent corruption.

Strengthening civil society and encouraging public participation in governance are equally crucial. A strong and active civil society, comprised of independent watchdog groups, investigative journalists, and human rights organizations, can play a vital role in exposing corruption and holding those responsible accountable. Citizens need to be empowered to participate in governance processes, ensuring that their voices are heard and their concerns addressed.

International cooperation is also essential in combating corruption. International organizations and agreements can facilitate the sharing of information and best practices, helping to strengthen the capacity of countries to combat corruption. International pressure and sanctions can also be effective in encouraging countries to implement reforms and hold those responsible for corruption accountable. The establishment of international mechanisms for asset recovery can also help to reclaim stolen assets and reinvest them in development projects.

Education and awareness campaigns are critical in fostering a culture of integrity and accountability. Educating citizens about the harmful effects of corruption and their rights to demand transparency and accountability can help to empower them to combat this pervasive problem. Educating young people about ethical behaviour and the importance of civic engagement is crucial in shaping a future generation that is committed to fighting corruption.

The fight against corruption is a long and arduous struggle, requiring sustained commitment and a collective effort from governments, civil society, and international organizations. However, the potential rewards are immense. By tackling corruption effectively, we can create a more just and equitable society, one where resources are used for the benefit of all, not just a select few. Ultimately, the fight against corruption is a fight for justice, a fight for the very soul of our democratic institutions and the well-being of all humanity. It is a fight that we must win.

Human Rights

The erosion of democratic principles often manifests in the systematic suppression of human rights, a profound injustice with far-reaching consequences. This suppression, frequently perpetrated by those in power, undermines the fundamental freedoms and dignity of individuals and communities. It manifests in diverse forms, ranging from subtle limitations on freedoms to outright brutality and state-sponsored violence. Understanding the mechanisms of this oppression and its devastating impact is crucial to fostering a more just and equitable world.

One of the most egregious violations of human rights is torture. This cruel and inhuman treatment, often inflicted to extract confessions, punish dissidents, or instil fear, leaves lasting physical and psychological scars on victims. The systematic use of torture by state actors constitutes a grave breach of international human rights law and undermines the rule of law itself. Impunity for those responsible for such acts further emboldens such abuses. Numerous reports from human rights organizations document the prevalence of torture in various regions globally, highlighting the need for increased accountability and prevention measures. Specific instances, meticulously documented with evidence, reveal the horrifying realities of torture chambers and the systematic dehumanization of victims. The long-term effects of torture extend beyond the physical pain, impacting mental health, family structures, and societal trust in institutions.

Extrajudicial killings, the deliberate killing of individuals without due process, represent another devastating manifestation of human rights abuse. These killings, often carried out by state security forces or armed groups, are frequently perpetrated with impunity, exacerbating cycles of violence and creating a climate of fear. Such actions violate fundamental rights to life and due process, undermining the very fabric of a just society. Investigations into such incidents are often hampered by lack of access to information, corruption, and intimidation of witnesses, making it exceedingly difficult to bring perpetrators to justice. The emotional and societal trauma inflicted by such acts, coupled with the devastating impact on families and communities, demands stringent measures to prevent and punish these violations.

The suppression of freedom of speech, a cornerstone of democratic societies, represents another significant human rights violation. This can take many forms, from censorship and media control to the intimidation and persecution of journalists, bloggers, and activists.

The restriction of free expression stifles debate, limits access to information, and hinders social progress. Governments may employ a range of tactics to suppress dissent, from legal restrictions on expression to the use of violence and intimidation against those who dare to speak out. Independent media outlets are often targeted for censorship or closure, while online platforms may be subject to surveillance and control. The chilling effect of these restrictions limits open discussion on critical issues, hindering social change and promoting a climate of conformity.

Beyond these specific violations, we see systematic abuses of power that undermine human rights in less overt, but equally damaging ways. Discriminatory laws and policies targeting specific groups based on race, religion, gender, or sexual orientation, create a climate of marginalization and inequality. These systemic injustices deny individuals equal opportunities, access to essential services, and participation in public life. The cumulative effect of these subtle forms of oppression can be profound, leading to widespread inequality and social unrest. The lack of access to justice for marginalized communities exacerbates the situation, ensuring that perpetrators often escape accountability for their actions.

The struggle to protect human rights often involves facing powerful interests and entrenched systems of oppression.

International human rights law provides a framework for protecting fundamental freedoms, but its enforcement remains challenging. International organizations and human rights groups play a vital role in documenting abuses, advocating for reform, and providing support to victims. However, their efforts are often hampered by lack of resources, political interference, and resistance from state actors.

This subject needs a multifaceted approach involving international cooperation, national legislation, and the active engagement of civil society organizations. Case studies illuminate the devastating human cost of these abuses. Reports from regions experiencing widespread human rights violations reveal the devastating impact on individuals, families, and communities. Narratives of victims provide powerful testimony to the suffering inflicted by these actions, underscoring the urgent need for redress. The resilience and resistance demonstrated by victims and human rights defenders in the face of oppression offer a beacon of hope in the fight for justice. Their work provides crucial insight into the effectiveness of different strategies in the protection of human rights, illuminating both success and shortcomings. Such analysis is crucial in informing future strategies and actions.

The fight for human rights is a continuous and complex struggle. It requires sustained efforts from individuals, civil society, and governments to uphold fundamental freedoms and ensure accountability for human rights violations. Strengthening international mechanisms for justice and accountability, promoting the rule of law, and fostering a culture of respect for human rights are essential steps toward a more just and equitable world.

Education and awareness raising about human rights are central in shaping a culture of respect and responsibility, empowering individuals to defend their own rights and the rights of others. The journey towards realizing universal human rights is ongoing, demanding constant vigilance and renewed commitment to the principles of justice, equality, and dignity for all. The fight is far from over, but the stories of resilience and the tireless work of human rights defenders offer a glimmer of hope for a future where human rights are not merely ideals, but lived realities for everyone.

Access to Justice Inequality in Legal Representation and Resources

Access to justice itself remains a significant hurdle, particularly for marginalized communities. This inequality in legal representation and resources further entrenches the cycle of injustice, perpetuating disparities and hindering redress for those most in need. The very structure of the legal system, intended to uphold justice, often contributes to this inequality, creating a system where the wealthy and powerful enjoy significantly better access to legal recourse than the vulnerable and disadvantaged.

One of the most critical factors impacting access to justice is the availability and effectiveness of legal aid programs. Ideally, these programs should provide essential legal services to those unable to afford them, ensuring equality before the law. In reality, many legal aid systems are chronically underfunded and understaffed, struggling to meet the overwhelming demand. This leads to long waiting lists, limited scope of representation, and a system that often fails to provide adequate support to those who desperately need it. The quality of representation offered by overburdened legal aid organizations can also suffer, leaving individuals feeling abandoned and their cases inadequately addressed. Furthermore, eligibility criteria for legal aid often exclude many who are struggling financially but technically fall above the poverty line, leaving a significant gap in access to justice for those teetering on the edge of financial stability.

Public defenders, often the last line of defence for indigent individuals facing criminal charges, frequently confront overwhelming caseloads and inadequate resources. The sheer number of cases assigned to a single public defender often necessitates rushed preparations and limited client interaction, potentially jeopardizing the quality of representation and hindering the ability to build a strong defence. Funding shortages result in insufficient training opportunities for public defenders, limiting their ability to stay abreast of legal developments and to effectively advocate for their clients. The adversarial nature of the criminal justice system, coupled with the inherent power imbalance between the prosecution and the defence, already stacks the deck against defendants. The under-resourcing of public defenders significantly exacerbates this imbalance, potentially resulting in wrongful convictions and unjust sentences. Moreover, the stigma associated with public defenders and the perception that they provide subpar legal representation can further disadvantage clients who depend on their services.

The cost of litigation, both civil and criminal, represents another substantial barrier to access to justice. Court fees, filing costs, expert witness fees, and attorney fees can quickly accumulate, rendering the pursuit of legal recourse prohibitively expensive for many. Even seemingly minor legal disputes can bankrupt individuals and families, forcing them to abandon their claims and accept unfair outcomes. This financial barrier disproportionately affects low-income individuals and communities, effectively silencing their voices and reinforcing existing inequalities. For example, victims of domestic violence, facing insurmountable legal costs, often find themselves unable to obtain restraining orders or pursue legal action against their abusers, leaving them vulnerable to continued harm. Similarly, individuals facing wrongful termination or discrimination often lack the financial resources to engage in lengthy and costly employment litigation, leading to unjust outcomes and economic hardship.

Beyond the direct financial costs, the complex and often opaque nature of the legal system presents additional challenges to accessing justice. Going through bureaucratic procedures, understanding legal jargon, and comprehending the intricacies of legal processes can be discouraging for individuals lacking legal expertise. This lack of legal literacy contributes to a power imbalance, leaving individuals vulnerable to manipulation and exploitation by those with greater legal knowledge. Many are unaware of their legal rights, unable to identify avenues for redress, or intimidated by the formal and intimidating environment of courtrooms. This creates a situation where individuals may forfeit their rights simply due to a lack of understanding or fear of the legal process.

The problem of access to justice extends beyond the financial and procedural barriers. Implicit bias within the legal system, including amongst judges, lawyers, and jurors, can further disadvantage marginalized communities. Studies have repeatedly shown that unconscious biases can influence decisions regarding bail, sentencing, and the overall outcome of cases. Racial, ethnic, and gender biases can impact every stage of the legal process, from arrest to trial to sentencing, leading to disparities in outcomes and contributing to the overrepresentation of minority groups in the criminal justice system. These biases are often subtle and difficult to detect, yet they have a profoundly negative impact on the fairness and impartiality of the legal system.

Addressing this complex problem requires a multi-pronged approach. Increased funding for legal aid programs is crucial, ensuring that these organizations are adequately equipped to provide quality representation to those who cannot afford it.

Reforming public defender systems, including increasing their salaries, reducing their caseloads, and providing access to better training and resources, is equally essential. Streamlining the court system and simplifying legal procedures can increase accessibility for those lacking legal expertise. Initiatives focused on legal literacy and community education can empower individuals to understand their legal rights and navigate the legal system more effectively.

Finally, addressing implicit bias through training, education, and systemic reforms is critical to achieving true equality before the law. Ultimately, ensuring equal access to justice demands a fundamental shift in the mindset, acknowledging that the current system falls short of its ideal and requires comprehensive and transformative reform to eliminate the systemic inequalities that prevent many from securing justice. Until these systemic inequities are addressed, the promise of equal justice under the law remains elusive for too many. The fight for justice extends beyond the courtroom, encompassing a broader struggle for equitable access to resources and the dismantling of systemic barriers that hinder the pursuit of justice for all. The pursuit of justice must be accessible, affordable, and free from bias. Only then will the scales of justice truly be balanced.

Access to a Health System

The pursuit of justice demands a critical examination of societal structures that perpetuate inequality, particularly in areas impacting fundamental human rights like access to healthcare. The stark reality is that healthcare is not a universal right, but rather a privilege often dictated by factors entirely outside an individual's control. Race, ethnicity, socioeconomic status, and geographic location all play significant roles in determining an individual's access to quality medical care, leading to profound and often life-threatening health disparities. This inequality is not a mere statistical anomaly; it's a systemic failure with devastating consequences for millions.

Studies consistently demonstrate that individuals from marginalized racial and ethnic groups face significant barriers to accessing adequate healthcare. These disparities manifest in various ways, from unequal access to insurance and timely appointments to differences in the quality of care received. For example, research has shown that Black patients are less likely to receive timely diagnosis and treatment for conditions like heart disease and cancer compared to their white counterparts, even when controlling for socioeconomic factors. This disparity is often attributed to implicit biases among healthcare providers, leading to misdiagnosis, delayed treatment, and ultimately, poorer health outcomes. The legacy of systemic racism within healthcare systems, including historical segregation and discriminatory practices, continues to cast a long shadow, perpetuating these inequalities. Beyond race, socioeconomic status is another powerful determinant of healthcare access. Individuals from low-income backgrounds frequently face insurmountable barriers to accessing healthcare, including lack of health insurance, limited access to transportation to medical facilities, and inability to afford the cost of medical care.

The uninsured population often delays seeking medical attention until conditions become critical, resulting in more complex and costly treatment. This delay in care can have life-altering implications, leading to preventable hospitalizations, long-term disabilities, and even premature death. Furthermore, those living in poverty often lack access to preventative care, increasing their risk of developing chronic conditions that could have been avoided or managed with early intervention. This cycle of poverty and poor health underscores the inextricable link between socioeconomic status and healthcare access.

Geographic location also plays a crucial role in determining healthcare access. Rural communities often face a significant shortage of healthcare providers, resulting in limited access to essential medical services. This "healthcare desert" phenomenon leaves rural residents with fewer options for care, longer travel distances to medical facilities, and decreased access to specialized care. The scarcity of specialists in rural areas means individuals may have to travel great distances for routine checkups or emergency care, creating significant financial burdens and logistical challenges. This disparity in access to care disproportionately affects vulnerable populations in rural areas, exacerbating existing health inequalities.

The consequences of these healthcare disparities are far-reaching and devastating. Inequitable access to healthcare translates to poorer health outcomes, higher rates of chronic diseases, and increased mortality rates among marginalized groups. Studies have documented significant differences in life expectancy, infant mortality rates, and rates of chronic conditions like diabetes and hypertension among different racial and socioeconomic groups.

These disparities not only impact individual health but also have significant societal ramifications, leading to decreased productivity, increased healthcare costs, and social and economic instability. The cost of ignoring these disparities is immense, both in human suffering and financial terms. Addressing these inequalities requires a multi-pronged approach that tackles the systemic issues driving them. Expanding access to affordable health insurance is crucial, ensuring that all individuals have the financial means to access healthcare services. Investing in community-based healthcare initiatives can improve access to care, particularly in underserved areas. The expansion of telehealth services can also play a significant role in bridging the geographic gap in healthcare access, providing remote access to medical professionals. Furthermore, addressing implicit bias within healthcare through training and education can promote culturally sensitive and equitable care for all patients.

Beyond these immediate solutions, a fundamental shift in our approach to healthcare is necessary. Healthcare must be recognized as a fundamental human right, not a commodity driven by market forces. This paradigm shift requires a commitment to equitable resource allocation, ensuring that healthcare resources are distributed fairly across all communities, regardless of race, ethnicity, socioeconomic status, or geographic location. Moreover, promoting health equity necessitates addressing the broader social determinants of health, such as poverty, housing insecurity, and food insecurity, which significantly impact health outcomes.

Addressing these underlying social factors is essential for creating a truly equitable healthcare system. The fight for equitable healthcare access requires sustained advocacy and political engagement. Raising awareness about the pervasive nature of healthcare disparities is essential in galvanizing support for policy changes that promote health equity. Holding policymakers accountable for enacting and enforcing policies that address healthcare disparities is vital in achieving meaningful change.

By advocating for a just and equitable healthcare system, we can strive to ensure that every individual, regardless of their background or circumstances, has access to the high-quality healthcare they deserve. This is not just a moral imperative, but a crucial step towards building a more just and equitable society, where health is a right and not a privilege. The journey towards health equity is a continuous process, requiring persistent effort, sustained commitment, and a unwavering dedication to dismantling the systemic barriers that prevent millions from accessing the healthcare they need and deserve.

Research consistently shows that racial and ethnic minorities are more likely to receive misdiagnoses or delayed diagnoses compared to white patients, even when presenting with similar symptoms. This disparity is particularly alarming in conditions such as heart disease and cancer, where timely diagnosis and treatment are crucial for optimal outcomes. This delay in diagnosis is often linked to a combination of factors, including implicit bias among healthcare providers who might attribute symptoms to other factors, leading to insufficient investigation and delayed referrals to specialists. The consequences of misdiagnosis extend far beyond individual suffering. Misdiagnosis can lead to unnecessary procedures, ineffective treatments, and increased healthcare costs. The financial burden of these errors disproportionately affects marginalized communities, further exacerbating their already precarious financial situations. The cumulative effect of these errors undermines trust in the healthcare system, contributing to health disparities and creating a cycle of disadvantage. Furthermore, the lack of culturally sensitive care adds another layer of complexity to this issue.

Understanding and addressing the unique health needs and cultural perspectives of diverse populations is paramount in providing equitable and effective healthcare. Socioeconomic status plays a significant role, with low-income individuals often facing barriers to accessing specialized medical care. This includes a lack of access to specialists, expensive medications, and advanced diagnostic tools.

Geographic location further complicates matters, with individuals living in rural or underserved areas often facing significant challenges in accessing timely and appropriate medical care. These limitations frequently lead to delayed diagnoses and treatment, resulting in poorer health outcomes and increased mortality. The cumulative effect of these interlocking disadvantages creates a system where individuals' access to essential medical services is not determined by their health needs, but rather by their race, economic status, and location.

The unequal access to specialized medical care is another critical area of medical discrimination. Individuals from marginalized communities often face greater difficulties in accessing specialists, such as cardiologists, oncologists, and neurologists. This disparity contributes to delayed diagnoses and treatments for serious conditions, leading to poorer health outcomes. Moreover, the availability and affordability of advanced medical technologies and treatments also often vary across different communities, further widening the gap in health outcomes. This disparity necessitates a critical evaluation of healthcare resource allocation and a commitment to equitable distribution of advanced medical services across all communities.

Addressing medical discrimination demands a multi-pronged approach. It requires increased awareness and education among healthcare providers to identify and mitigate implicit biases. Implementing implicit bias training programs can help healthcare professionals recognize and address their unconscious biases in their interactions with patients. Furthermore, promoting cultural competency within healthcare institutions is crucial in creating a more welcoming and equitable environment for patients from diverse backgrounds. This involves providing healthcare providers with the necessary tools and resources to understand and effectively communicate with patients from diverse cultural backgrounds.

Moreover, structural changes are necessary to dismantle systemic barriers to healthcare access. This includes improving access to affordable health insurance, expanding community-based healthcare initiatives in underserved areas, and investing in telehealth services to overcome geographic barriers to care.

Furthermore, addressing the social determinants of health – such as poverty, housing insecurity, and food insecurity – is essential in creating a more equitable healthcare system. These social factors significantly impact health outcomes and contribute to health disparities, making it critical to address these broader societal issues to truly achieve health equity.

Beyond individual efforts, policy changes are crucial. Mandating data collection on racial and ethnic disparities in healthcare can shed light on the extent of medical discrimination and guide the development of targeted interventions. Enacting legislation to protect patients from discrimination and ensure equitable access to care is also necessary. This can include policies that require healthcare providers to actively address implicit bias and provide culturally sensitive care. Holding healthcare institutions accountable for ensuring equitable access to care is also crucial in driving meaningful change.

The fight against medical discrimination is a complex and ongoing struggle. It requires a multifaceted approach that tackles implicit bias, addresses systemic inequalities, and promotes cultural competency within the healthcare system. It demands a commitment to recognizing the inherent value and dignity of every individual, regardless of their background or circumstances. This is not merely a matter of improving healthcare outcomes; it is a fundamental human rights issue. By actively dismantling the systems that perpetuate medical discrimination, we can pave the way for a more just and equitable healthcare system, where every individual has the opportunity to access the highest quality of care, regardless of race, ethnicity, socioeconomic status, or geographic location. Only through continuous vigilance, systemic change, and unwavering advocacy can we truly achieve health equity and ensure that healthcare is a right, not a privilege, for all.

Mental Health Disparities Stigma and Lack of Access to Care

The preceding sections illuminated the stark realities of healthcare disparities based on race, socioeconomic status, and geographic location. However, the pervasive issue of mental health disparities demands its own focused examination. This is not merely a subset of the broader healthcare crisis; it represents a unique and devastating form of injustice, deeply rooted in societal stigma and compounded by unequal access to care. The consequences are far-reaching, affecting individuals, families, and communities, and hindering overall societal progress.

The stigma surrounding mental illness remains a formidable barrier to seeking help. For many, particularly within marginalized communities, admitting to struggling with mental health is fraught with fear of judgment, discrimination, and social isolation. This fear is often well-founded. The pervasive societal stereotypes portraying individuals with mental illness as unstable, dangerous, or simply "weak" create a climate of silence and shame, preventing individuals from seeking the care they desperately need. This stigma is particularly pronounced in communities already burdened by systemic inequalities, where existing societal biases further amplify the negative consequences of disclosing mental health struggles.

The lack of culturally competent mental healthcare exacerbates this problem. Effective mental healthcare requires an understanding of an individual's cultural context, beliefs, and experiences. For example, the expression and understanding of mental distress can vary significantly across different cultural groups. What might be viewed as a symptom of depression in one culture may be interpreted differently in another, leading to misdiagnosis and ineffective treatment. Failure to integrate cultural understanding into treatment plans undermines the therapeutic relationship and can lead to patients feeling misunderstood and alienated, further reinforcing their reluctance to seek help. This lack of cultural sensitivity is particularly acute in immigrant and refugee communities, where individuals may grapple with trauma, language barriers, and the added stress of adapting to a new culture, all while navigating a mental healthcare system that may not adequately address their unique needs.

The disparities in access to mental healthcare resources are equally alarming. Marginalized communities frequently lack access to adequate mental healthcare services, including qualified professionals, affordable treatment options, and culturally appropriate interventions. This shortage is especially pronounced in rural and underserved areas, where geographical limitations further restrict access to specialists and specialized care. The scarcity of culturally competent professionals adds another layer of difficulty.

Finding a therapist or psychiatrist who understands the specific challenges faced by a particular community can be incredibly difficult, leading to delays in treatment and poorer health outcomes. This inequality in access is not merely an inconvenience; it is a significant contributor to the disproportionately higher rates of mental illness and suicide among marginalized groups.

The financial burden of mental healthcare is another significant barrier, particularly for individuals with low socioeconomic status. The cost of therapy, medication, and hospitalization can be prohibitive for many, forcing them to forgo treatment or delay seeking help until their condition worsens. This financial barrier disproportionately affects low-income individuals and families, compounding their existing struggles and reinforcing the cycle of inequality. The lack of affordable insurance coverage, coupled with the high cost of mental healthcare services, creates a system where access to care is determined by financial resources, rather than clinical need.

Addressing these disparities requires a multi-pronged approach. First, we need to actively combat the stigma surrounding mental illness through public awareness campaigns, educational initiatives, and media representation that challenges negative stereotypes and promotes understanding. This requires a concerted effort from healthcare professionals, policymakers, educators, and the media to create a more accepting and supportive environment for individuals struggling with mental health issues. Furthermore, increasing funding for mental healthcare services is vital, particularly in underserved communities. This includes investing in training and recruiting more culturally competent mental health professionals, expanding access to affordable treatment options, and improving the availability of mental healthcare services in rural and underserved areas.

Improving access to culturally competent care requires dedicated training for healthcare providers. This training must go beyond superficial awareness of cultural differences and delve deeply into the specific needs and experiences of diverse populations. It must also involve creating partnerships with community leaders and organizations to understand the unique challenges and perspectives within those communities. Building trust and rapport with patients is paramount, and achieving this requires sensitivity, respect, and a genuine effort to understand the patient's lived experience.

Furthermore, policies that expand access to affordable healthcare, including mental healthcare, are critical. Expanding access to mental health coverage through insurance reforms, increasing funding for community-based mental health services, and implementing telehealth services to overcome geographic barriers can improve access to care. Legislation that protects individuals with mental illness from discrimination in employment, housing, and other areas of life is equally important in reducing the stigma and creating more equitable opportunities.

The fight against mental health disparities is not just a healthcare issue; it is a social justice issue. It requires a comprehensive approach that addresses the systemic inequalities that contribute to this crisis. This means challenging societal biases, expanding access to care, and creating a more inclusive and supportive environment for individuals struggling with mental health. Only by dismantling the systems that perpetuate inequality can we truly achieve mental health equity and ensure that everyone has the opportunity to access the care they need, regardless of their background or circumstances. The long-term consequences of inaction are profound, both for individuals and for society as a whole. Ignoring this crisis perpetuates a cycle of suffering and reinforces the very inequalities we claim to oppose.

The stark realities of healthcare disparities manifest profoundly in disparate health outcomes. Life expectancy, a fundamental indicator of overall population health, reveals a deeply troubling pattern of inequality. Across the globe, and particularly within nations boasting advanced healthcare systems, significant gaps in life expectancy persist along racial, ethnic, and socioeconomic lines. Individuals from marginalized communities frequently experience substantially shorter life spans compared to their more privileged counterparts. This disparity isn't simply a matter of individual choices; it is a direct consequence of systemic inequalities embedded within healthcare access, quality of care, and broader societal determinants of health.

Chronic diseases further exacerbate these inequalities. Conditions such as heart disease, stroke, diabetes, and cancer account for a significant portion of mortality and morbidity worldwide. However, the prevalence of these diseases varies dramatically across different populations, mirroring the patterns observed in life expectancy. Marginalized communities frequently bear a disproportionately higher burden of chronic diseases, often experiencing earlier onset, more severe complications, and higher mortality rates. This disparity arises from several interconnected factors, including genetic predispositions, environmental exposures, lifestyle choices, and most importantly, access to healthcare.

The lack of access to preventative care plays a crucial role. Regular checkups, screenings, and early detection of chronic diseases are essential for effective management and improved outcomes.

However, individuals from low-income communities and marginalized groups often face significant barriers to accessing these services, including lack of health insurance, financial constraints, geographical limitations, and difficulties navigating complex healthcare systems. This lack of preventative care allows chronic diseases to progress unchecked, leading to more severe health complications and reduced life expectancy.

The economic consequences of health disparities are substantial, extending far beyond the immediate costs of healthcare. Reduced life expectancy translates to lost productivity, decreased workforce participation, and increased financial burdens on individuals, families, and society as a whole. The high prevalence of chronic diseases places an enormous strain on healthcare systems, leading to increased healthcare expenditures and reduced overall economic output. The cumulative impact of these economic burdens significantly hinders societal progress and reinforces the cycle of inequality.

Infant mortality rates serve as another poignant indicator of healthcare disparities. These rates, which measure the number of infant deaths per 1,000 live births, consistently reveal dramatic differences between various populations. Low-income communities and racial and ethnic minorities often experience significantly higher infant mortality rates than more affluent groups. This disparity stems from several contributing factors, including limited access to prenatal care, inadequate maternal nutrition, exposure to environmental toxins, and socioeconomic stressors during pregnancy. These disparities highlight the crucial role of healthcare access and social determinants of health in ensuring positive infant outcomes.

Addressing these disparities demands a multifaceted approach. It requires significant investment in public health initiatives aimed at improving access to affordable and quality healthcare, particularly in underserved communities. This includes expanding access to health insurance, increasing funding for community health centres, and addressing the social determinants of health that contribute to health disparities, such as poverty, lack of education, and environmental injustice. Furthermore, tackling implicit bias within the healthcare system is paramount; this necessitates comprehensive training for healthcare professionals to address unconscious biases and promote culturally competent care. Finally, policymakers must prioritize policies that promote health equity and address the root causes of these disparities. Only through a concerted and comprehensive effort can we hope to achieve health equity and ensure that everyone has the opportunity to live a long, healthy life, regardless of their race, ethnicity, or socioeconomic status. The societal cost of inaction is immeasurable, both in human suffering and economic terms. The time for decisive change is now.

Addressing the multifaceted challenge of healthcare disparities demands a comprehensive and multifaceted strategy, moving beyond mere symptom treatment to tackle the systemic roots of inequality. This requires a concerted effort from policymakers, healthcare providers, communities, and individuals, all working in unison towards a shared goal of health equity. A central pillar of this strategy is improving access to healthcare services, particularly for marginalized and underserved populations. This isn't simply about increasing the number of hospitals or clinics; it requires a fundamental shift in how healthcare is delivered and financed.

One crucial step is expanding access to affordable health insurance. Millions worldwide lack access to essential healthcare due to the prohibitive cost of insurance premiums and medical care. Universal healthcare models, where the government plays a central role in ensuring access for all citizens, offer a pathway towards greater equity. Such systems, while varying in specifics, prioritize affordability and accessibility, minimizing the financial burden of illness on individuals and families. Even within systems that are not universally accessible, government subsidies and assistance programs can be implemented to mitigate the cost barrier for low-income individuals and families. The design of these programs is crucial, ensuring they are easy to navigate and free from bureaucratic hurdles that disproportionately affect less-advantaged populations. Furthermore, public awareness campaigns can help individuals understand their rights and options when it comes to accessing affordable healthcare.

Beyond insurance, geographic access is another critical component. Many underserved communities are located in rural areas or urban deserts, far removed from medical facilities. Addressing this challenge requires strategic investments in telehealth technologies, expanding the reach of remote healthcare consultations and monitoring. Mobile clinics, which bring healthcare services directly to underserved areas, offer another valuable approach. These clinics can offer essential preventative care, screenings, and treatment for acute illnesses, reducing the need for lengthy and costly travel to distant hospitals. Investing in the infrastructure required for these mobile clinics, as well as training the personnel to operate them effectively, requires significant commitment but offers substantial returns in terms of improved access and health outcomes. The location of new healthcare facilities must also be carefully considered, with a deliberate effort to establish services in underserved areas, prioritizing those communities with the greatest need.

Addressing medical discrimination, a persistent and insidious barrier to equitable healthcare, is also crucial. This requires a multi-pronged approach that tackles both overt and subtle forms of bias.

Overt discrimination, such as overt refusal of care based on race, ethnicity, or sexual orientation, must be met with swift and decisive legal action. Strong anti-discrimination laws, vigorously enforced, are essential to deter such behaviour and ensure accountability for those who engage in it. However, addressing subtle forms of bias, which can be even more pervasive and damaging, is a greater challenge. Implicit bias, often unconscious and unintentional, can lead to disparities in treatment, diagnosis, and access to care. For example, studies have repeatedly shown that racial and ethnic minorities often receive less aggressive treatment for certain medical conditions compared to white patients, even when factors such as severity of illness are controlled for.

Combating implicit bias requires comprehensive training for healthcare professionals. This training should focus on raising awareness of these biases, developing strategies for identifying and mitigating them in clinical settings, and promoting cultural competency. Cultural competency goes beyond simple awareness; it requires healthcare providers to actively seek to understand the cultural beliefs, values, and health practices of their patients, ensuring that care is delivered in a culturally sensitive and respectful manner. This includes training healthcare providers to communicate effectively with patients who may have different communication styles or linguistic barriers. Furthermore, incorporating diverse perspectives in the design and implementation of healthcare services is crucial, ensuring that the needs of all communities are addressed. This can involve establishing community advisory boards that give local voices a role in shaping healthcare policies and practices.

Promoting culturally competent care goes hand-in-hand with addressing language barriers. Many marginalized communities struggle to access healthcare because they lack access to interpreters or healthcare providers who speak their native language. Investing in language access services, including providing interpreters for appointments and translating patient education materials into multiple languages, is vital for ensuring effective communication and understanding. Furthermore, recruiting and retaining a diverse healthcare workforce is essential. Having a healthcare system that reflects the diversity of the communities it serves is crucial not just for delivering culturally competent care but also for building trust and ensuring that marginalized communities feel comfortable seeking and receiving healthcare. This includes actively recruiting individuals from diverse backgrounds to medical schools and other healthcare training programs, addressing systemic barriers that may prevent these groups from entering the profession.

Policymakers have a critical role to play in ensuring that strategies to address healthcare disparities are effectively implemented. This starts with adequate investment in public health programs aimed at promoting health equity. This includes funding for community health centres, which provide accessible and affordable care to underserved populations; supporting initiatives to address the social determinants of health, such as poverty, housing insecurity, and food insecurity, which significantly impact health outcomes; and enacting policies that promote health equity across all areas of healthcare.

Data collection and analysis are crucial tools for policymakers. Accurate and reliable data, disaggregated by race, ethnicity, socioeconomic status, and other relevant factors, can illuminate the patterns and extent of healthcare disparities, providing policymakers with the evidence needed to formulate effective strategies. This data should inform the allocation of resources and policies that target the specific needs of communities most affected by healthcare disparities. The use of this data is critical to holding healthcare providers accountable for delivering equitable care and ensuring that the policies and programs implemented are truly effective in achieving their aims.

The role of communities themselves is indispensable in this endeavour. Community-based organizations, working in partnership with healthcare providers and policymakers, can play a vital role in advocating for improved access to care, educating community members about health issues, and providing culturally appropriate health promotion and disease prevention programs. Community engagement is crucial in understanding the specific needs and priorities of these communities. This can involve conducting focus groups, community surveys, and other participatory research methods to ensure that programs and initiatives are tailored to the specific cultural contexts and needs of the target populations. By fostering strong partnerships between healthcare providers and community leaders, trust can be built, improving the uptake of healthcare services and promoting health equity within communities.

The Fight Against Injustice

The fight against injustice isn't solely the domain of lawmakers, activists, or large organizations. It begins with each individual, with the everyday choices we make and the actions we take—or fail to take—in the face of unfairness. Recognizing injustice is the first crucial step. This isn't always straightforward; injustice often cloaks itself in subtle forms, disguised as "tradition," "efficiency," or even "common sense." It manifests in micro aggressions, systemic biases embedded in institutions, and the unequal distribution of resources and opportunities. Recognizing these subtle forms requires critical self-reflection and a willingness to question the status quo. We must examine our own biases, privileges, and complicity in perpetuating systems of injustice.

Beyond the workplace, consider the pervasive issue of unequal access to quality education. Schools in affluent neighbourhoods often boast better resources, smaller class sizes, and more experienced teachers than those in impoverished areas. This disparity, though rarely explicitly stated as discriminatory, perpetuates a cycle of disadvantage, limiting opportunities for children from less privileged backgrounds. Similarly, unequal access to healthcare, as discussed in the previous chapter, isn't simply a matter of insufficient resources; it's a complex interplay of systemic factors, including discriminatory practices and implicit biases within the healthcare system itself.

Recognizing injustice involves educating oneself. This means actively seeking out information from diverse sources, challenging your own preconceived notions, and critically analyzing the information you consume. It requires actively listening to the experiences of marginalized groups and understanding the historical and systemic forces that have shaped their lives. For example, understanding the legacy of colonialism and its ongoing impact on global inequality necessitates delving into historical texts, documentaries, and personal narratives that expose the enduring effects of past injustices.

Once injustice is recognized, the next step is to challenge it. This can be daunting, especially when facing powerful institutions or entrenched social norms. However, even small acts of defiance can have a ripple effect, inspiring others to speak out and creating a climate of accountability. One effective approach is to speak up when witnessing discrimination or injustice. This might involve challenging a racist joke, confronting a sexist comment, or reporting discriminatory behaviour to the appropriate authorities. This act of speaking out, while potentially uncomfortable, is a vital step in dismantling systems of oppression.

However, it's central to approach such challenges with careful consideration. Direct confrontation might not always be the most effective strategy, particularly if it puts oneself or others at risk. A more nuanced approach may be needed, depending on the context and the power dynamics involved. This could involve seeking support from allies, organizing collective action, or employing more indirect methods of challenging injustice, such as writing letters to elected officials or engaging in peaceful protests. The key is to find a method that aligns with one's comfort level and maximizes impact while ensuring personal safety.

Supporting social justice initiatives is another powerful way to combat injustice. This could involve donating time or resources to organizations working to address specific forms of inequality or organizations fighting for economic equality. Participation in these organizations not only provides valuable support but also exposes one to a wider network of individuals committed to social justice, fostering collaboration and amplifying the impact of individual efforts. Moreover, supporting businesses and organizations that champion ethical practices and social responsibility demonstrates a commitment to aligning one's actions with one's values.

Engaging in respectful dialogue is also essential in challenging injustice. This involves communicating with individuals who hold differing perspectives, seeking to understand their viewpoints, and finding common ground where possible. This doesn't mean compromising one's principles or accepting unjust systems, but rather fostering constructive communication that seeks to bridge divides and promotes understanding. It's important to remember that dialogue doesn't always lead to immediate agreement, but it can create opportunities for shifting perspectives, building empathy, and fostering more meaningful engagement with the issue at hand.

The process of challenging injustice is not always linear or easy. There will be setbacks, moments of frustration, and occasions when progress seems slow or nonexistent. Maintaining resilience and perseverance is critical. Learning from past experiences, adapting strategies, and continuing to engage in the struggle are crucial for making sustained progress. The fight for justice requires a commitment to long-term engagement, a willingness to confront personal biases and privileges, and a dedication to creating a more equitable world.

Furthermore, individuals can advocate for policy changes at both local and national levels. This could involve contacting elected officials to express concerns about specific issues, participating in public forums or hearings, or supporting legislation that promotes social justice. Lobbying efforts, although often perceived as the domain of professional lobbyists, are also accessible to ordinary citizens who can collectively exert significant influence. Organized collective action through petitions, public demonstrations, and letter-writing campaigns can hold policymakers accountable and advocate for significant reforms.

Beyond formal political action, individual actions can have a profound impact on promoting social justice within communities.

Volunteering at local community centres, mentoring underprivileged youth, or engaging in community organizing efforts can create meaningful change at the grassroots level. These actions build bridges between different communities, foster empathy and understanding, and create opportunities for shared experiences that promote social cohesion and cooperation in addressing local injustices.

One often-overlooked aspect of combating injustice lies in making conscious choices in our everyday lives. Choosing to support businesses that prioritize ethical labour practices, reducing our environmental footprint to address environmental injustice, and advocating for fair trade practices all contribute to a larger movement toward a more just and sustainable world. These seemingly small acts, when aggregated, become a powerful force for positive change.

In addition, actively participating in the civic life of one's community fosters a climate where social justice can flourish. This can involve running for local office, participating in community meetings, joining neighbourhood watch programs, or simply engaging in respectful dialogue with neighbors to address issues of concern. Active civic engagement strengthens the bonds of community, promotes collaboration, and enhances the capacity of communities to address shared challenges, including those that stem from injustice. These actions help create a community where everyone feels a sense of belonging and where collective efforts are focused on creating a fairer and more equitable society.

Finally, recognizing and challenging injustice is a continuous process of learning, reflection, and action. There will be moments of doubt, setbacks, and challenges. Yet, it is crucial to maintain hope and persevere in the fight for a more just and equitable world. The struggle against injustice requires courage, empathy, and resilience.

It is a journey that demands continuous self-assessment, a willingness to learn from mistakes, and a commitment to building a better future for all. By acknowledging our own limitations, remaining open to new perspectives, and engaging with others who share the commitment to social justice, we collectively create a society where human rights are upheld, and fairness prevails. The path to justice is long and arduous, but the pursuit itself is a testament to the enduring human spirit and our collective capacity for creating positive and lasting change.

Collective Action - Organization and Defence of Causes

Collective action is the lifeblood of social change. While individual actions are crucial, the power to dismantle systemic injustice lies in the collective mobilization of people demanding reform. History is replete with examples of social movements that have reshaped societies, from the abolition of slavery to the women's suffrage movement to the Civil Rights movement. These movements, driven by the collective will of ordinary citizens, demonstrate the transformative potential of organized action.

The effectiveness of collective action hinges on several key factors. Firstly, strong leadership is vital. Leaders are not necessarily those who hold formal positions of power but rather individuals who can inspire, motivate, and organize others around a common goal. Effective leaders possess strong communication skills, the ability to build consensus, and the strategic acumen to navigate complex challenges. They understand the need for clear messaging, focusing on a shared vision and achievable goals.

Secondly, a well-defined strategy is essential for success. This involves identifying the target of the action, articulating clear objectives, and developing a plan to achieve those objectives. The strategy should consider the available resources, potential obstacles, and the overall political landscape. A robust strategy may involve several tactics, from peaceful protests and civil disobedience to lobbying and legal action. The choice of tactics will depend on the specific context and the aims of the movement.

Thirdly, building broad-based coalitions is vital for increasing the reach and impact of collective action. This involves bringing together diverse groups with shared interests to create a powerful collective voice. Coalitions can amplify the message, enhance resource mobilization, and provide a wider platform for advocacy.

The challenge lies in managing diverse perspectives and finding common ground among groups with varying priorities. The success of any coalition rests on its ability to build trust, foster collaboration, and maintain a shared sense of purpose.

For instance, the environmental justice movement successfully broadened its base of support by demonstrating how environmental degradation disproportionately impacts marginalized communities. This strategy brought together environmental activists, community organizers, and representatives from affected communities, creating a powerful coalition focused on achieving environmental justice and equity.

Furthermore, effective communication is vital in mobilizing collective action. This goes beyond simply spreading information; it involves crafting a compelling narrative that resonates with the target audience and persuades them to participate in the movement.

It requires using various communication channels—social media, traditional media, community events—to reach a broad audience and foster a sense of collective identity and shared purpose. The rise of social media has revolutionized the ability of social movements to organize, communicate, and mobilize support.

Consider the Arab Spring uprisings, where social media played a critical role in coordinating protests, disseminating information, and mobilizing popular support for regime change. The ability to bypass traditional media outlets allowed activists to organize rapidly and effectively, despite government attempts to suppress dissent.

Advocacy groups play a critical role in supporting collective action. These organizations, dedicated to advancing specific causes, provide vital resources, expertise, and infrastructure to social movements. They offer legal support, conduct research and advocacy, and assist in organizing campaigns. The expertise and resources they provide are often crucial in ensuring the success of social movements.

Effective advocacy groups are also skilled in navigating the complexities of political systems, building relationships with policymakers, and influencing public opinion.

Successful advocacy campaigns often employ a multi-pronged approach, combining various methods to maximize impact. This might involve grassroots mobilization, media advocacy, lobbying, litigation, and public education. The choice of tactics will depend on the specific issue, the political context, and the resources available.

Community organizing plays a vital role in fostering collective action at the grassroots level. It involves building relationships within communities, empowering residents to address local issues, and creating networks of support. Community organizers work with residents to identify problems, develop solutions, and implement strategies for change. They often serve as a bridge between communities and larger advocacy organizations, facilitating collaboration and resource mobilization.

Moreover, the digital age presents both challenges and opportunities for collective action. Social media platforms, while enabling rapid mobilization and information dissemination, also present challenges related to misinformation, online harassment, and the potential for manipulation. Understanding these complexities is essential for building effective digital strategies that maximize the benefits of technology while mitigating its risks.

Finally, maintaining momentum in collective action requires sustained commitment and perseverance. Social movements often face setbacks, internal disagreements, and opposition from powerful interests. The ability to overcome these obstacles, adapt to changing circumstances, and maintain a long-term perspective is crucial for achieving lasting change. Celebrating small victories along the way helps keep the movement energized and focused on the larger goals.

The fight for justice is often a marathon, not a sprint; staying the course requires dedication, resilience, and a steadfast belief in the power of collective action to overcome injustice. It's the enduring belief in the power of unity and the persistent pursuit of a more equitable world that ultimately fuels the movement's strength and lasting impact.

Policy Reform - Systemic Change and Structural Solutions

Policy reforms represent a crucial battleground in the fight against injustice. While grassroots movements and collective action are essential for raising awareness and mobilizing public opinion, lasting change necessitates systemic shifts achieved through legislative and policy interventions. These reforms must address the root causes of inequality, not simply its symptoms, and must be designed to be both effective and equitable. A piecemeal approach will fail; comprehensive, interconnected reforms are needed to tackle the complex web of injustices that permeate our societies.

One critical area demanding reform is education. The persistent achievement gap between children from different socioeconomic backgrounds reveals a systemic flaw in educational systems worldwide. Many under-resourced schools, particularly those located in marginalized communities, lack the funding, resources, and qualified teachers necessary to provide quality education.

Policy reforms should prioritize equitable funding formulas that distribute resources based on student need, not solely on property taxes or local funding levels. This means investing in infrastructure improvements, providing access to advanced technology, and recruiting and retaining highly qualified educators in underserved communities. Furthermore, curriculum reforms are needed to address systemic biases and ensure that all students have access to a diverse and inclusive education that reflects their backgrounds and experiences. Initiatives promoting early childhood education and after-school programs can also significantly mitigate the effects of socioeconomic inequality on educational outcomes. Investing in mentorship programs and providing scholarships for students from disadvantaged backgrounds are additional critical policy measures to ensure equitable access to higher education opportunities.

The employment landscape is another arena rife with injustice. Wage disparities based on gender, race, and ethnicity remain pervasive, reflecting deep-seated systemic biases in hiring, promotion, and compensation practices. Policy reforms should strengthen equal pay legislation, ensuring that women and minorities receive equal compensation for equal work. Robust enforcement mechanisms are vital, including independent audits and penalties for discriminatory practices. Furthermore, measures to address occupational segregation, where certain professions are disproportionately dominated by specific demographic groups, are essential. This could involve initiatives to encourage women and minorities to enter traditionally male-dominated fields, such as STEM careers, through targeted mentorship programs, apprenticeships, and scholarships. Policies promoting work-life balance, such as paid parental leave and flexible work arrangements, can also help reduce gender inequality in the workplace. Moreover, strengthening anti-discrimination laws and providing robust mechanisms for reporting and addressing workplace harassment are crucial steps in creating more equitable workplaces. Finally, governments should actively promote policies that encourage the creation of high-quality jobs in underserved communities, addressing the historical patterns of economic disenfranchisement that have disproportionately impacted certain groups.

Housing is another fundamental human need often denied to marginalized communities. Systemic racism and discriminatory housing practices have historically resulted in residential segregation and limited access to affordable housing for minorities and low-income individuals. Policy reforms must address these historical injustices through initiatives promoting fair housing practices, combating redlining and other discriminatory lending practices, and investing in the development of affordable housing in underserved communities. Rent control measures and policies to protect tenants from eviction can also safeguard vulnerable populations from homelessness and housing insecurity.

Furthermore, government investment in public housing and subsidized housing programs is essential for ensuring access to safe and decent housing for all. Addressing the lack of housing affordability through a combination of regulatory measures and direct government investment is a crucial step toward greater equity.

The criminal justice system is another area where systemic injustice is starkly apparent. Racial and ethnic disparities in arrests, convictions, and sentencing are well-documented, reflecting inherent biases in policing, prosecution, and judicial processes.

Policy reforms are desperately needed to address these systemic issues. This includes reforming policing practices to reduce racial profiling and police brutality, enhancing police accountability, and investing in community-oriented policing strategies that build trust between law enforcement and the communities they serve.

Moreover, sentencing reforms are decisive to address disparities in prison sentences for similar offenses committed by people of different races and socioeconomic backgrounds. Investing in restorative justice initiatives and expanding access to legal representation for indigent defendants are also vital steps towards creating a fairer and more equitable criminal justice system.

Additionally, reforming parole and probation systems to reduce recidivism and facilitate successful reintegration into society is necessary. The focus must shift from punishment to rehabilitation and addressing the underlying social and economic factors that contribute to criminal behaviour.

Healthcare disparities are a stark reflection of broader societal inequalities. Access to quality healthcare remains a privilege, not a right, for many, particularly for marginalized communities. Policy reforms should prioritize universal healthcare coverage, ensuring that all individuals have access to affordable and quality healthcare services, regardless of their socioeconomic status or insurance coverage.

Investing in preventative care and addressing social determinants of health, such as poverty, food insecurity, and lack of access to safe housing, can also significantly improve health outcomes. Additionally, reforms must tackle the pervasive racial and ethnic disparities in healthcare provision, including implicit biases among healthcare providers and the lack of cultural competency in healthcare settings. Addressing these disparities requires a comprehensive approach involving legislation, education, and increased investment in healthcare infrastructure in underserved communities.

Environmental injustice further exposes the deep-seated inequalities in our societies. Marginalized communities are disproportionately burdened by environmental hazards, such as air and water pollution, toxic waste sites, and climate change impacts. Policy reforms must address these inequalities through stricter environmental regulations, investment in environmental remediation in affected communities, and policies promoting environmental justice and equity. This requires meaningful engagement with affected communities in environmental decision-making and the development of policies that reflect their priorities and needs. Moreover, a transition to a more sustainable and equitable economy is essential, one that minimizes the environmental footprint of industrial activities and prioritizes environmental protection and sustainable development.

Addressing systemic injustice requires a multi-pronged approach encompassing policy reforms, collective action, and individual responsibility. These policy recommendations, while ambitious, represent essential steps toward creating more just and equitable societies. The ultimate goal is to dismantle the structures that perpetuate inequality and build a world where everyone has the opportunity to thrive, regardless of their race, gender, socioeconomic status, or other arbitrary characteristics. The path toward justice is not easy; it demands sustained commitment, political will, and unwavering dedication to building a more inclusive and equitable future for all. The fight for justice is a continuous process of reform, adaptation, and relentless pursuit of a better world. It is only through persistent efforts, encompassing both large-scale systemic changes and small, individual acts of kindness and empathy that we can hope to create a society worthy of the ideals of fairness and equality for all.

Promoting Education and Awareness

Promoting education and awareness is vital in the fight against injustice. It's not enough to simply identify and condemn acts of unfairness; we must cultivate a societal understanding that fosters empathy, critical thinking, and a commitment to dismantling the systems that perpetuate inequality. This requires a fundamental shift in how we approach education, from early childhood through higher learning and beyond, and a broader engagement with information dissemination and media literacy. An educated populace, equipped with the tools to critically analyze information and understand diverse perspectives, is better positioned to identify and challenge injustice in all its forms.

The foundation for combating injustice is laid in early childhood education. Curricula should actively incorporate lessons on diversity, equity, and inclusion, moving beyond tokenistic mentions to a deep engagement with the lived experiences of marginalized groups. Children need to learn about the historical and ongoing struggles for social justice, including the civil rights movement, the fight for women's suffrage, and the ongoing battle for LGBTQ+ rights. This education should not simply be a recitation of facts but should foster critical analysis and encourage children to question power structures and systemic biases. Interactive learning methods, incorporating storytelling, role-playing, and group discussions, can be particularly effective in promoting empathy and understanding.

Furthermore, early exposure to diverse cultures and perspectives through literature, art, and music can broaden children's horizons and challenge preconceived notions. The goal is not just to create awareness but to develop a generation of critical thinkers who actively challenge injustice.

Moving beyond early childhood education, primary and secondary schools must play a crucial role in fostering social justice awareness. The focus should be on equipping students with the tools to analyze social issues critically, recognizing the historical and systemic roots of inequality. Students should learn to identify biases in media representations and develop strategies to counter misinformation. Moreover, the integration of social-emotional learning into the curriculum is essential. This approach emphasizes the development of skills such as empathy, self-awareness, social responsibility, and conflict resolution—all crucial in addressing injustice effectively. Schools should actively create inclusive learning environments where students from diverse backgrounds feel safe, respected, and valued, thereby promoting a culture of empathy and understanding.

Higher education institutions bear a significant responsibility in fostering critical thought and social justice activism. University curricula should incorporate courses that explore the theoretical and practical aspects of social justice, examining the historical context of injustice and its contemporary manifestations. Students should be encouraged to engage in research and fieldwork, allowing them to directly interact with affected communities and gain a firsthand understanding of the challenges they face. Furthermore, universities should provide opportunities for students to participate in community-based projects that address social justice issues, such as mentoring programs, voter registration drives, and advocacy campaigns. This hands-on experience can be invaluable in transforming theoretical understanding into effective action.

Beyond the formal curriculum, universities must create spaces for open dialogue and debate on social justice issues, fostering a campus culture that values critical thinking, dissent, and social responsibility.

However, formal education alone is insufficient. We must also address the pervasive influence of misinformation and biased narratives in the media. Media literacy education is central in combating the spread of false or misleading information and developing critical consumption habits. This involves teaching individuals how to identify bias, evaluate sources, and recognize propaganda techniques. It also requires developing skills in discerning credible information from unreliable sources and understanding the implications of biased reporting on social justice issues. Critically engaging with media, including social media platforms, is essential in combating the perpetuation of harmful stereotypes and misconceptions. The goal is to empower individuals to become informed and discerning consumers of information, capable of critically evaluating narratives surrounding issues of justice.

Beyond formal education and media literacy, the creation of spaces for open and honest dialogue is crucial. Community forums, workshops, and public discussions can provide platforms for individuals to share their experiences, express their perspectives, and engage in constructive conversations about justice. These spaces must be designed to be inclusive and welcoming, ensuring that the voices of marginalized groups are heard and valued.

Facilitated dialogue can encourage empathy and understanding by providing a safe environment for individuals to confront their biases and preconceptions. These conversations should not shy away from difficult topics but should instead strive for meaningful engagement with complex social issues.

The role of art and culture in promoting empathy and understanding should not be underestimated. Art, in all its forms, has the power to communicate complex ideas and emotions in a way that transcends language barriers. Stories, songs, films, and visual art can effectively convey the experiences of marginalized groups, fostering empathy and promoting understanding among wider audiences. Supporting and promoting artists who address social justice themes can be a powerful way to encourage dialogue and raise awareness. Furthermore, the integration of art and culture into education and community initiatives can be a particularly effective means of promoting social justice awareness and action.

Combating injustice requires a long-term commitment to education and awareness-building that spans all levels of society. It requires transforming our educational systems, fostering media literacy, promoting open dialogue, and leveraging the power of art and culture to cultivate empathy and understanding. By investing in these initiatives, we lay the groundwork for a more just and equitable future. The challenge is not just to educate individuals but to reshape the societal consciousness, fostering a widespread commitment to challenging and dismantling the structures that perpetuate inequality. This is not a task that can be accomplished overnight; it requires sustained efforts, ongoing dialogue, and a steadfast dedication to creating a world where everyone has the opportunity to thrive, regardless of their background or circumstances. The fight for justice is a collective endeavor, requiring the active participation of individuals, communities, and institutions. Only through a concerted and sustained commitment to education, awareness, and action can we hope to achieve a truly equitable and just society.

Building a Just Future for a More Equitable World

Building a just future necessitates a fundamental shift in our collective mindset, moving beyond simply reacting to injustices to proactively building systems and structures that prioritize equity and fairness. This requires a multi-pronged approach, engaging individuals, communities, governments, and international organizations in a sustained and collaborative effort.

One key element is the reformation of the legal and political systems. Laws must be reviewed and reformed to eliminate discriminatory practices and ensure equal access to justice for all. This includes addressing biases in the criminal justice system, such as racial profiling and wrongful convictions, and ensuring fair representation for marginalized communities in legal proceedings. Political systems must be made more transparent and accountable, reducing the influence of corruption and promoting participatory democracy. This demands not only legal reforms but also a cultural shift towards greater transparency and accountability in governance.

Independent oversight bodies, strengthened judicial systems, and robust mechanisms for citizen engagement are crucial in building a truly just political landscape. Furthermore, international cooperation is vital in addressing transnational injustices, such as human trafficking, arms trade, and environmental degradation that transcend national borders.

International legal frameworks must be strengthened and enforcement mechanisms improved to hold perpetrators accountable and prevent future abuses. Beyond legal and political reforms, economic justice is fundamental.

Addressing systemic economic inequality requires a multifaceted approach that includes fair wages, accessible healthcare, affordable housing, and quality education for all. This necessitates policies that redistribute wealth and resources more equitably, empowering marginalized communities and providing opportunities for social mobility. Progressive taxation, robust social safety nets, and investments in public goods and services are vital in creating a more just and equitable economic system. Furthermore, the promotion of ethical business practices, including fair labor standards, environmental sustainability, and responsible sourcing, is crucial in ensuring that economic development does not come at the expense of social justice. Supporting worker cooperatives, social enterprises, and other alternative economic models that prioritize social good over profit maximization can further contribute to building a more equitable economy.

Environmental justice is intrinsically linked to social justice. The disproportionate impact of environmental degradation on vulnerable communities underscores the need for equitable environmental policies and practices. This requires addressing issues like pollution, access to clean water and sanitation, and the impact of climate change on marginalized communities. Investing in renewable energy sources, promoting sustainable agriculture, and protecting biodiversity are not only crucial for environmental sustainability but also for ensuring environmental justice for all.

Moreover, incorporating the perspectives and knowledge of indigenous and local communities in environmental decision-making is essential for achieving truly equitable and sustainable outcomes. International cooperation is vital in addressing global environmental challenges, such as climate change, which disproportionately affects vulnerable nations and populations.

Healthcare justice demands that everyone has access to quality healthcare, regardless of their socioeconomic status, race, ethnicity, or geographic location. This requires addressing the systemic barriers to healthcare access, including affordability, geographical limitations, and discrimination. Investing in public health infrastructure, expanding access to affordable healthcare insurance, and addressing healthcare disparities are essential in ensuring healthcare justice for all. Furthermore, promoting preventative healthcare, addressing social determinants of health, and fostering a culturally competent healthcare system are crucial in improving health outcomes for all populations. Universal health coverage, as advocated by international organizations like the World Health Organization, is a key goal in achieving healthcare justice globally.

The fight against religious persecution demands a recognition of the fundamental human right to freedom of religion or belief. This requires legal protections against discrimination and violence based on religious affiliation, ensuring that individuals can practice their faith freely without fear of reprisal. Addressing religious intolerance necessitates fostering mutual respect and understanding between different religious communities, promoting interfaith dialogue, and countering hate speech and discrimination. International cooperation is vital in protecting religious minorities and addressing religious persecution globally. This includes working with governments and civil society organizations to promote religious freedom and hold perpetrators of religious persecution accountable.

Combating injustice is not a solely governmental or institutional responsibility; it necessitates a broad, collective effort. This necessitates the active participation of civil society organizations, community groups, faith-based organizations, and individuals in advocating for social justice and holding those in power accountable. Engaging in peaceful protests, advocating for policy change, and supporting organizations working to advance social justice are all critical in achieving a more equitable world. Furthermore, promoting dialogue and understanding across different groups and communities is essential in building bridges and fostering collaboration towards a common goal.

Building a just future requires hope, resilience, and a commitment to ongoing action. While the challenges are significant, the potential for progress is immense. By working together, acknowledging past injustices, and actively building a more just and equitable world, we can create a society where everyone has the opportunity to thrive. This is not a destination, but a journey that requires continuous engagement, adaptation, and a willingness to learn and grow. The path to justice is paved with the collective efforts of individuals and organizations committed to creating a more just and equitable future for all. This requires a continued commitment to education, awareness, advocacy, and collaborative action, always striving for a world where human dignity and rights are respected and upheld. The fight for a just world is ongoing, but with sustained effort and collaboration, a more equitable and hopeful future is within our reach. The journey towards justice is a continuous process of learning, adapting, and evolving, and requires sustained engagement and collaboration.

COMMON GOOD

Concept

The vibrant political ideology of ancient Greece, specifically in Athens during the 6th to 4th centuries BC, was driven by the convergence of philosophy, science, and culture towards a singular focus - politics. Being a part of the polis was not only essential for the Greek citizen of classical antiquity, but it also granted them a life of honour and dignity. It went beyond just residing in an urban centre; it meant being an integral member of a well-organized political and social unit, with defined territorial boundaries. The Greek man found his true sense of self and individuality in the plural existence of the "polis", a crucial foundation for his personal and political identity, setting him apart from those who lacked this status. The freedom to engage in political action, as emphasized by Hannah Arendt, was considered a fundamental requirement for leading a life of dignity and humanity. Among all human activities that could guarantee such a life, the commitment to the affairs of the polis held a position of utmost significance.

The Athenian democracy, for two centuries, was a crucial period in the history of political thought. It was during this time that the concept of the polis, or city-state, became central to the idea of freedom and citizenship for the Greek people. The Greek citizen's life was divided into two distinct spheres: the private and the public.

The private sphere encompassed matters related to property, marriage, and family, while the public sphere involved participation in political debates and decision-making. The public sphere was seen as the realm where the Greek citizen could fully exercise their virtues of political coexistence and demonstrate their effectiveness as a member of the polis. This duality of existence, with both individual and communal dimensions, was essential to the Greek understanding of a dignified life. Furthermore, the Athenian democracy was not just a political system but a way of life. The citizens were expected to actively participate in the governance of the polis, making political action a central aspect of their lives. This emphasis on political engagement was based on the belief that it was through the collective effort of citizens that the polis could thrive and ensure a dignified life for all its members. Therefore, for the Greek people, the commitment to the affairs of the polis was not just a duty but a way of fulfilling their human potential and leading a life of true freedom and dignity.

The "Common Good" for Platonic thought was built upon the pillars of education, morality, and politics, making it the foundation for the ideal City. It was believed that a city governed by philosophers, specifically a philosopher- king, would create a hierarchy of homogeneous classes. This hierarchy would consist of heads of government, auxiliaries or warriors, and craftsmen or peasants. Thus, creating social stability and ensuring a dignified life for all its members. Education, morality, and politics were not just mere duties for the Greek people, but rather a way of fulfilling their human potential and leading a life of true freedom and dignity. Justice, according to Plato, was the idea that required everyone to respect the social and political hierarchy. This concept would result in social stability as individuals would understand their personal and selfish renunciations imposed by reason. By controlling their individual passions in favour of the balance of the social totality, the polis could thrive and ensure a dignified life for all its members. This was seen as the ultimate goal for the Greek people, who were committed to the affairs of the polis.

The concept of "good" as an "Idea" is a central theme in Plato's book "Republic". It is seen as the ultimate goal and guiding principle for the Greek people, who were deeply committed to the affairs of the polis. The philosopher presents the "Idea of the good" as the absolute norm that serves as the basis for philosophy, which is seen as the supreme "art of measurement". This concept is present throughout Platonic thought, from the very beginning until the end. Plato uses a metaphor of light and the sun to explain the function of the "Idea of the good". Just as light reveals things in the physical world, the good reveals truth and knowledge in the intelligible world. It is the perfect ideal form that grants truth to known things and the power to know them. In this way, the good is seen as the foundation for justice, moderation, courage, and wisdom. However, the philosopher argues that the most important thing to be understood is the "Idea of good" itself, as it is through reference to it that other virtues become truly useful and beneficial.

The philosopher's emphasis on the "Idea of good" reflects the belief that by controlling their individual passions and striving for balance in society, the polis could thrive and ensure a dignified life for all its members. This was seen as the ultimate goal for the Greek people, who were deeply invested in the well-being of their city-state. The "Idea of good" serves as a guiding light, providing a moral compass for individuals and society as a whole. It is the ultimate standard of truth and knowledge, and its pursuit is seen as the key to a just and virtuous life.

This concept is deeply rooted in Platonic philosophy, where the "common good" is believed to be the highest good for every human being. However, this notion is not limited to personal gain, as it is also intertwined with the greater good of the community. The "common good" is not just a mere concept, but rather a metaphysical foundation of the political dimension of human reality. It is the driving force behind the creation of political systems and the need for individuals to come together and form a society. This is due to the fact that humans have needs that they cannot fulfil on their own, and thus, require the collective effort of a community. The pursuit of the "Idea of good" is therefore not only an individual endeavour but also a collective responsibility towards the greater good of society. In integration with the highest possible and real good of all others, politics arises from the need for each human individual to strive for goods that cannot be attained individually. This highlights the importance of the "common good" in shaping the political landscape of a society. It serves as a moral compass, guiding individuals towards a just and virtuous life, while also promoting the well-being of the community as a whole.

The notion of the common good based on living together in the polis is recovered and re-dimensioned by Aristotle (384 - 322 BC). In the first paragraph of Book One of Politics, the philosopher argues that "every city is a kind of association, and that every association is formed with some good in mind; because man only works for what he has in mind", and that all "societies, therefore, aim at some good - especially the most important of them, since it aims at a greater good, involving all the others: the city or political society"

Aristotle, the celebrated Greek philosopher, held a distinct viewpoint on the concepts of a "fulfilling life" and "noble deeds" that deviated from the popular beliefs of his era. He saw the purpose of a political community as more than just a place for coexistence - it was a platform for the fostering of virtues and the advancement of the collective welfare. According to Aristotle, the "common good" was not tied to material possessions or individual desires, but rather to the moral character and actions of the community as a whole.

According to Aristotelian theory, there is a clear distinction between authentic or constitutional governments and degenerate or despotic ones. This distinction is based on the concept of the "common good", which is a fundamental principle shared by constitutional governments but foreign to despotic governments, as they prioritize the well-being of the ruling class. However, Aristotle's understanding of the common good cannot be reduced to an idealistic or universal model that is disconnected from reality. It is not a timeless and metaphysical principle, but rather a complex and multi-faceted concept that is as diverse and elusive as the category of "being" and its endless implications. In fact, the philosopher argued that the very nature of "good" is indeterminate, and therefore cannot be confined to a single definition. Similarly, just as there can be no single scientific perspective for understanding all objects that are derived from a particular idea, there can also be no single science for comprehending the various forms of good that exist in the world.

In the work of Cicero (106 - 43 BC), the concept of common utility (utilitas communis) is introduced. Cicero argues that the reason for organizing men into society is not due to their weakness, but rather their innate instinct for sociability. He explains that the human species is not meant to live in isolation and wander, but rather to seek common support even in times of abundance. Cicero goes on to say that the Republic should be a collective of people, not just any group of men, but a gathering that is founded on legal consent and common utility. This means that the people must come together and agree on a set of laws and principles that benefit the common good. By doing so, they create a sense of unity and cooperation, rather than competition and conflict. This idea of common utility is important because it highlights the idea that humans are inherently social beings who thrive in communities. It also emphasizes the importance of working together for the greater good, rather than pursuing individual interests. Cicero's perspective challenges the notion that self-interest is the driving force of human behavior, instead suggesting that a sense of communal benefit is what truly motivates us.

The concept of the "common good" in Thomas Aquinos' political theory is fundamental to understanding his perspective on communal living. His belief in the divine origin of power, coupled with its realization through human nature, highlights the importance of individuals working together for the solidification of society. This idea of communal benefit is a central theme in Aquinos' theory, and it challenges the traditional belief that self-interest drives human behaviour. Aquinos' emphasis on the common good also suggests that individuals are not solely motivated by their own desires, but rather by a sense of duty to their community. This goes against the individualistic mindset that is often associated with human nature. By prioritizing the well-being of the community over individual interests, Aquinos promotes a more balanced and harmonious society. Furthermore, Aquinos' theory of the common good highlights the interconnectedness of individuals within a community. He believed that each person has a role to play in achieving the common good, and that no one can truly flourish without the support and cooperation of others. This idea further reinforces the notion that humans are social beings who are meant to live in communities, and that working together for the greater good is essential for a prosperous and fulfilling life.

Machiavelli's "realism" states that people are inherently selfish and their actions are driven by self-interest. He believed that political leaders should be pragmatic and focused on the preservation of their power and the state's interests. This can be seen in his book "The Prince", where he argues that leaders should not be bound by moral principles, but rather should do whatever is necessary to maintain their power. Furthermore, Machiavelli's ideas suggest that human nature is inherently flawed and that people are motivated by their own self-interest. He believed that individuals are unable to thrive without the support and cooperation of others, and that this support is necessary for the greater good of society. This highlights the importance of community and working together for the better of all. It can be argued that Machiavelli's ideas have had a lasting impact on political philosophy, as they challenge traditional notions of morality and divine providence. His emphasis on pragmatism and the pursuit of self-interest has influenced modern political thinking and continues to shape the way leaders govern and make decisions. Ultimately, Machiavelli's doctrine highlights the complex and often conflicting dynamics of human nature and the role it plays in shaping our political systems.

Rousseau's belief that man joins society to better face the forces of nature highlights the inherent need for cooperation and interdependence within human society. This concept of socialization, while necessary for survival, also creates a delicate balance between individual freedom and collective responsibility. The two "ideal models" of contract that arise from this process serve as a warning against the pitfalls of societal formation. An iniquitous contract, one that deprives individuals of their freedom and equality, ultimately results in an unjust society. On the other hand, a legitimate contract, one that prioritizes the natural foundations of the individual and fosters egalitarianism and the common good, has the potential to create a just and harmonious society.

Rousseau's emphasis on the social contract and the importance of balancing individual liberties with societal responsibilities continues to be a relevant and influential concept in modern political thinking. It highlights the complexities of human nature and the constant struggle to find a balance between self-interest and the greater good. Ultimately, Rousseau's ideas serve as a reminder of the ever-evolving nature of society and the need for constant reflection and adaptation in the pursuit of a just and equitable world.

The "particular will" refers to the individual self-interests that drive human behaviour. Rousseau recognized that this innate desire for self-preservation and personal gain could lead to conflict and inequality within society. However, he also believed in the potential for humans to overcome these selfish impulses and work towards the common good. This is where the concept of the general will comes into play.

The "corporate will" refers to the interests of specific groups within society, such as the wealthy or the ruling class. These groups may act in their own self-interest, but Rousseau argued that their actions should be aligned with the general will in order to maintain social harmony. This highlights the delicate balance between individual and collective interests that Rousseau sought to address in his theory.

Lastly, the "will of all" includes the opinions and desires of all individuals within society. Rousseau believed that the general will should reflect the collective interests and values of the majority, rather than catering to the desires of a select few. This emphasis on the greater good over individual gain serves as a reminder of the importance of cooperation and compromise in achieving a just and equitable society.

The traditional idea of public policy as a technical issue ignores the complex and dynamic nature of societal problems. By solely relying on scientific research to provide solutions, this linear approach neglects the need for collaboration between different disciplines and the importance of ethical considerations. As society becomes more interconnected and interdependent, it is increasingly clear that a holistic and multi-faceted approach is necessary for progress. This requires not only the systematic application of knowledge but also a high sense of mission to contribute to the common good and an understanding of the broader ethical implications of policy decisions. Furthermore, the traditional conception of the relationship between science and public policy fails to acknowledge the role of individual virtues and good governance in achieving a better society. A focus on technical solutions and scientific measurements can overlook the human aspect of policy-making and the importance of values such as empathy, compassion, and fairness. Without these virtues, policies may not truly serve the common good and could even perpetuate inequality and injustice. Additionally, good governance, which includes transparency, accountability, and citizen participation, is crucial for ensuring that policies are effective and ethical. Thus, a more comprehensive approach that incorporates both scientific knowledge and ethical considerations is necessary for creating a better society for all.

The post-World War II period marked a significant shift in economic policies, with the Keynesian model of public intervention gaining prominence. This approach was characterized by a strong state intervention, a centralized and sectorized hierarchy of policies, and a focus on income redistribution for economic stability. Public spending was seen as a decisive element in this process, and public policies were expected to not only fulfil welfare functions but also serve economic policy objectives. During this period, the Keynesian state played a crucial role in the production of goods and services. In addition to the already existing public services such as roads, ports, education, and security, the state began to provide even more generously.

Furthermore, new areas of public provision were established, including health, housing, higher education, and social services. This expansion of public services was accompanied by a system of benefit payments, which covered citizens of all ages and ensured a strong social contract in a time of economic prosperity.

However, despite its successes, the Keynesian model also had its flaws. The centralized and top-down approach often led to unequal distribution of resources and perpetuated social inequalities. In addition, the focus on economic growth and stability often came at the expense of ethical considerations and citizen participation. Therefore, a more comprehensive approach that incorporates both scientific knowledge and ethical considerations is needed to create a better society for all. Good governance, which includes transparency, accountability, and citizen participation, must be prioritized in order to ensure that policies are effective and just.

Over the years, the concept of a more liberalized approach to governance has gained momentum, with the belief that private management is more efficient and effective than government control. This led to the idea that the state should take a backseat in the provision of goods and services, and instead focus on regulating and stimulating private initiatives. This shift in ideology had a profound impact on public policy formulations across Europe, as governments began to prioritize making their administrations more flexible and reducing the role of the state.

One of the ways this was achieved was through privatization of services, with the assumption that the state was not equipped to effectively manage them. This was followed by subcontracting of certain strategic functions, under the belief that they could not be privatized but could be delegated to external parties. In addition, various partnerships were formed between public and private entities, leading to a mix of management styles.

These changes were seen as a way to streamline the government and improve efficiency, but they also had ethical implications and raised concerns about citizen participation in decision-making processes. As a result, there is a growing understanding that a more comprehensive approach is needed to create a better society for all. This includes not only scientific knowledge, but also ethical considerations and good governance practices. Transparency, accountability, and citizen participation have become key priorities in ensuring that policies are both effective and just. Without these principles in place, the potential for abuse of power and lack of consideration for societal needs increases. Therefore, it is crucial to strike a balance between private management and good governance in order to promote a fair and equitable society.

The importance of the common good is often overlooked in today's society. With the emphasis on individualism and self-gain, the idea of distributing goods and resources for the benefit of everyone has been forgotten. However, it is essential to remember that a society can only thrive when its members work together towards the common good. This means that certain resources and benefits should be shared and distributed in a way that benefits everyone, rather than just a select few. One of the key aspects of the common good is fairness. It is essential for resources to be allocated in a way that ensures fairness for all individuals. This ensures that everyone has an equal opportunity to succeed and live a good life. When resources are distributed unfairly, it can lead to inequality, which can have far-reaching consequences on society as a whole.

The common good also promotes the idea of solidarity, where individuals work together for the greater good, rather than just for their own personal gain. This creates a sense of community and fosters a more harmonious and cohesive society. In order to achieve the common good, it is important for individuals to look beyond their own interests and think about the well-being of others. This requires a collective effort and a willingness to sacrifice personal gains for the greater good. It also means that those in positions of power and influence have a responsibility to make decisions that benefit society as a whole, rather than just themselves. When everyone works towards the common good, it creates a more equitable and just society, where all individuals have the opportunity to thrive and prosper.

In order to create a fair and just society, it is important for those in positions of power and influence to prioritize the common good rather than their own personal interests. This includes following the principle of equality, which calls for the equal distribution of resources in order to promote cooperation and harmony. By prioritizing this principle, can be created a more equitable society where all individuals have the opportunity to thrive and succeed. However, it is also important to recognize that different social contexts may require different principles of fairness in order to achieve the common good.

In situations where cooperation and harmony are not the primary goals, the principle of equity may be more appropriate. This principle calls for resources to be distributed in a way that takes into account individual needs and circumstances. By recognizing and applying the appropriate principles of fairness in different social contexts, we can ensure that decisions are made for the betterment of society as a whole. Ultimately, promoting distributive justice requires a deep understanding of the various principles of fairness and how they apply to different social contexts.

By prioritizing the common good and being mindful of the principles of equality and equity, those in positions of power and influence can work towards creating a more just and equitable society for all individuals. This requires a strong sense of responsibility towards the well-being of society and a commitment to making decisions that benefit the greater good.

The principle of equality, which is rooted in the belief that all individuals should have the same opportunities and rights, is a crucial aspect of creating a just and equitable society. However, it is important to recognize that equality does not necessarily mean treating everyone exactly the same. In fact, the principle of equity recognizes that different individuals may require different resources in order to achieve equal outcomes. This can be seen in the idea that individuals should receive resources in proportion to their relative contributions, which is known as distributive justice. By taking into account the principle of equity in addition to equality, those in positions of power and influence can work towards creating a more just and equitable society. This requires a deep sense of responsibility towards the well-being of society, as well as a commitment to making decisions that benefit the greater good. This means considering the needs of marginalized and underprivileged communities, and actively working towards addressing systemic inequalities. Ultimately, by understanding and implementing both principles of equality and equity, can be created a society where all individuals have equal opportunities and are able to thrive.

Expanding on the concept of equity and its role in creating a just society, it is important to recognize that true equity goes beyond simply treating everyone the same. It involves actively addressing and rectifying systemic inequalities that have historically disadvantaged marginalized and underprivileged communities. This includes providing resources and opportunities to these communities in order to level the playing field and create equal access to success.

However, the idea of meritocracy, where individuals are rewarded based on their talents and efforts can often be seen as conflicting with the principle of equity. This is because meritocracy assumes that everyone has equal opportunities to succeed, which is not always the case. In order for meritocracy to truly work, there must be a level playing field for all individuals, regardless of their background or circumstances. Thus, the concept of equity serves as a necessary foundation for a functioning meritocracy. Without addressing systemic inequalities and actively working towards creating equal opportunities for all, meritocracy cannot truly exist.

It is only by understanding and implementing both principles of equality and equity that we can create a society where all individuals have equal chances to thrive.

The significance of the collective well-being is often disregarded in modern times. However, equity plays a vital role in attaining the common good. Not only is fairness a moral principle, but it is also a fundamental element in establishing a fair society.

In his book "A Theory of Justice," John Rawls presents the concept of justice as fairness, which highlights equity as a cornerstone. According to Rawls, fairness entails that every individual should have equal personal rights and liberties, regardless of their social position or background. Furthermore, it also demands equal and just opportunities for all individuals, regardless of their circumstances. Rawls believed that efforts to reduce economic disparities should aim to maximize the benefits for the most disadvantaged individuals.

This means that any economic policies or measures should prioritize helping those who are the least privileged in society. By doing so, a just and equitable society can be created, where everyone has an equal opportunity for success and prosperity. Therefore, the concept of fairness is crucial in promoting the common good and establishing a more just society for all individuals.

Utilitarianism is a doctrine that posits that actions are deemed right and justifiable if they are beneficial and serve the interests of the majority. This is because such actions promote happiness, and the well-being of the greatest number of people should be the guiding principle for societal conduct and policies. On the other hand, actions that diminish the overall welfare of society are considered bad.

In his 1789 publication, "An Introduction to the Principles of Morals and Legislation," Jeremy Bentham, an English philosopher, jurist, and social reformer, argues that the utilitarian approach to distributive justice focuses on the outcomes of social actions, without considering the means used to achieve them. Although the core concept of utilitarianism may seem straightforward, there is great debate surrounding the definition and measurement of "welfare". He initially defined welfare through the hedonistic calculus, a method for calculating the level of pleasure an action is likely to induce. As a moralist, Bentham believed it was possible to quantify units of pleasure and pain for all those affected by a particular action, and use this balance to determine its overall potential for good or evil.

Egalitarianism, a moral ideology, is founded on the belief that all individuals should be treated with the same level of respect and fairness, regardless of their individual differences. This principle demands that every person has an equal right to opportunities and resources, regardless of their race, gender, religion or economic status.

This philosophy is of extreme importance in shaping economic and political systems, as it emphasizes the importance of equality and fairness in ensuring the well-being of all individuals. One of the primary concerns of egalitarianism is addressing income inequality and the distribution of wealth. This means that individuals with varying occupations should receive equal compensation for their work. This is a crucial step towards achieving egalitarianism, as it promotes equal treatment and opportunities for all individuals.

Ultimately, egalitarianism is not just about achieving equality as an end result, but also about the processes and policies that lead to it. The ultimate goal of this ideology is to create a community where everyone is treated as equals and has an equal standing in relation to others. It serves as a guiding principle in creating a fair and just society where every individual has the opportunity to thrive and succeed.

The ideology of distributive justice strives to create a society where all individuals are treated equally and have equal opportunities to succeed. This is achieved through fair and just government programs that distribute basic benefits to those who are unable to provide for themselves. These programs are designed to ensure that every member of society has the necessary resources to meet their basic human needs and fulfil their desires.

The concept of distributive justice is constantly evolving, as it is shaped by the political processes of society. This means that the frameworks and systems in place to achieve distributive justice may differ across different societies and may also change over time within a society. The success of these frameworks is essential as they directly impact the lives of individuals through the distribution of benefits and burdens, such as taxation. Therefore, debates over which distributions are morally just and preferable are at the core of the concept of distributive justice.

Ultimately, the goal of distributive justice is to create a community where every individual has the opportunity to thrive and succeed. It serves as a guiding principle in building a fair and just society where no one is left behind and everyone has equal standing in relation to others. By providing essential resources and addressing inequalities, distributive justice aims to create a more equitable and harmonious world for all.

Governance and the Rule of Law

Governance and the rule of law are not mere buzzwords, but rather the backbone of a functioning society. The symbiotic relationship between the government and its citizens is one of mutual responsibility and trust. The government is tasked with creating and enforcing laws that promote fairness and equality, while citizens must adhere to these laws and hold their leaders accountable for any transgressions. However, this relationship is not always harmonious, and it is during such times that the principles of governance and the rule of law are put to the test.

The concept of justice and equality is at the heart of governance and the rule of law. These principles serve as a safeguard against abuse of power and discrimination. They ensure that every member of society is treated with respect and dignity, regardless of their social status or background. This creates a sense of stability and security within a society, as every individual knows that they are protected by the law. Without these principles, a society can quickly spiral into chaos and oppression, leaving its citizens vulnerable and marginalized.

Governance and the rule of law are not just abstract concepts, but rather the foundation of a well-functioning society. They promote accountability, fairness, and equality, and serve as a safeguard against abuse of power. Both the government and its citizens have a vital role to play in upholding these principles, and only when they work together can a society truly thrive. It is the responsibility of every individual to understand and uphold the principles of governance and the rule of law, for the better of society as a whole.

Government institutions are a fundamental component of any society, working diligently to uphold the principles of governance and the rule of law. They are an integral part of the system, ensuring that laws are implemented fairly and that the rights of individuals are protected. Through their collective efforts, they play a vital role in maintaining societal order and stability. These institutions work in conjunction with one another, each having its own unique responsibilities and duties.

* The executive branch is responsible for enforcing laws and managing the day-to-day operations of the government.

* The legislative branch is responsible for creating laws and policies that guide the actions of the government.

* The judicial branch, on the other hand, is responsible for interpreting and upholding the laws of the land.

Together, these institutions form the backbone of society, providing a framework for a just and equitable society to thrive. Effective governance requires the active participation of every individual in upholding these principles and ensuring the success of these institutions.

It is the responsibility of every citizen to understand and support these institutions, as they are vital to the prosperity of society as a whole. By working together, government institutions and individuals can create a strong and prosperous society, where the rule of law is upheld and the rights of all are protected. Only through this collective effort can a society truly thrive and reach its full potential.

Public Administration is a vital aspect of any government, as it is responsible for the implementation of policies and programs that aim to improve the overall wellbeing of society. Through this system, governments can ensure that public services are delivered efficiently and effectively to the people, ensuring that their needs are met and their rights are protected.

This, in turn, leads to the prosperity of society as a whole. The role of public administration extends beyond just the execution and delivery of public services. It also involves the management of resources, both human and financial, to ensure that they are utilized in the most effective way possible. This requires collaboration and coordination between government institutions and individuals, as well as a strong understanding of the needs and priorities of the community.

With the joint effort of all stakeholders, public administration can create a strong and prosperous society where the rule of law is upheld and the rights of all are protected. In today's world, the importance of public administration cannot be overstated. It plays a central role in shaping the future of a nation, as well as the lives of its citizens.

By working together and utilizing the principles of good governance, public administration can help societies reach their full potential and succeed. It is a constantly evolving field, adapting to the changing needs of society and finding innovative solutions to complex problems. With the right leadership, public administration can open the way for a brighter and more prosperous future for all.

Principles of Good Governance are essential in public administration. They provide a framework for effective decision-making and ensure transparency and accountability. Good governance is based on principles such as fairness, equity, and responsiveness, which help societies reach their full potential and succeed. These principles guide administrators in making decisions that benefit the greater good and promote social and economic development.

Public administration is an ever-evolving field, constantly adapting to the changing needs of society. As such, the principles of good governance also evolve to address new challenges and find innovative solutions to complex problems. With the right leadership and a commitment to these principles, public administration can open the way for a brighter and more prosperous future for all. Good governance ensures that public resources are used efficiently and effectively, fostering trust and confidence in government institutions.

The principle of transparency in public administration is vital for building trust and confidence in government institutions. By promoting openness and accessibility, citizens can have a better understanding of how their tax money is being used and hold their leaders accountable. This is especially important in today's digital age, where information can easily be shared and accessed by the public.

Through transparency, citizens can have a clearer picture of how their government operates and be more engaged in the decision-making process. An important aspect of good governance is inclusivity. This means ensuring that all segments of society are represented and have a voice in the decision-making process. By including diverse perspectives, public administration can find innovative solutions to complex problems that may have been overlooked otherwise. Inclusivity also promotes equity and fairness, creating a more inclusive and just society. With the right leadership and commitment to these principles, public administration can pave the way for a brighter and more prosperous future for all.

Accountability is a crucial aspect of public administration that ensures that individuals and institutions are held responsible for their actions and decisions. This not only promotes transparency and integrity but also helps in finding innovative solutions to complex problems. With accountability, there is a greater focus on addressing issues and rectifying mistakes, rather than simply passing blame. It creates a culture of learning and improvement, leading to more effective and efficient public administration.

Inclusivity is another essential principle that can greatly enhance public administration. By involving diverse perspectives and voices, inclusivity can help in identifying problems and finding solutions that may have been overlooked otherwise. It also promotes equity and fairness, creating a more inclusive and just society. Inclusivity also helps in building trust and increasing public participation, which is crucial for the success of any administration.

The key components of a successful endeavour are effectiveness and efficiency. These two elements are vital for making progress towards a goal in a timely and resource-efficient manner. Effectiveness refers to the ability to attain desired outcomes, while efficiency focuses on achieving those outcomes with the optimal use of resources. Both are equally essential for the successful completion of any task or project.

To be effective and efficient, one must have a thorough understanding of the desired outcomes and the necessary steps to reach them. This requires meticulous planning and attention to detail. Without a well-crafted plan, even the most skilled individual may face challenges in achieving their desired outcomes efficiently. Hence, it is critical to invest time and effort in creating a solid plan before embarking on any endeavor. When one can achieve their desired outcomes in a timely and resource-efficient manner, it not only brings a sense of accomplishment but also saves valuable time and resources. This is particularly significant in a business setting where time and resources are often limited. By striving for both effectiveness and efficiency, businesses can enhance their productivity and ultimately, their success. Therefore, it is crucial to prioritize effectiveness and efficiency in all aspects of life to achieve desired outcomes and make the most of available resources.

Democratic governance is a form of government that places great importance on involving all individuals in the decision-making process. Central to this concept is representation, which not only ensures that diverse viewpoints are heard, but also taken into account when making crucial choices. This means that individuals from different backgrounds, regardless of race, gender, socioeconomic status, or other factors, have the opportunity to contribute to the governance of their country.

Through representation, democratic governance strives to create a society that is fair and just, where the opinions and needs of all are valued. This not only fosters a sense of inclusivity and belonging, but also leads to more effective and well-rounded decision-making.

By considering a variety of perspectives, policies and laws are more likely to reflect the needs and values of the entire population. Additionally, representation serves as a key tool in promoting social equality and justice. By granting a platform for underrepresented groups to voice their concerns and ideas, democratic governance works towards addressing systemic inequalities and discrimination. It also encourages the engagement of marginalized communities in the political process, empowering them to shape their own future. In essence, representation is a fundamental aspect of democratic governance, promoting fairness, inclusivity, and social progress.

Instead of centralizing decision-making power, local governance involves delegating authority to local governments and communities. This empowers them to make decisions that align with their unique values and preferences, resulting in more efficient and effective decision-making. Compared to centralized approaches, local governance is often preferred due to the intimate understanding local entities have of their community's challenges and concerns. By actively involving them in the decision-making process, decisions are more likely to meet the specific needs of the community. Additionally, the concept of local governance promotes a sense of ownership and collaboration within the community, leading to better outcomes and a stronger sense of community. Ultimately, local governance is a crucial tool in promoting inclusive and impactful decision-making at the community level.

When it comes to decision-making, it is imperative that they are made at the most suitable level. This not only guarantees effectiveness, but it also fosters a more receptive atmosphere. For example, if decisions are made at the upper echelons of an organization, the implementation and adaptation process may be prolonged. However, when decisions are made at the lowest feasible level, they can be executed with greater speed and efficacy, thereby streamlining the entire process. Moreover, when decisions are made at the lowest level, it allows for a wider range of inputs and perspectives to be considered. This not only cultivates inclusivity and teamwork, but it also results in superior decision-making. When multiple viewpoints are taken into account, the resulting decision is often more comprehensive and successful. This also open the way for a more responsive environment, as diverse individuals may offer unique insights and solutions to problems. Ultimately, ensuring that decisions are made at the lowest possible level is important in establishing a thriving and efficient organization. It facilitates prompt and efficient decision-making, promotes inclusivity and teamwork, and leads to exceptional outcomes. By adopting this approach, organizations can create a more dynamic and responsive environment, which can fuel continuous growth and success.

Ensuring high ethical standards should be a top priority for public institutions in their efforts to prevent and combat corrupt practices. To achieve this, it is essential to implement effective policies and mechanisms that provide a framework for identifying and addressing corruption. These measures should be established to guarantee that the public sector operates with integrity, accountability, and transparency.

One vital policy that can be adopted is the establishment of an independent anti-corruption agency, equipped with the necessary resources and authority to investigate and prosecute corruption cases. Additionally, clear guidelines and procedures must be in place for reporting and handling corrupt activities, fostering a culture of openness and responsibility within public institutions.

Regular audits and reviews of public institutions are also vital mechanisms that can be employed to identify and address potential areas of corruption, enabling prompt corrective action.

Strict penalties and consequences for individuals found guilty of corrupt practices are essential to serve as a deterrent and send a strong message that corruption will not be tolerated in public institutions. By implementing these robust policies and mechanisms, we can strive towards a public sector that upholds the highest ethical standards and is worthy of public trust.

Building a successful society relies on ethical conduct in governance, which serves as its foundation. It is crucial to cultivate a culture of honesty and moral principles in all aspects of life. This begins with the leaders and individuals in positions of power serving as models for others to emulate. When leaders are transparent and sincere, it sets the tone for the rest of society to follow suit. This leads to a more dependable and trustworthy community where individuals can rely on one another.

Educating individuals on the significance of ethical behavior is vital in promoting a culture of integrity. This can be achieved through various methods, such as workshops, training programs, and incorporating it into the school curriculum. When individuals are aware of the impact of their actions and the importance of ethical behavior, they are more likely to uphold these values in their daily lives. This not only benefits the individual but also contributes positively to society as a whole.

However, educating individuals alone is not enough. It is equally important to establish proper checks and balances to ensure ethical conduct is practiced. This can include an independent body overseeing the actions of individuals in positions of power, as well as implementing strict consequences for those who engage in unethical behavior. By establishing a system that promotes and rewards integrity, we can create a society where ethical behavior is the norm, rather than the exception.

In the modern world we live in, clashes and disagreements are an inevitable aspect of life. However, what truly matters is our ability to handle these conflicts. It is not about evading them, but instead, finding peaceful solutions through negotiation. The development of effective methods for peaceful conflict resolution and negotiation is a crucial step towards achieving a more harmonious society. Resolving conflicts in a peaceful manner involves seeking common ground and comprehending both sides of the argument. It demands patience, empathy, and proficient communication. On the other hand, negotiation is the process of reaching a mutually beneficial agreement for all parties involved. It entails compromise, problem-solving, and a willingness to find a middle ground. Both approaches are vital for effectively managing conflicts in a peaceful and constructive manner.

However, developing these mechanisms is no easy task, and it requires constant effort and practice. It involves educating individuals and communities on the significance of conflict resolution and negotiation. It also involves creating a secure and inclusive environment for all parties to express their views and reach a resolution.

The growing recognition and significance of social justice and equity necessitate the alignment of policies and decisions with these principles. This involves not only advocating for equality and impartiality, but also actively striving to dismantle systemic barriers and prejudices. As an example: policies that aim to combat poverty and provide equitable opportunities for underprivileged communities can greatly contribute towards achieving social justice and equity. Additionally, decision-makers must take into account the repercussions of their choices on diverse groups of people. This requires having a profound understanding of the varied needs and perspectives of individuals and communities. By incorporating this perspective into policies and decisions, can be ensured that they are equitable and just for all. This also entails purposefully seeking and heeding the voices of marginalized and underrepresented individuals in the decision-making process.

Furthermore, policies and decisions that uphold social justice and equity also have a positive impact on society as a whole. By fostering a more inclusive and fair society, we can cultivate a sense of belonging and unity, and mitigate tensions and conflicts. Ultimately, this can lead to a more peaceful and harmonious society where everyone has the opportunity to succeed. Therefore, it is imperative for policies and decisions to actively contribute to social justice and equity in order to create a better world for all.

The Rule of Law is a fundamental principle that ensures that all citizens are equal under the law. This principle states that the law is above all individuals and institutions, and that everyone must adhere to it. Under the Rule of Law, no one is above the law, and everyone is subject to the same laws and consequences.

The Rule of Law is essential for maintaining a just and fair society. It guarantees that all individuals, regardless of their position or status, are held accountable for their actions. This principle promotes equality and prevents those in power from abusing their authority. Without the Rule of Law, society would descend into chaos and anarchy, as there would be no consequences for wrongful actions.

Furthermore, the Rule of Law is central for protecting individual rights and freedoms. It ensures that everyone is entitled to a fair trial and due process, and that their rights are not violated by the government or other individuals.

The Rule of Law also promotes transparency and accountability in government, as it holds those in power accountable for their actions.

The legality of any decision-making process is a critical aspect that cannot be overlooked. It is imperative that all actions and decisions are grounded in existing laws and legal jurisdiction in order to be deemed valid. This ensures that no one is exempt from the law and that all choices are made within a standardized framework.

Without legality, chaos would reign and there would be a higher risk of arbitrary decisions. Adhering to the law not only preserves the rights of individuals, but also ensures fairness for all. At the core of legality lies the concept of morality. This is where laws come into play, guiding our actions and decisions to ensure they fall within the confines of what is considered lawful. Without legal jurisdiction, wrongdoings may go unpunished and the balance of power could shift towards those with influence. To maintain a just society, it is crucial for everyone to comply with the law and make decisions based on legal authority.

Ignorance is not an excuse when it comes to legality. It is the responsibility of each individual to familiarize themselves with the law and understand its legal jurisdiction. This is especially important for those in positions of power, as their actions and decisions can have a greater impact on society. By ensuring that all actions and decisions are grounded in law and legal authority, we are able to establish a fair and just society for all.

In a society where laws and legal authority hold great weight, it is essential to prioritize transparency in all legal matters. This means making laws and legal proceedings easily accessible to the general public. By doing so, it promotes transparency and accountability among those in positions of power, as their actions will be subject to public scrutiny.

This transparency also allows for citizens to better understand and participate in the legal system, ensuring that their rights and voices are heard. Furthermore, legal transparency is especially important for those in positions of power, as their actions and decisions have the potential to greatly impact society.

By ensuring that all laws and legal proceedings are easily accessible and understood, can be established a fair and just society for all. This not only promotes trust in the legal system, but also serves to protect the rights and liberties of all individuals. In addition, with a transparent legal system, it becomes easier to identify and address any potential partiality or injustices within the system, leading to a more equitable society.

When a legal system is transparent, it not only promotes trust within the system, but also provides greater protection for the rights and liberties of all individuals who are subject to it. By making laws and legal proceedings open and accessible to the public, citizens can have confidence that they are being treated fairly and that their rights are being respected. This can lead to a more harmonious society, where people feel secure and valued. Furthermore, transparency within the legal system is crucial for identifying and addressing any potential biases or injustices that may exist. By making information readily available to the public, it becomes easier to recognize and rectify any systemic disparities or prejudices that may be present. This can lead to a more equitable society, where all individuals are given equal treatment and opportunity under the law. Ultimately, promoting transparency within the legal system is essential for creating a just and fair society for all.

In order to achieve a truly equitable society, it is decisive for the legal system to address and rectify any systemic disparities or prejudices that may be present. This means taking a proactive approach in promoting transparency and accountability within the legal system. By doing so, we can ensure that all individuals are given equal treatment and opportunity under the law, regardless of their race, gender, or socio-economic background.

This not only promotes fairness, but also helps to protect the fundamental rights and freedoms of all individuals. One key aspect of promoting transparency within the legal system is providing mechanisms for legal redress in case of rights violations. This means creating accessible and effective paths for individuals to seek justice if they feel their rights have been violated. By doing so, we can hold those in positions of power accountable and discourage any discriminatory or unjust practices. This, in turn, will lead to a more just and fair society for all, where individuals can trust in the legal system to protect their rights and freedoms. Overall, ensuring the protection of individual rights and freedoms and providing mechanisms for legal redress are crucial steps in creating a more equitable society.

Judicial and legal reforms are essential to promote accountability and transparency within the legal system. These reforms aim to strengthen the fundamental rights and freedoms of individuals and ensure that everyone is treated fairly and equally under the law. They are decisive for creating a just and democratic society where the rule of law is upheld and citizens can trust in the legal system. Reforms in the legal and judicial processes can bring about significant improvements in the way justice is administered. By addressing issues such as delays in court proceedings, corruption, and discrimination, these reforms can help increase the efficiency and accessibility of legal systems. This, in turn, can lead to the timely resolution of disputes and the protection of individual rights. By promoting fair and equal treatment for all individuals, judicial and legal reforms can contribute to building a society where everyone can live with dignity and respect.

The autonomy of the courts is essential for the effective functioning of a democratic community. It guarantees that the legal system maintains neutrality and remains unaffected by external pressures or influences, particularly from political factions. This independence ensures equal access to justice for all citizens, regardless of their social standing or political associations. Without this safeguard, the integrity of the legal system would be compromised, and many would be deprived of justice. Political interference in the courts can have severe repercussions, such as partial verdicts, resulting in miscarriage of justice and the erosion of public confidence in the judiciary. Therefore, it is imperative to have measures in place to prevent such interventions and preserve the independence of the courts.

This can be achieved by establishing robust legislative frameworks, ensuring the selection and appointments of judges are based on merit and honesty, and providing adequate resources and support to the legal system. Furthermore, safeguarding the autonomy of the courts also entails protecting the rights and freedoms of judges. They should be able to make decisions without fear of retaliation or retribution. Their judicial independence should remain untainted by external influences, ensuring a fair and unbiased judicial process.

This not only safeguards the rights of judges but also upholds the rights of citizens to a just trial. Overall, the independence of the judiciary is crucial for the proper functioning of a fair and democratic society, and it is the responsibility of each individual to uphold and defend it.

Public access to court records can also serve as a valuable resource for researchers and journalists, leading to a more informed and educated public. By maintaining transparency, the judiciary can continue to uphold its crucial role in a fair and democratic society. The independence of the judiciary is a vital aspect of a fair and just society. To uphold this independence, it is crucial for courts to prioritize and enhance transparency in their proceedings. By doing so, the rights of judges can be safeguarded, and the rights of citizens to a just trial can be upheld. This not only promotes trust and accountability in the justice system, but it also serves as a valuable resource for research and can aid in the prevention of discrimination and bias. By working together to maintain an independent and transparent judiciary, we can ensure the integrity of the justice system and uphold the principles of a democratic society.

Organizing educational initiatives is an essential method of promoting a well-informed public. These programs impart valuable knowledge and resources, cultivating heightened understanding and consciousness of legal entitlements and duties. By enabling individuals to comprehend their rights, these educational initiatives empower communities to effectively navigate the legal system. This not only benefits individuals, but also contributes to a more equitable society.

When people are knowledgeable about their rights and responsibilities, they are better equipped to safeguard themselves and others against injustice and mistreatment. Consequently, these programs serve as a potent instrument for advancing social justice and parity.

Furthermore, these educational initiatives often target marginalized communities, providing them with much-needed support and direction. In doing so, they not only enhance legal proficiency, but also address institutional disparities within the legal system. This results in a fairer and more accessible legal system, where all individuals can confidently seek justice and uphold their rights.

The legal system plays a vital role in every nation by upholding law and order. However, corruption within the legal system can erode trust in the judiciary and undermine faith in the justice system. To combat this issue, measures must be taken to combat corruption within the legal system.

These measures may include establishing oversight bodies to investigate and address any corrupt practices within legal institutions. These bodies would be responsible for investigating allegations of corruption and ensuring the legal system is free from any unethical conduct. Additionally, they would monitor the behavior of judges, lawyers, and other legal professionals to ensure compliance with ethical standards. This would promote transparency and accountability, essential for maintaining public trust.

Another fundamental aspect of preventing corruption within the legal system is ensuring law enforcement accountability. This would involve holding law enforcement agencies accountable for their actions and decisions through mechanisms like performance evaluations, audits, and disciplinary processes. By implementing these measures, law enforcement agencies would be deterred from engaging in corrupt practices, and citizens could be assured of fair and just treatment under the law. These steps are imperative for upholding the integrity of the legal system and fulfilling the principles of justice for all.

One way to promote accountability and transparency within law enforcement agencies is to establish clear protocols and procedures for handling complaints or reports of misconduct. This allows for a more structured and consistent approach to addressing issues and ensures that all complaints are taken seriously and investigated thoroughly. Additionally, implementing regular training and education on ethical standards and codes of conduct can help reinforce the importance of integrity and professionalism within the law enforcement community.

Another key step in promoting accountability and transparency is to establish an independent oversight body or commission that is responsible for monitoring and evaluating the performance of law enforcement agencies. This body can conduct investigations, issue recommendations, and hold agencies accountable for any instances of corruption or misconduct.

By having an independent body in place, citizens can have confidence that their complaints are being heard and addressed by a neutral party, rather than being handled internally by the same agency that may be the subject of the complaint. Overall, promoting accountability and transparency within law enforcement agencies is fundamental for maintaining public trust and confidence in the legal system. By implementing these measures, agencies can demonstrate their commitment to upholding the principles of justice for all and ensure that citizens are treated fairly and justly under the law. These steps are essential for creating a more accountable and transparent law enforcement system that serves and protects the community.

The ethical standards that govern legal professionals are imperative in maintaining the trust and integrity of the legal system. These codes of conduct and professional regulations act as a compass, guiding lawyers to uphold ethical principles and foster a culture of professionalism within the legal community.

These measures ensure that lawyers prioritize the best interests of their clients and the legal system as a whole. The codes of conduct outline the fundamental values and beliefs that lawyers must abide by, including honesty, regard, and confidentiality. They also provide guidance on potential conflicts of interest and the importance of maintaining objectivity during legal proceedings. Conversely, professional regulations establish the specific rules and requirements that lawyers must follow in their practice. These regulations span various aspects, such as advertising, billing, and handling client funds.

By reinforcing ethical standards, the legal profession maintains its credibility and trustworthiness, benefiting both clients and the overall fairness of the legal system. A strong culture of integrity and professionalism within the legal community also encourages lawyers to hold themselves and their colleagues accountable, ensuring the provision of high-quality legal services for all.

Encouraging collaboration between the legal sector and other sectors is central for addressing multidimensional challenges that impact our society. As the legal sector plays a significant role in creating policies and laws that affect various aspects of our lives, it is essential that they work closely with other sectors to ensure a holistic approach is taken when addressing complex issues. This collaboration can lead to more effective solutions that take into account different perspectives and expertise from various fields. For instance, collaboration between the legal sector and the education sector can help address the issue of access to justice for vulnerable and marginalized communities. By working together, they can develop educational programs that raise awareness of legal rights and empower individuals to seek legal assistance when needed. This can also help reduce the burden on the legal sector by providing individuals with the knowledge and resources to resolve disputes before they escalate into legal conflicts. Furthermore, collaboration between the legal sector and the health sector can help tackle issues related to health equity and access to healthcare.

By working together, they can address systemic barriers that prevent marginalized communities from accessing quality healthcare, such as discrimination and poverty. This can lead to improved health outcomes and reduce the need for legal interventions in health-related issues. Encouraging collaboration between different sectors is crucial for building a more equitable and just society, where multidimensional challenges are addressed effectively.

Social Justice

Social justice is a fundamental concept that strives to create a society where all individuals are treated fairly and have equal opportunities to succeed. It aims to eliminate discrimination and promote equality in all aspects of life.

This theory highlights the importance of addressing societal issues such as poverty, racism, and sexism, and creating a more just and equitable society for everyone. One of the main goals of social justice is to bridge the wealth gap and ensure that all individuals have equal access to resources and opportunities. This includes access to education, healthcare, and employment, regardless of their race, gender, or socio-economic status. It also advocates for the redistribution of wealth and resources to help those who are marginalized and disadvantaged.

Furthermore, social justice is not just about addressing inequalities, but also about creating a society where everyone is treated with dignity and respect. It recognizes the importance of diversity and inclusivity, and strives to eliminate discrimination and prejudice towards marginalized groups. By promoting fairness and equality, social justice plays a vital role in creating a more harmonious and cohesive society where everyone has a voice and is valued.

During the 20th century, social justice has evolved into a broader movement that encompasses not only economic equality, but also political, cultural, and social equality. This includes addressing issues such as gender and racial discrimination, access to healthcare and education, and equal representation in government and decision-making processes. Social justice recognizes that every individual deserves to be treated fairly and with dignity, regardless of their background or circumstances.

In recent years, the concept of social justice has gained more recognition and support from individuals and organizations around the world. This is due in part to the increasing awareness of social injustices and inequalities, as well as the growing movement towards promoting diversity and inclusivity. By acknowledging and addressing these issues, social justice plays a crucial role in creating a more cohesive and harmonious society where everyone is valued and has the opportunity to thrive. The fight for social justice is ongoing, and there is still much work to be done to ensure that all individuals are treated with dignity and respect. However, the progress made towards promoting fairness and equality is a testament to the importance and impact of social justice in creating a more just and inclusive world for all.

In order to uphold the concept of the common good, it is essential to recognize and address systemic issues and structural inequalities that often prevent certain groups from accessing the same resources and opportunities as others. This requires a collective effort to dismantle systems of oppression and advocate for policies that promote fairness and equality. It also means acknowledging and working to eliminate biases and prejudices that may contribute to these barriers.

In today's world, the idea of the common good is more crucial than ever. With the rise of globalization and interconnectedness, it is important to understand that the well-being of one individual or group cannot be isolated from the well-being of others. In order for society to thrive, we must prioritize the needs of the community as a whole, rather than just focusing on individual success. This means working towards creating a society where basic necessities such as food, shelter, and healthcare are accessible to all, regardless of their socioeconomic status. By striving towards the common good, we can create a more inclusive and equitable world for all. This requires a shift in mindset from individualism to collectivism, where the success of one is tied to the success of all. It also means recognizing that the common good encompasses not just the present generation, but also future generations. This requires us to consider the impact of our actions on the environment and work towards sustainability for the benefit of all. Ultimately, the common good is about creating a just and fair society where everyone has the opportunity to live a fulfilling life and reach their full potential.

The concept of social justice is rooted in the belief that every individual has the right to live a life free from discrimination and inequality. To achieve this, we must recognize the importance of human rights, ensuring that every person is treated with dignity and respect. Additionally, access to basic necessities such as education, healthcare, and employment must be guaranteed to all members of society, regardless of their background or circumstances. It involves engaging individuals and communities in decision-making processes that directly impact their lives. By involving all members of society in these discussions, we can ensure that their voices are heard and their needs are addressed. This leads to a more equitable and just society, where everyone has the opportunity to contribute and thrive. Finally, equity is essential in creating a society where social justice can thrive. This means recognizing and addressing systemic barriers that prevent certain groups from reaching their full potential. By promoting equity, we can create a fair and just society where everyone has equal opportunities to succeed. In summary, social justice requires us to uphold human rights, provide access and participation, and promote equity for all members of society.

The Universal Declaration of Human Rights, adopted by the United Nations in 1948, emphasizes the importance of social justice. It recognizes that without social justice, human rights cannot be truly upheld. This connection is crucial because it highlights the integral role that social justice plays in creating a fair and just society for all. In essence, human rights and social justice go hand in hand, and one cannot be fully achieved without the other. Moreover, promoting equity is a key component of social justice. By ensuring that all members of society have equal opportunities to succeed, we can create a more just and equitable society. This means breaking down barriers and addressing systemic inequalities that prevent certain groups from reaching their full potential. By promoting equity, we can create a level playing field where everyone has a fair chance to succeed and thrive. This is essential for achieving social justice and creating a society where everyone's human rights are respected and protected.

A just society is one where every individual has equal opportunities to access the essentials needed for a dignified life. This includes access to basic needs like shelter, food, and healthcare, as well as access to education and other opportunities. Without this access, certain groups are prevented from reaching their full potential and are at a disadvantage compared to others. This creates a cycle of inequality that is detrimental to the well-being of individuals and the society as a whole. Promoting equity is crucial in breaking this cycle and creating a more just society. By prioritizing equal opportunities for all, regardless of their gender, race, or class, we can create a level playing field where everyone has a fair chance to succeed and thrive. This not only benefits individuals, but also contributes to a more harmonious and cohesive society.

It is the responsibility of society to ensure that everyone's human rights are respected and protected, and promoting equity is an essential step in achieving this goal.

Social justice is a fundamental aspect of a functioning society, but one that is not always easy to achieve. It requires a concerted effort from all members of society to ensure that everyone is given a fair chance to succeed and thrive. This not only benefits individuals, but also contributes to a more harmonious and cohesive society. When everyone's human rights are respected and protected, it creates a sense of equity and fairness that is essential for a healthy and functioning society. However, achieving social justice is not a one-time task. It requires ongoing effort and dedication to promote and maintain equity for all individuals. This means actively listening to and uplifting the voices of marginalized and vulnerable communities. It also means actively working to break down systemic barriers and biases that may prevent certain groups from fully participating in society.

As members of society, it is our responsibility to ensure that everyone's human rights are respected and protected. This includes promoting equity and actively working towards social justice. By giving a voice to those who have been silenced and providing opportunities for participation, we can create a more just and fair world for all. This means not only addressing major societal problems, but also actively listening to and uplifting the voices of those most affected by these issues. Only by working together can we achieve true social justice and create a more equitable society for all.

Equity goes beyond simply treating everyone the same, but rather takes into account the effects of discrimination and aims for an equal outcome. This is critical in creating a more just and fair world for all. It means actively addressing systemic issues and inequalities that have long been ingrained in our society. By acknowledging and understanding the unique challenges faced by marginalized communities, we can work towards creating a more equitable society.

On the other hand, "equity" takes into consideration the different starting points and provides resources accordingly. In this scenario, the tallest person's box is given to the shortest person, allowing them to finally see the game. This is a powerful visual representation of how equity can create a more just and fair world for all. Creating a more equitable society requires actively listening to and uplifting the voices of those most affected by social issues. By working together and acknowledging the different starting points and needs of individuals, we can achieve true social justice. It is not enough to simply address the major societal problems, but we must also strive for equity in all aspects of life. Only then can we truly create a more just and fair world for all.

Social justice is not just about addressing the major societal problems, but also striving for equity in all aspects of life. It means creating a society where everyone's human rights are respected, protected, and promoted. Achieving social justice is not a one-size-fits-all solution. It requires a deep understanding of the issues and challenges faced by different communities. It also means actively dismantling systemic barriers, prejudice, and discrimination that hinder individuals from reaching their full potential. This could include implementing policies and programs that promote diversity and inclusivity, and actively addressing issues such as income inequality and access to education and healthcare. Ultimately, true social justice is a continuous process that requires a commitment to principles such as participation and equity. It is not a destination, but a journey towards creating a more just and fair world for all. By valuing social justice and remaining dedicated to its principles, we can make progress towards a more equal and inclusive society.

In recent years, there has been a tremendous surge in the attention given to personal well-being. Whether it is through self-help books, workplace policies, or commercial products, the focus on subjective well-being has become ever-present. The rise of questionnaires evaluating one's feelings and mindfulness exercises has shown an increased interest in the topic. However, it has become clear that individual well-being is not solely dependent on one's actions. While personal growth and development are essential, it is also necessary to recognize the role of interactions with others in our lives. People are social beings, and as such, our well-being is also influenced by our relationships with those around us. How we grow, act, think, and feel is heavily dependent on the persons we surround ourselves with. Therefore, it is important to consider our well-being not only in the context of ourselves but also in relation to others. Our well-being is not just about being well as individuals; it is also about being well together. The quality of our relationships plays a significant role in our overall well-being. The support and connections we have with others can greatly impact our mental and emotional state. As such, it is crucial to not only focus on our personal well-being but also on nurturing and maintaining healthy relationships with those around us. After all, we are not meant to go through life alone, and our well-being is greatly intertwined with the well-being of those we interact with.

It is a common misconception that personal well-being is solely the responsibility of the individual. In fact, our well-being is greatly influenced by the one of those around us. This is why it is essential to not only focus on our own individual well-being, but also on development and maintaining healthy relationships with the communities we are a part of. The concept of community well-being recognizes the importance of the intermediate scale between the individual and the nation. It highlights the crucial role that communities play in our overall well-being. However, there is often confusion about what exactly constitutes a community. While some may define it as a residential neighbourhood, others may view it as a group of people with shared interests and values. In this way, community well-being can encompass both physical and virtual communities. Ultimately, community well-being can be defined as a combination of various factors, including social, economic, environmental, cultural, and political conditions. These conditions are not only identified by individuals, but also by their communities. This working definition emphasizes the importance of not only personal well-being, but also the well-being of the communities we are a part of. By recognizing and prioritizing community well-being, we can create a more holistic approach to overall well-being for both individuals and society as a whole.

The well-being of the community can be achieved when everyone is working together to help each other. This is because the community is a group of people with a shared interest and goals. By prioritizing the common good over individual interests, the community can succeed and improve the overall quality of life for its members. This means that when making decisions, it is important to consider how it will impact the community as a whole, rather than just one person.

In order to contribute to the common good, individuals must recognize the importance of their actions and how they can affect others. This requires selflessness and empathy, understanding that the well-being of the community is interconnected with individual well-being. By working together and making decisions for the greater good, the community can create a positive and supportive environment for all its members. This can lead to a stronger and more resilient community with a higher quality of life. It is essential for individuals to understand that their actions and decisions can have a lasting impact on the community. By prioritizing the common good, individuals can contribute to the growth and development of their community. This creates a community where everyone feels valued and supported, leading to a better quality of life for all. When individuals understand the importance of working together for the common good, the community can thrive and become a place where everyone can flourish.

Well-being is a central aspect of a successful community. It encompasses not only physical health, but also emotional and psychological well-being. It goes beyond just the absence of illness and includes the presence of social-emotional coping skills that help individuals maintain a state of health and happiness. When individuals within a community prioritize their well-being, it creates a positive ripple effect that benefits everyone. In addition to its connection to health, well-being is also closely linked to the quality of life within a community. When individuals have a strong sense of well-being, they are more likely to have a strong sense of identity and are able to attain personal goals. They are also better equipped to pursue spiritual meaning and prevent maladaptive behaviours.

Furthermore, well-being includes the development of competencies and skills, which can contribute to the overall growth and development of the community. The existence of social support is another important aspect of well-being. When individuals feel valued and supported within their community, it leads to a better quality of life for all. This support can come in various forms, such as having a sense of belonging, receiving emotional and practical support from others, and having a sense of control over events in one's life.

In order to achieve a true sense of belonging within a community, individuals must undergo a process of conscientisation. This involves developing critical thinking skills and a heightened awareness of societal issues. Through this, individuals are able to challenge and re-evaluate their perspectives, leading to a more inclusive and supportive community.

By, by engaging in dialogue and developing a shared understanding, members of the community can renegotiate their collective social identity. This process fosters a sense of unity and encourages individuals to adopt healthier behaviours. By creating a safe and open space for discussion, people are able to develop a deeper understanding of themselves and others, ultimately strengthening the community as a whole. Lastly, as individuals gain a sense of control over their own lives, they are empowered to make positive changes. This includes taking control of their health, as well as other aspects of their lives. By prioritizing their well-being and working together for the common good, a flourishing community is created where individuals feel supported and empowered to make positive changes in their lives.

By actively participating in their community, individuals not only gain a sense of fulfilment and pride, but also a feeling of connection and purpose. This involvement becomes an integral part of their lives, and they are unable to imagine living any other way. However, their efforts are often met with challenges, such as difficulty accessing information and resources, and facing suspicion and even intimidation from professionals. This can make it difficult for them to continue their work and make positive changes. - Despite these challenges, community activists are seen as both problem solvers and part of the authorities in their community. They are constantly balancing the needs and opinions of different community members, and their actions are often met with a mix of reactions, including suspicion, hostility, and gratitude.

Ethical Considerations

The concept of ethical issues is not something that can be easily categorized or generalized as it holds various perspectives, making it a complex matter. As a leader, it is essential to have a clear understanding of your own values and beliefs in order to make ethical decisions. However, what may seem like the right decision for one person may not be the same for another. In today's society, there are many factors that can influence one's ethical decision-making. From personal experiences to cultural and societal norms, these can all play a role in shaping one's perspective. As a leader, it is important to take all of these factors into consideration when making decisions that can impact both oneself and others. Being actively involved in organizational life can also present ethical challenges. As a student, spouse, child, sibling, employee, and leader, one may encounter situations where their ethical decision-making skills will be put to test. It is essential to constantly reflect on one's values and beliefs in order to make the right decisions, even in the most challenging of circumstances.

It is essential to recognize that what one may consider to be a moral principle may not hold the same significance for someone else. This is why it is important to constantly evaluate and re-evaluate our own values, as well as the values of others, in order to make the most ethical decisions. In doing so, we can understand that there may be varying perspectives and beliefs that need to be taken into account. This requires a deep understanding of one's own values and beliefs, as well as being open to considering the values and beliefs of others.

Pursuing the common good often involves making decisions and engaging in actions that align with ethical principles. It encourages responsible and moral behaviour that benefits the greater community. This can be accomplished by helping those in need, standing up against injustice, and promoting equality for all. This not only benefits the individual, but also contributes to the collective good of society.

It also requires individuals to take into consideration the impact of their actions on others and the environment. This means being mindful of the consequences of our choices and actively seeking ways to minimize harm and promote positive change. It involves being empathetic, compassionate, and understanding towards others, and actively working towards creating a fair and just society for all.

Persons have to look beyond their own self-interests and work towards the better of their communities and the world. It is a continuous effort that requires collaboration, open-mindedness, and a willingness to take action. By pursuing the common good, can be generated a more harmonious and equitable society for present and future generations.

When it comes to making the world a better place, everyone has a responsibility to do its part. Pursuing the common good means actively seeking out opportunities to make positive changes in our communities and society as a whole. This can involve making difficult decisions and taking action that aligns with our personal moral code and ethical principles. One of the most important aspects of pursuing the common good is being mindful of how our actions affect others.

It's considering the well-being of those around us. This can mean making sacrifices and putting the needs of others before our own. Pursuing the common good also requires a deep understanding of our own values and beliefs. It's important to constantly reflect on our actions and decisions to ensure they align with our personal ethical principles. By staying true to our values, we can create a more just and compassionate world for all. Ultimately, pursuing the common good is a continuous journey, but one that is essential for creating a better future for everyone.

One way to ensure that our decisions align with our personal ethical principles is to constantly reflect on and evaluate our actions. This involves considering the potential impact of our decisions, both positive and negative, and weighing them against our own values and beliefs. By doing so, we can make more informed and conscientious choices that are in line with our moral compass. Moreover, it is important to remember that our actions have a ripple effect on the world around us. Actions can inspire and influence those around us, creating a domino effect of positive change. In this way, pursuing the common good is not just a personal endeavour, but a collective one that can have a far-reaching impact. Ultimately, the pursuit of the common good is a continuous trip that requires constant reflection and evaluation. It is not a one-time accomplishment, but a lifelong commitment to making ethical decisions in all aspects of everybody lives.

Along through life, everybody is faced with countless decisions that will impact not only themselves, but those around as well. It is essential that it is understood the ethical implications of choices, as they can have far-reaching consequences. By cultivating a mindset of ethical decision-making, it is created a brighter and more just future for all. Making ethical decisions is not a one-time event, but rather a continuous process. It requires a deep understanding of the own personal ethics and values, as well as the ability to critically assess the potential outcomes of actions. This commitment to ethical decision-making extends beyond personal lives, but also applies to people's contributions in the workplace and society as a whole. With advancements in technology and globalization, actions have the power to reach and impact others on a global scale.

Ethics is a complex and subjective concept, often influenced by personal beliefs and values. When discussing ethics, it is important to recognize that there may be conflicting viewpoints. However, by focusing on the common benefits of aligning personal values with actions, can be reduced these conflicts and created a more harmonious environment. One of the main benefits of this alignment is increased operational efficiency. When individuals and organizations make ethical decisions, they are able to work together more smoothly and effectively. This can lead to improved productivity and better overall performance.

In addition, aligning values with actions can also help to reduce risk. Ethical decision-making takes into account potential consequences and strives to mitigate any negative impacts, resulting in a more stable and secure environment. Furthermore, by aligning values with actions, it's created a space for individual contributions. When individuals feel that their values are in line with those of the organization, they are more likely to feel motivated and engaged in their work. This can lead to innovative ideas and a stronger sense of purpose within the organization.

Additionally, ethical decision-making can also improve external relationships. When an organization operates ethically, it builds trust and credibility with its stakeholders, leading to stronger partnerships and a positive reputation in the global community. In summary, aligning our values with our actions not only benefits individuals and organizations, but also has a positive impact on a global scale.

Ethical Considerations

The concept of ethical issues is not something that can be easily categorized or generalized as it holds various perspectives, making it a complex matter. As a leader, it is essential to have a clear understanding of your own values and beliefs in order to make ethical decisions. However, what may seem like the right decision for one person may not be the same for another. In today's society, there are many factors that can influence one's ethical decision-making. From personal experiences to cultural and societal norms, these can all play a role in shaping one's perspective. As a leader, it is important to take all of these factors into consideration when making decisions that can impact both oneself and others. Being actively involved in organizational life can also present ethical challenges. As a student, spouse, child, sibling, employee, and leader, one may encounter situations where their ethical decision-making skills will be put to test. It is essential to constantly reflect on one's values and beliefs in order to make the right decisions, even in the most challenging of circumstances.

It is essential to recognize that what one may consider to be a moral principle may not hold the same significance for someone else. This is why it is important to constantly evaluate and re-evaluate our own values, as well as the values of others, in order to make the most ethical decisions. In doing so, we can understand that there may be varying perspectives and beliefs that need to be taken into account. This requires a deep understanding of one's own values and beliefs, as well as being open to considering the values and beliefs of others.

Pursuing the common good often involves making decisions and engaging in actions that align with ethical principles. It encourages responsible and moral behaviour that benefits the greater community. This can be accomplished by helping those in need, standing up against injustice, and promoting equality for all. This not only benefits the individual, but also contributes to the collective good of society.

It also requires individuals to take into consideration the impact of their actions on others and the environment. This means being mindful of the consequences of our choices and actively seeking ways to minimize harm and promote positive change. It involves being empathetic, compassionate, and understanding towards others, and actively working towards creating a fair and just society for all.

Persons have to look beyond their own self-interests and work towards the better of their communities and the world. It is a continuous effort that requires collaboration, open-mindedness, and a willingness to take action. By pursuing the common good, can be generated a more harmonious and equitable society for present and future generations.

When it comes to making the world a better place, everyone has a responsibility to do its part. Pursuing the common good means actively seeking out opportunities to make positive changes in our communities and society as a whole. This can involve making difficult decisions and taking action that aligns with our personal moral code and ethical principles. One of the most important aspects of pursuing the common good is being mindful of how our actions affect others.

It's considering the well-being of those around us. This can mean making sacrifices and putting the needs of others before our own. Pursuing the common good also requires a deep understanding of our own values and beliefs. It's important to constantly reflect on our actions and decisions to ensure they align with our personal ethical principles. By staying true to our values, we can create a more just and compassionate world for all. Ultimately, pursuing the common good is a continuous journey, but one that is essential for creating a better future for everyone.

One way to ensure that our decisions align with our personal ethical principles is to constantly reflect on and evaluate our actions. This involves considering the potential impact of our decisions, both positive and negative, and weighing them against our own values and beliefs. By doing so, we can make more informed and conscientious choices that are in line with our moral compass. Moreover, it is important to remember that our actions have a ripple effect on the world around us. Actions can inspire and influence those around us, creating a domino effect of positive change. In this way, pursuing the common good is not just a personal endeavour, but a collective one that can have a far-reaching impact. Ultimately, the pursuit of the common good is a continuous trip that requires constant reflection and evaluation. It is not a one-time accomplishment, but a lifelong commitment to making ethical decisions in all aspects of everybody lives.

Along through life, everybody is faced with countless decisions that will impact not only themselves, but those around as well. It is essential that it is understood the ethical implications of choices, as they can have far-reaching consequences. By cultivating a mindset of ethical decision-making, it is created a brighter and more just future for all. Making ethical decisions is not a one-time event, but rather a continuous process. It requires a deep understanding of the own personal ethics and values, as well as the ability to critically assess the potential outcomes of actions. This commitment to ethical decision-making extends beyond personal lives, but also applies to people´s contributions in the workplace and society as a whole. With advancements in technology and globalization, actions have the power to reach and impact others on a global scale.

Ethics is a complex and subjective concept, often influenced by personal beliefs and values. When discussing ethics, it is important to recognize that there may be conflicting viewpoints. However, by focusing on the common benefits of aligning personal values with actions, can be reduced these conflicts and created a more harmonious environment. One of the main benefits of this alignment is increased operational efficiency. When individuals and organizations make ethical decisions, they are able to work together more smoothly and effectively. This can lead to improved productivity and better overall performance.

In addition, aligning values with actions can also help to reduce risk. Ethical decision-making takes into account potential consequences and strives to mitigate any negative impacts, resulting in a more stable and secure environment. Furthermore, by aligning values with actions, it's created a space for individual contributions. When individuals feel that their values are in line with those of the organization, they are more likely to feel motivated and engaged in their work. This can lead to innovative ideas and a stronger sense of purpose within the organization.

Additionally, ethical decision-making can also improve external relationships. When an organization operates ethically, it builds trust and credibility with its stakeholders, leading to stronger partnerships and a positive reputation in the global community. In summary, aligning our values with our actions not only benefits individuals and organizations, but also has a positive impact on a global scale.

Public Goods

Public goods are the pillars of a well-functioning society. They are the building blocks that enable progress and growth, and are indispensable to the well-being of its citizens. Education, healthcare, and infrastructure are some of the key public goods that are crucial for the common good. These goods are not only essential for individual development, but also for the overall advancement of a nation. In today's interconnected world, knowledge has become a public good with a global reach. It is no longer confined to a single country or region, but rather it is shared and utilized by people all around the world. As such, the responsibility for creating and disseminating knowledge for development falls not just on individual nations, but on the international community as a whole.

The importance of knowledge as a public good for development has been recognized by many. It is through education that individuals can acquire the skills and knowledge necessary for personal growth and contribution to society. Healthcare ensures the well-being of citizens and enables them to lead productive lives. And infrastructure, such as roads and utilities, provides the foundation for economic growth and progress. Thus, investing in these public goods is crucial for the success and prosperity of a nation.

Governments play a crucial role in the provision of public goods such as healthcare and infrastructure. Strong institutions enable governments to effectively enforce regulations and taxation, mobilizing resources to provide for the well-being of their citizens. This not only eliminates the free rider problem, but also ensures that all individuals, regardless of their economic status, have access to essential services that enable them to lead productive lives. An inclusive government, one that values the welfare of all its citizens, has the ability to balance the needs of present and future generations. By investing in public goods, such as healthcare and infrastructure, these governments are able to create a more prosperous and sustainable society. This is because public goods not only benefit individuals, but also have spill over effects that contribute to overall societal progress and development. As a result, investing in public goods is vital for the success and prosperity of a nation, and for creating a better future for all its citizens.

Public goods are investments that benefit the entire society, rather than just individuals. The provisions of public goods, such as water, are essential for the success and prosperity of a nation. Water is not only essential for drinking, but also for agriculture, livestock, electricity generation, and industry. These services provided by water have spill over effects that contribute to overall societal progress and development. In addition to its direct benefits, water also plays a central role in creating a better future for all citizens. By providing clean and accessible water, public goods can improve the health and well-being of individuals. This, in turn, can lead to increased productivity and economic growth. Furthermore, investing in public goods like water can also help to reduce inequalities and promote social cohesion. When everyone has access to the same essential resources, it can create a more equitable society where all citizens have the opportunity to thrive. Overall, investing in public goods like water is not only necessary for the functioning of society, but it also has far-reaching impacts on the well-being and development of a nation. By recognizing the importance of public goods and making investments in them, it is build a better future for all citizens, and contribute to the progress and prosperity of society.

Education

Education is the foundation of a prosperous society. It equips individuals with the necessary skills and knowledge to contribute to the economy and society. By investing in education, the government is investing in the future of its citizens and the nation as a whole. It is considered to be the backbone of modern society. It acts as a catalyst for growth and development, providing individuals with the tools they need to succeed both professionally and personally. Education is not just about acquiring knowledge, but also about developing critical thinking and problem-solving skills that are essential for a prosperous society. By investing in education, the government is not only investing in the future of its citizens, but also in the growth and stability of the nation.

Education is a fundamental human right that should be accessible to all individuals regardless of their background. It is the key to breaking the cycle of poverty and creating equal opportunities for all. With education, individuals are empowered to make informed decisions and actively participate in the economy and society. This, in turn, leads to a more stable and prosperous nation. Moreover, education plays a crucial role in promoting social cohesion and reducing social inequalities. It allows individuals from diverse backgrounds to come together and learn from each other, promoting tolerance and understanding. Investing in education is not just about building schools and providing resources, but also about training and supporting educators. Teachers play a vital role in shaping the minds of future generations and preparing them for the challenges they will face. By investing in their training and development, the quality of education provided to students will improve, leading to a more skilled and knowledgeable workforce. Ultimately, education is the key to creating a brighter future for individuals, society, and the nation as a whole.

Healthcare

Healthcare is a fundamental public good that ensures the physical and mental well-being of individuals. Access to quality healthcare is crucial for a healthy and productive population. It is a basic human right that should not be compromised, and investing in education is a key factor in providing individuals with the necessary knowledge and skills to improve the quality of healthcare.

By investing in the training and development of healthcare professionals, it is ultimately investing in the well-being of society as a whole. Furthermore, quality education is essential in addressing the challenges that the healthcare industry will face in the future. With the constant advancements in technology and medicine, healthcare professionals must continuously improve their skills and knowledge to provide the best possible care for patients. This is where education plays a crucial role, as it provides healthcare professionals with the necessary tools and resources to adapt to these changes and challenges. Ultimately, this will lead to a more skilled and knowledgeable workforce, resulting in improved healthcare services for individuals and society. In conclusion, education is the key to creating a brighter future for individuals, society, and the nation as a whole. Those public goods are part of the fundamental Human Right.

Infrastructure

Investing in infrastructure is necessary for the proper functioning of a society. It not only supports the economy but also promotes social well-being and a better quality of life. The government plays a crucial role in providing and maintaining infrastructure, as it is a key factor in promoting economic growth and development. Overall, public goods are essential for the common good, and it is the responsibility of the government to provide and maintain them for the benefit of society. This is especially important in times of national insecurity, as the government must take steps to prevent the appropriation of public goods by other states. National insecurity can be caused by a variety of factors, including the actions of other states. When one country seeks to appropriate the public goods of another, it can create tension and instability between the two nations. This can lead to economic struggles and can even result in conflict. As such, it is central for the government to not only provide and maintain public goods, but also to protect them from outside threats. In addition to maintaining and protecting public goods, the government must also ensure that they are accessible to all members of society. This includes marginalized and underprivileged communities who may not have the means to access these essential resources on their own. By providing public goods and ensuring their accessibility, the government not only promotes economic growth and development, but also works towards creating a more equitable society.

Representation

The common good, a term often used in conjunction with democratic values, is a fundamental belief in society. This concept emphasizes the importance of participation, representation, and decision-making processes, which are all vital in any democratic society.

It is believed that the common good takes into account the diverse needs and perspectives of the population, ensuring that no individual or group is left behind. One of the key aspects of the common good is the idea of participation. In order for a society to thrive, all members must have the opportunity to actively participate in decision-making processes not only ensuring that everyone's voices are heard, but also helping to create a sense of ownership and responsibility among the population. Decision-making that takes into account the diverse needs and perspectives of the population are decisive in promoting equality and fairness within a society.

Representation is another important aspect of the common good. It is essential that all members of a society are represented in decision-making processes, regardless of their race, gender, socioeconomic status, or any other factor. This ensures that the needs and perspectives of all individuals are taken into account, creating a more inclusive and just society. Overall, the common good is a vital concept that promotes democratic values and strives for a society where everyone's needs and perspectives are valued and considered.

Social Inclusion

Social integration is a key aspect of promoting the common good in society. It involves actively promoting and protecting the rights and dignity of every individual, regardless of their background or circumstances. This includes valuing diversity, promoting equality, and ensuring equal opportunities for all members of society. By doing so, social integration aims to create a more inclusive and just society where everyone's needs and perspectives are considered and respected.

The process of social integration is ongoing and requires the participation of all individuals and institutions in society. It involves promoting values such as non-discrimination, non-violence, solidarity, and participation, while also fostering a sense of community and belonging for all members of society. By actively engaging in this process, societies can become more stable, safe, and just for everyone, including disadvantaged and vulnerable groups and individuals. Social integration is a vital concept that helps to build a more cohesive and equitable society for the betterment of all its members.

Social integration and inclusion are essential for creating a stable and safe society for everyone. It involves actively engaging in efforts to provide equal opportunities for all, regardless of their background. This process aims to create a more cohesive and equitable society where everyone can reach their full potential in life. It is not just about providing equal rights and opportunities, but also ensuring that all members of society can actively participate in all aspects of life.

It helps to build a society where disadvantaged and vulnerable groups and individuals are not left behind. It promotes active participation in decision-making processes, allowing everyone's voices to be heard. By including everyone in society it comes to be a more just and fair environment for all. Social integration is not just a one-time event, but an ongoing process that requires continuous efforts from all members of society. By promoting social integration, it will be a society where everyone feels included and valued. It allows for a more diverse and inclusive community, where individuals from different backgrounds can come together and learn from one another. This not only benefits the marginalized groups but also benefits society as a whole. When everyone is included, we can work towards building a better future for all. Therefore, it is crucial to actively engage in the process of social integration to create a more cohesive, just, and equitable society for the betterment of all its members.

In modern society, it is important to foster a sense of social harmony in order to maintain a stable and tranquil community. This entails fostering belonging, active participation, inclusivity, recognition, and legitimacy. When all members and factions of a community feel a sense of belonging and are given the opportunity to participate and be included, it cultivates a feeling of unity and solidarity. A socially cohesive society does not necessarily imply uniformity or shared beliefs. In fact, by embracing diversity and respecting differing ideas, perspectives, and abilities, a community can thrive and harness the potential that comes with diversity. This means that even when competing interests arise, there is a reduced likelihood of tension and conflict. Instead, a socially cohesive society values and celebrates diversity, resulting in a more harmonious and empathetic community.

It is vital for societies to continuously make every effort towards achieving social cohesion. This can be accomplished through promoting inclusivity and diversity, as well as addressing any underlying issues that may create divisions within a community. By constantly working towards social cohesion, societies can create a sense of unity and understanding, ultimately creating a more peaceful and gratifying environment for all individuals to reside in.

Expanding upon the idea of social participation, it is important to recognize the impact it has on promoting inclusivity and diversity within a community. When individuals are given the opportunity to actively engage in society's activities and have a say in decision-making processes, it creates a sense of empowerment and belonging. This, in turn, leads to a more inclusive and diverse community as people from all backgrounds can come together and contribute to the betterment of society. Furthermore, social participation also allows for the addressing of underlying issues that may create divisions within a community.

By giving individuals a voice and the ability to influence decisions, it opens up avenues for discussions and resolutions to issues that may have otherwise gone unnoticed. This not only promotes a sense of unity within the community but also fosters a deeper understanding of each other's perspectives and experiences.

Overall, the constant work towards social cohesion through promoting inclusivity and diversity, as well as addressing underlying issues, creates a harmonious and peaceful environment for all individuals to reside in. It is a crucial aspect of building a strong and thriving community, where everyone feels valued and their voices are heard. By encouraging social participation, societies can create a more equitable and gratifying environment for all to live in.

Sustainability

Sustainable practices and environmental awareness are essential components of a sustainable future. They contribute to the common good by prioritizing the well-being of both current and future generations. Sustainable practices aim to preserve our planet's resources and mitigate the negative impacts of human activity on the environment. By prioritizing sustainability, we can ensure that our planet remains healthy and thriving for generations to come.

Environmental awareness is a critical aspect of sustainability. It involves taking responsibility for the impact of our actions on the environment and actively working towards preserving and protecting it. This can include reducing our carbon footprint, conserving resources, and implementing sustainable practices in our daily lives. By practicing environmental stewardship, we can minimize our negative impact on the environment and promote a more sustainable way of living. In today's world, sustainable practices and environmental awareness are more important than ever. With the increasing threat of climate change and the depletion of natural resources, it is crucial that we prioritize sustainability in all aspects of our lives. By doing so, we can ensure that future generations will have access to a healthy and thriving planet, and fulfil our responsibility to be good stewards of the environment. Let us all do our part in promoting sustainability and environmental stewardship for a better future.

Environmental awareness is a responsibility that should be shared by all, as we all play a role in shaping the environment. This can be reflected through the choices we make as individuals, the practices of companies and communities, and the actions of government organizations.

It is important to recognize that we all have unique environmental, social, and economic interests, but it is our shared responsibility to ensure a healthy and prosperous planet for future generations. The concept of environmental awareness is deeply ingrained in our society and has been for many years. From traditional farming practices to spiritual beliefs, there has always been a sense of appreciation for the natural resources that surround us. Work towards a more sustainable future, it is vital to incorporate environmental awareness into our daily lives. This can help to preserve natural resources and achieve sustainable outcomes for all.

In order to become a more sustainable society, it is important to consider the different natural resource systems and the desired outcomes for each one. This includes sustaining clean and healthy air, protecting and restoring ecosystems, generating clean energy, supporting ecologically sensitive land management, consuming less and reducing waste, and sustaining water resources. By focusing on these outcomes, we can work towards a more sustainable future and ensure the availability and quality of these resources for generations to come. It is also important to take care not to degrade the resources we do use and to restore and rehabilitate them whenever possible. This will help to create a more harmonious relationship between humans and the environment.

Sustainable development emphasizes the importance of meeting the needs of the present while also considering the needs of future generations. This means taking a holistic approach towards development that not only focuses on economic growth but also prioritizes social inclusion and environmental protection. By harmonizing these three core elements, we can work towards creating a more sustainable and resilient future for both people and the planet. In order for sustainable development to be achieved, there must be a balance between economic growth, social inclusion, and environmental protection. These elements are interconnected and must be addressed simultaneously in order to achieve true sustainability. This requires a shift in mindset and practices, where economic growth is not the sole indicator of development, but rather a more comprehensive approach that considers the well-being of individuals and societies as a whole. This includes eradicating poverty, promoting inclusive economic growth, reducing inequalities, and promoting sustainable management of natural resources and ecosystems.

Environmental consciousness is a critical component of sustainable development, and must be embraced by individuals, communities, and governments worldwide in order to ensure the longevity of our resources. This can take on many forms, such as creating protected areas, replanting trees, limiting harvests, reducing pollution, and purchasing sustainable products. These actions can be carried out at various scales, from local community efforts to global initiatives, and in both rural and urban areas. Despite the global nature of many environmental issues, local actions are still crucial in addressing these challenges and promoting sustainability.

One of the key aspects of environmental consciousness is the involvement and empowerment of local communities. By engaging in stewardship actions, individuals can utilize their own expertise and knowledge to care for the environment that directly impacts them. This can be especially important for communities whose livelihoods and subsistence needs are reliant on the health of their environment. By taking ownership and responsibility for the stewardship of their surroundings, these communities can play a significant role in promoting sustainability and responding to external drivers of change. Furthermore, environmental awareness encompasses a wide range of actions, from strict conservation efforts to active restoration projects. This highlights the diverse ways in which individuals and communities can contribute to the protection and management of our resources. By actively engaging in awareness actions, can be ensured the availability and quality of resources for future generations, and work towards a more equitable, prosperous, and sustainable world for all.

Solidarity

Solidarity is a key aspect of building strong communities. It is the idea that members of a community are interconnected and share a sense of responsibility towards one another. This creates a strong foundation of mutual support and care, promoting the common good. Solidarity encourages individuals to put the needs of the community above their own, fostering a sense of unity and cooperation. In today's society, the concept of solidarity is more important than ever. With various social and political issues dividing communities, it is crucial to promote a sense of togetherness and interconnectedness.

By fostering solidarity, individuals are encouraged to collaborate and work towards the betterment of the community as a whole. This not only benefits the common good but also promotes a sense of belonging and purpose for individuals within the community. However, building solidarity within a community is not always easy. It requires individuals to prioritize the needs of the community over their own, which can be challenging. It also requires open communication, understanding, and a willingness to support and care for one another. By continuously promoting the concept of solidarity, can formed stronger and more resilient communities that can overcome any challenges that may arise.

The concept of civic solidarity is central in building and maintaining strong and resilient communities. It entails citizens coming together and supporting each other in times of need, putting the well-being of the community over their own. This can be challenging as it requires individuals to be selfless and prioritize the greater good. However, with open communication, understanding, and a willingness to care for one another, this can be achieved. The promotion of civic solidarity has countless benefits for communities. It fosters a sense of belonging and unity among citizens, leading to a stronger and more cohesive society. It also promotes a culture of mutual support and assistance, where individuals can rely on each other during difficult times. This can lead to the development of social networks and the creation of a safety net for community members. Furthermore, civic solidarity plays a crucial role in overcoming challenges that may arise within a community. By working together and supporting each other, citizens can tackle issues such as economic instability, natural disasters, and social injustices. This not only helps in finding solutions but also strengthens the bond between community members. In essence, civic solidarity is the foundation for building sustainable and resilient communities that can thrive in the face of adversity.

The concept of civic solidarity is a powerful one, especially when it comes to dealing with external forces that may threaten the unity of a nation. It is in times of struggle that citizens are called upon to come together and tackle issues such as economic instability, natural disasters, and social injustices. Through this collective effort, not only can solutions be found, but the bond between community members can also be strengthened. This connection is what forms the foundation for building sustainable and resilient communities that can thrive in the face of adversity. Solidarity is not just about standing together in times of crisis, but it is also about shared identification with an "imagined community." This community is not defined by class or social position, but rather by a common way of life, folkways, and a shared history of struggle. This sense of shared identity and purpose is what brings people together and allows them to work towards a common goal. It is in this sense of belonging and unity that can help a nation overcome external forces and emerge stronger and more resilient. Civic solidarity is not just a concept, but a way of life. It is about citizens coming together to support and uplift each other, and in doing so, creating a stronger and more cohesive society. It is through this solidarity that a nation can overcome any challenges that come its way and emerge as a united and resilient force.

By actively promoting and practicing civic solidarity, we can create a better future for ourselves and our communities. It not only brings people together but also helps in overcoming challenges and obstacles that a nation may face. By promoting and practicing civic solidarity, people can create a supportive and inclusive community for themselves and future generations. This, in turn, opens the path towards a better and more resilient society.

Additionally, solidarity also plays a key role in addressing social issues and injustices. When individuals come together in solidarity and stand up against oppression, they can bring about meaningful change. This is evident in the history of many social movements, where people from different walks of life joined forces to fight for a common cause.

Solidarity is not just a concept, but a practice that can bring about real and positive change in our world. It is a powerful tool for promoting social justice and creating a better future for all. By recognizing the value of solidarity and actively practicing it, we can build a society that is more compassionate, inclusive, and resilient.

Together, we can create a world where everyone's needs and voices are heard and where no one is left behind. Solidarity is not just about coming together and standing in unity, but it also involves actively working towards a common goal. This means recognizing and addressing systemic issues and inequalities that exist in our society. By promoting solidarity, we can create a more equitable and just world for all. It requires us to not only acknowledge our shared humanity, but also actively work towards dismantling barriers and promoting equal opportunities for all individuals, regardless of their race, gender, religion or socio-economic status. Not only supporting each other in times of need, but also actively advocating for the rights and well-being of others.

Expanding on the concept of trust, it is an important element in building solidarity. Trust is built on mutual understanding, shared values, and a sense of community. When we trust each other, we are more likely to work together towards a common goal, and this is where solidarity comes into play. In today's world, where there is so much division and conflict, trust and solidarity are even more important. It is through trust that people can bridge the gaps between individuals and groups, and come together to create a better future for generations to come.

Trust is the foundation on which empathy, compassion, and a shared vision for a better world can be built. Besides, trust is not just limited to personal relationships, but it also plays a vital role in society. A strong healthcare system, for example, requires trust between individuals and the government or healthcare organizations. Trust can also enhance cooperation between different communities and ensure the well-being of the entire society. However, trust can be easily broken, especially when social distance increases and expectations of strangers are unknown. Therefore, it is essential to build and maintain trust to strengthen solidarity and create a better world for all.

Trust is the foundation of any successful society. It allows for cooperation, solidarity, and the well-being of all members. However, trust is fragile and can easily be broken, especially when individuals are distanced from one another and do not know what to expect from strangers. In such situations, building and maintaining trust becomes essential in order to strengthen solidarity and create a better world for everyone.

Altruism, or the act of selflessly living for others, is a key component in building and maintaining trust within a society. It involves placing the good of others above one's own self-interest and sacrificing time, energy, or possessions for the collective good. This moral obligation to the community is the opposite of selfishness and requires individuals to act voluntarily and intentionally. French sociologist Émile Durkheim argued that altruism and shared values should be the basis of social solidarity, as it helps to prevent selfish behaviour and encourages individuals to consider their duties to the community. However, altruism can only thrive in a society where trust has been established.

It is essential to cultivate a sense of trust within a community before expecting altruistic behaviour to flourish. This can be achieved through open communication, mutual respect, and a willingness to work towards the collective good. By doing so, it can enhance cooperation between different communities and ensure the well-being of the entire society.

Civic Engagement

In social and political theory, the common good refers to the well-being of all members of society. It is not about the interests of one group or individual, but rather the interests of all. This concept is often linked to the idea of a social contract, where individuals agree to form a society and follow certain rules and principles for the benefit of everyone. This agreement is essential for maintaining a functioning and just society. The concept of the common good is often seen as a key element in creating a fair and equal society. It recognizes that the well-being of each individual is interconnected and that the success of one person is dependent on the success of others. This idea is especially important in today's globalized world, where the actions of one country can have a significant impact on the rest of the world.

By promoting the common good, persons can work towards creating a more just and sustainable world for all. However, achieving the common good is not always easy. It requires individuals to put aside their own interests and work towards the greater good. This can be a difficult task, as people naturally tend to prioritize their own needs and desires. Additionally, determining what is truly in the common good can be a complex and ongoing process. It requires constant communication, compromise, and a willingness to listen and understand different perspectives. Despite these challenges, striving towards the common good is crucial for creating a better society for all.

Living together in society means that individuals must steer complex relationships with others and constantly make decisions that balance their own desires with the common good. This can be a daunting task, as the concept of "the common good" is multifaceted and ever-evolving. It requires ongoing communication, compromise, and a willingness to understand and respect different perspectives. Despite the challenges, striving towards the common good is essential for creating a better society for all. Without a shared understanding of what is morally just and acceptable, chaos and conflict would reign.

This is why Hobbes argues that the establishment of a social contract is crucial for maintaining order and promoting a sense of morality within society. By agreeing to live under a sovereign with absolute authority, individuals are able to create a framework for living together that promotes cooperation and allows for a "commodious" way of life. However, this does not mean that morality and justice are fixed and unchanging. Rather, they are constantly being negotiated and re-evaluated as society evolves. The social contract serves as a foundation, but it is up to individuals to continually strive towards the common good and adapt to changing circumstances. This ongoing process of determining what is truly in the common good requires a deep understanding of others and a willingness to work together for the betterment of all.

The common good is the foundation of society and governments, and its maintenance is the responsibility of the people. This requires an understanding of others and working together for the better of all.

In the case of a tyrannical government, the people have a right to resist and even dissolve the social contract to start a new. Locke's concept of the social contract is based on the idea that individuals enter into society to protect their property and well-being. However, when the government fails to fulfil this duty, either by becoming tyrannical or by neglecting its duty to protect the people, it nullifies the compact and puts itself in a state of war with the people. It is then the people's right, and perhaps even their duty, to resist and overthrow the government. This highlights the importance of continually striving towards the common good in order to maintain a just and stable society.

Jean-Jacques Rousseau was a prominent figure during the Enlightenment, a time of intellectual growth in France. He contributed to major works and engaged in discussions that delved into the pressing issues of his era. Rousseau had two social contract theories - one that outlined the moral and political development of humans, and the other that provided a solution to the problems faced in modern society. In his essay, "Discourse on the Origin and Foundations of Inequality Among Men," commonly known as the Second Discourse, Rousseau presents a naturalized account of the social contract. He believes this theory to be problematic, as it portrays the evolution of humans from a State of Nature to society. The second theory, presented in "The Social Contract," is his idealized view on how to address the issues created in modern society.

Rousseau's theories highlight the importance of understanding others and working together for the common good. He believed that when a government fails to uphold the well-being and property of its people, it goes against the social contract and creates a state of war with its citizens. This emphasizes the need for a deep understanding of others and a willingness to work together to ensure the common good is upheld for the betterment of all. Rousseau's ideas provide a valuable perspective on the role of society and government in promoting a fair and just society for all its citizens.

Rawls' theory of justice emphasizes the importance of fairness and equality in society. It goes beyond traditional social contract theories by outlining the fundamental principles that should govern our actions and decisions. These principles act as a guide for constructing a just and well-ordered society, ensuring that everyone's rights and freedoms are respected and protected. Rawls' theory serves as a reminder that our society should be built upon a deep understanding of others and a willingness to work together for the common good.

In addition, Rawls' theory sets limits on the ways in which we can organize society. By prioritizing justice and fairness, it prevents any form of discrimination or oppression that may arise in the pursuit of power or wealth. This ensures that everyone, regardless of their background or social status, has an equal opportunity to prosper and contribute to society. Rawls' principles serve as a reminder that society and government should work together to create a fair and just world for all its citizens. It highlights the need for a deep understanding of others and a willingness to work together to ensure the common good is upheld.

This theory has become deeply ingrained in our societal structures, influencing our daily interactions and shaping our perceptions of ourselves and others. Its impact extends far beyond the realm of philosophy, permeating into our cultural and social systems. As such, it is essential for us to constantly reflect on and evaluate the validity and effectiveness of this theory in promoting a fair and just society. Moreover, the ongoing critiques of social contract theory serve as a reminder of the complexities and nuances involved in creating an equitable and harmonious society. These critiques challenge us to consider the diverse perspectives and experiences of individuals within our communities, promoting a deeper understanding and empathy for others.

By actively engaging in dialogue and discourse, we can work towards a more inclusive and equitable social contract that benefits all members of society. In essence, the principles of social contract theory call for a collective effort towards the common good, emphasizing the importance of cooperation and collaboration. This requires a willingness to listen, learn, and adapt in order to create a society that truly serves the needs and rights of all individuals, rather than a select few. By staying vigilant and continuously examining and improving our social contract, we can strive towards a fair and just society that upholds the values of equality, justice, and empathy.

Though individual rights and freedoms hold significance, the notion of the common good suggests that there may arise situations where individual interests must be reconciled with the wider interests of the community. This belief stems from the understanding that society as a whole thrives when its members prioritize the greater good over their own individual needs. This is particularly evident in times of public health crises, where personal liberties may have to be temporarily curtailed for the sake of safeguarding the well-being of the larger population. In such cases, the common good takes precedence over individual liberties. While it may seem like an encroachment upon personal rights, it is crucial to recognize that for a society to function effectively, there must be a balance between individual and collective interests. This is why democratic systems and the rule of law exist, to ensure that the common good is upheld while also protecting individual rights. Despite the perceived conflict between individual rights and the common good, they are actually interdependent and rely on each other for the smooth functioning of society. By striking a balance between individual and community needs, a healthy and harmonious society can be achieved. This delicate equilibrium requires continual communication and compromise between citizens and the government, along with a mutual understanding and respect for each other's rights and responsibilities. Ultimately, the concept of the common good serves as a reminder that we are all interconnected and must work together for the greater good of society.

The concept of the common good highlights the importance of balancing individual and collective interests in a society. While individuals have their own rights and responsibilities, it is fundamental to also consider the well-being of the community as a whole. This requires continual communication and compromise between citizens and the government, as well as a mutual understanding and respect for each other's perspectives. It is inevitable that individuals have differing perspectives on what constitutes the common good. Some may prioritize universal rights and values, while others may take into account contextual factors and prioritize certain rights over others. This diversity of thought can lead to dynamic interpretations of the common good, as it is constantly evolving and adapting to the changing needs and values of a society. Ultimately, the concept of the common good serves as a reminder that we are all interconnected and must work together for the greater good of society. It requires a balance between individual and collective interests, and recognition of the importance of compromise and understanding in achieving this balance. Only by continually engaging in communication and respecting each other's perspectives can we truly strive towards a society that upholds the common good for all its members.

In any society, there will always be inherent conflicts between individual and collective rights. These conflicts often raise complex legal and moral issues that require careful consideration and nuanced solutions. It is essential for individuals to recognize the importance of balancing their personal interests with the greater good of the collective.

This balance can only be achieved through open and respectful communication, as well as a willingness to compromise and understand different perspectives. Without this, conflicts may escalate and lead to further division and harm within a society. Achieving a balance between individual and collective interests is crucial for the common good of all members of a society. It requires a deep understanding of the complexities and nuances of each individual's rights and the impact they have on the collective. This recognition allows for the creation of culturally sensitive solutions that can address conflicts in a fair and just manner. It also highlights the importance of continuous engagement and open communication between individuals, as this is the key to finding common ground and reaching compromises that benefit everyone.

The balance between individual interests and the common good is a constant struggle in our society. It is a debate that has far-reaching consequences and can greatly impact how we perceive and apply rights, both at an individual and collective level. This ongoing discussion has led to the development of various implementation strategies that aim to respect cultural differences while upholding fundamental human rights. This is essential for creating a harmonious coexistence between individuals and the collective. The importance of communication and mutual understanding cannot be overstated in this debate. By continuously engaging in open and respectful dialogue, we can bridge the gap between personal interests and the common good. It is through this exchange of ideas and perspectives that we can find compromises and solutions that benefit both the individual and the collective. This approach also allows for the recognition and respect of each other's rights, opening the way towards a society that values the common good and embraces diversity. The willingness to compromise and understand different perspectives is fundamental in finding a balance between individual and collective rights.

It requires a level of empathy and open-mindedness that allows for the recognition and respect of diverse beliefs and values. By valuing the common good and working towards a society that embraces inclusivity and diversity, we can create a more just and harmonious world for all. This ongoing discussion and exchange of ideas will continue to shape our understanding and implementation of rights, ultimately leading to a more equitable and peaceful society.

The discourse surrounding individual and collective rights is an essential aspect of human rights on a global scale. This ongoing discussion reflects not only the diverse cultural norms and values held by different societies, but also the deep philosophical divides that exist when it comes to understanding and implementing human rights. By acknowledging and engaging in this debate, persons can gain a more comprehensive understanding of the complexities and nuances involved in human rights issues. Moreover, the conversation around individual versus collective rights has significant implications for how we define, respect, and implement human rights. It forces us to question whether certain rights should take precedence over others, and how we can strike a balance between the needs and interests of the individual and the collective. This ongoing exchange of ideas and perspectives is crucial in shaping our understanding of human rights and working towards a more equitable and peaceful society for all. Ultimately, the individual versus collective rights debate serves as a reminder that human rights are not a one-size-fits-all concept.

Civic engagement and active participation in the community are critical for creating a healthy society. This involves actively being involved in the community, whether it is by volunteering at local events, advocating for social issues that matter to you, or contributing in any way that makes a positive impact on society as a whole. These actions may seem small, but they can have a huge impact on the community and the people within it.

Volunteering is one of the most common forms of civic engagement. It allows individuals to give back to their community and make a difference in the lives of others. By volunteering, individuals can gain a sense of fulfilment and purpose, as well as develop new skills and build relationships with others. Additionally, advocating for social issues is another important aspect of civic engagement. This involves using one's voice to bring attention to important causes and promoting positive change in society. By actively participating in these activities, individuals can play a crucial role in promoting the common good and creating a better world for everyone. Furthermore, contributing to the overall betterment of society can take many forms. It can range from simple acts of kindness, such as helping a neighbor in need, to larger actions like participating in community clean-up projects or donating to charitable organizations. Every contribution, no matter how big or small, can make a positive impact and help create a more cohesive and supportive community. By actively engaging in the community and working towards the common good, individuals can play a vital role in shaping the world around them and creating a better future for all.

Individuals engaging in civic participation can make a significant impact on their community, both small and large. By actively participating in the community, individuals can work towards creating a more supportive and cohesive environment for all. This not only benefits the community in the present, but also sets the foundation for a better future.

Civic engagement involves addressing public concerns and taking action to protect public values, whether through political or non-political means. It is not limited to group activities alone; individuals can also make a difference on their own. By actively participating in their community, individuals can help shape the world around them and create a positive impact. This can involve volunteering, participating in community events, or even simply being a responsible and engaged citizen. Each individual's contribution, no matter how small, can make a significant difference in creating a better and more harmonious society.

By actively engaging in their community and addressing public issues, individuals can make a positive impact and contribute to the betterment of society. This not only benefits the community as a whole, but also fosters a sense of belonging and unity among its members. In a world where individual actions can often feel insignificant, civic engagement empowers individuals to make a meaningful difference and create a more cohesive and supportive community.

Civic engagement goes beyond just participating in community events and volunteer work. It requires a set of valuable skills that can positively impact society. Empathy allows individuals to understand and connect with others, while active listening helps build relationships and foster understanding.

Furthermore, the ability to lead helps guide and mobilize others towards a common goal. These skills are essential for creating a strong and inclusive community.

It also involves being physically present in our cities and communities. This means actively participating in local government and decision-making processes, as well as being aware and involved in issues that affect the community. By being present, individuals can voice their opinions and make a tangible impact in shaping the place they call home. This sense of ownership and responsibility not only benefits the community, but also creates a sense of belonging and unity among its members. In a world where individual actions can sometimes feel small and insignificant, civic engagement empowers individuals to make a meaningful difference. It provides a platform for individuals to use their skills and voices to create positive change in their communities. By coming together and working towards a common goal, individuals can create a more cohesive and supportive society for all.

By being aware of one's surroundings, individuals are able to take part in civic engagement and make a difference. Events within their local communities serve as catalysts for individuals to use their skills and voices to create positive change. It is through civic participation that individuals are able to come together and work towards common goals, thus creating a more cohesive and supportive society for all.

Whether it is through volunteering, voting, or advocating for important issues, civic engagement empowers individuals to make a meaningful difference in their communities. Civic engagement not only benefits the community, but also the individuals themselves. By actively participating in their communities, individuals are able to gain a sense of purpose and fulfilment. They are able to see the direct impact of their actions and feel a sense of pride in contributing to the betterment of society. Additionally, civic engagement provides individuals with the opportunity to connect with like-minded individuals and build relationships within their communities. This sense of unity and belonging can have a positive impact on mental health and overall well-being. In a society where individuals often feel insignificant and powerless, civic engagement serves as a platform for individuals to have their voices heard and make a difference. It allows for individuals to take ownership of their communities and work towards creating a better future for themselves and others. By coming together and utilizing their skills and passions, individuals can create a more inclusive and equitable society for all.

Citizen engagement and participation are essential components of a thriving democracy, as they enable individuals to actively participate in the decision-making process and hold elected officials accountable. However, despite the significant benefits of citizen engagement, there are several challenges that hinder its effectiveness. One of the major issues related to citizen engagement is the lack of awareness and understanding among citizens about their rights and responsibilities. Many citizens are not aware of their role in the decision-making process, and therefore, they do not participate in it. This lack of understanding results in a limited pool of individuals that can be engaged and mobilized, ultimately leading to a loss of diversity in voices and perspectives in the decision-making process. In addition, the lack of citizen engagement can also lead to a lack of accountability and transparency in the decision-making process.

When citizens are not actively involved, there is a risk of decisions being made without proper checks and balances, allowing for potential corruption and bias to influence the outcomes. Additionally, a lack of citizen engagement can also lead to a disconnect between the government and its citizens, as decisions are made without considering their needs and concerns. This can ultimately result in a breakdown of trust and confidence in the government, hindering future attempts at citizen engagement. In order to overcome these challenges and promote effective citizen engagement, it is vital to educate and empower individuals about their rights and responsibilities as citizens. This can be achieved through various means, such as civic education programs and accessible information resources. By equipping citizens with the necessary knowledge and resources, they can actively participate in the decision-making process and ensure that their voices are heard. This not only promotes a more inclusive and equitable society but also strengthens the foundations of a thriving democracy.

The Judiciary

Defining Judicial Independence in a Democratic Society

Judicial independence, a cornerstone of any functioning democracy, is more than a mere aspiration; it's a fundamental structural guarantee ensuring the fair and impartial administration of justice. Its absence invariably leads to the erosion of human rights, the undermining of the rule of law, and the weakening of democratic institutions. Understanding its true meaning, however, requires a careful distinction between judicial independence and judicial impartiality. While often used interchangeably, they represent distinct, yet complementary, concepts. Judicial impartiality refers to the procedural and ethical obligation of judges to remain unbiased in their decisions, free from prejudice or external influence during the specific adjudication of a case.

This requires judges to apply the law fairly to all parties, regardless of their background, status, or political affiliations. It's a personal commitment to fairness demonstrably displayed in every courtroom interaction.

Judicial independence, conversely, is a structural and institutional guarantee safeguarding the judiciary's autonomy from undue influence by other branches of government or powerful private interests. This protection is not focused on individual judges' behaviour during a specific case but on the broader institutional framework that surrounds the judiciary. It ensures the judiciary operates free from external pressures which could compromise its ability to make impartial decisions consistently, across the spectrum of cases that come before the court. This protection is achieved through a complex interplay of constitutional provisions, legislative safeguards, and procedural mechanisms that insulate the judiciary from political machinations and corrupting forces.

The absence of judicial independence means that courts are vulnerable to manipulation, potentially rendering their judgments arbitrary and unjust, fundamentally eroding public trust in the legal system.

The historical evolution of judicial independence offers valuable insights into its importance and fragility. In many countries, the struggle for an independent judiciary has been long and arduous, often intertwined with broader struggles for democracy and human rights. The theoretical underpinnings of judicial independence are rooted in the fundamental principles of the rule of law, due process, and the separation of powers. The rule of law demands that all individuals, including those in power, are subject to and accountable under the law. An independent judiciary plays a critical role in ensuring the rule of law by interpreting and applying the law impartially and without fear or favour. Due process ensures fairness and equity in legal proceedings.

Judicial independence is essential for guaranteeing due process, as only an impartial and unbiased judiciary can ensure fair trials and protect individuals' rights. The separation of powers prevents the concentration of power in any single branch of government, protecting individual liberty and promoting accountability. An independent judiciary serves as a vital check on the power of the executive and legislative branches, preventing abuse of power and upholding the principles of democratic governance. This checks and balances system ensures no single entity controls the entirety of governmental functions and the ability to interpret, and potentially manipulate, the law.

The concept of judicial independence is frequently challenged by competing interests and pressures. The delicate balance between ensuring judicial independence and maintaining public accountability necessitates a nuanced understanding of the various threats to judicial autonomy.

Political interference, ranging from subtle pressures to blatant intimidation, can severely compromise the integrity and impartiality of the judiciary. Governments may seek to influence judicial decisions through appointments, budget allocations, or public pronouncements criticizing court rulings. This can create a chilling effect, discouraging judges from rendering decisions that may be unpopular with the ruling power. Such political meddling not only undermines individual cases but also erodes public trust in the fairness of the legal system as a whole, fostering cynicism and distrust.

Corruption within the judiciary itself presents another grave threat to judicial independence. Bribery, favouritism, and other forms of misconduct can compromise the integrity of judicial decisions and undermine public faith in the legal system. Such corruption can manifest in various forms, from direct bribes influencing judicial outcomes to more subtle forms of favouritism shown towards certain individuals or groups. This corruption undermines the rule of law and erodes the public's trust in the fairness of the justice system, potentially leading to decreased faith in democratic institutions more broadly. The fight for judicial independence, therefore, necessitates a multifaceted approach addressing not only external pressures but also the internal vulnerabilities of the judiciary itself. Transparent processes, strong ethics codes, and robust disciplinary mechanisms are essential to address these challenges, ensuring the judiciary's integrity is maintained to the highest standards.

Furthermore, the tension between judicial independence and accountability is a critical aspect that requires careful consideration. While judicial independence necessitates protection from external influence, it does not imply immunity from scrutiny or accountability. Judges, like all public officials, must be accountable for their actions. This accountability is not meant to undermine their independence, but rather to ensure that they exercise their powers responsibly and within the bounds of the law. Appropriate mechanisms for accountability include judicial review, appeals processes, ethical codes, and disciplinary procedures. These mechanisms provide checks and balances, ensuring that judicial power is not abused and that judges are held responsible for their decisions. The effectiveness of these mechanisms hinges on their transparency and impartiality, thus protecting both judicial independence and public trust.

The insidious erosion of judicial independence often begins subtly, masked under the guise of legitimate governance. Political interference, however, rarely manifests as overt coercion; instead, it adopts more nuanced and insidious tactics. One of the most potent instruments of political control is the manipulation of judicial appointments.

Governments, through their control over the nomination and confirmation processes, can subtly shape the composition of the judiciary, favouring candidates who align with their ideological perspectives or political agendas. This isn't always a blatant act of selecting judges based on partisan loyalties; rather, it can involve a more sophisticated strategy of prioritizing candidates who have expressed certain judicial philosophies or have a history of rulings sympathetic to the government's position, even if ostensibly within the bounds of existing legal frameworks.

This subtle form of manipulation can have far-reaching consequences. A judiciary subtly skewed in favour of a particular ideology may be less inclined to challenge government actions, even when those actions contravene fundamental constitutional principles or established legal precedents. This creeping influence can gradually erode public trust in the fairness and impartiality of the justice system, leaving citizens feeling vulnerable to the whims of political power. The consequences are particularly acute in areas involving fundamental rights, where judicial review serves as a crucial bulwark against government overreach. A judiciary lacking genuine independence will be ill-equipped to uphold these rights effectively, leaving vulnerable populations exposed to unchecked governmental power.

Beyond appointments, budgetary control represents another potent weapon in the arsenal of political interference.

Governments wielding control over judicial funding can exert influence by strategically allocating resources. Reduced funding for courts or specific judicial functions, for instance, can lead to delays, understaffing, and an overall decline in the efficiency and effectiveness of the justice system. Such resource constraints can indirectly compromise judicial independence by creating a dependence on the executive branch for the necessary resources to perform judicial duties. The threat isn't necessarily the outright denial of funding; it's the power to withhold or selectively allocate resources to shape the judiciary's operations and, ultimately, its decisions.

Public criticism, while seemingly a hallmark of a transparent and accountable system, can also become a tool of political pressure. Governments or their allies may launch sustained campaigns of public condemnation against judges who issue rulings perceived as unfavourable. The goal isn't always to directly influence a specific ruling; rather, it's to create an atmosphere of intimidation that discourages judges from making independent decisions in the future. This can manifest as coordinated media attacks, public statements from government officials, or even orchestrated protests targeting judges and their families. The cumulative effect of such actions is to create a chilling effect, making judges hesitant to issue rulings that may invite such public scrutiny.

The insidious nature of this pressure is that it rarely crosses the explicit line of direct interference. Governments can typically claim that criticism is merely an exercise of freedom of speech or a response to public concern, masking the true intention of chilling judicial independence. This tactic necessitates a robust and independent media landscape capable of providing balanced coverage and critically examining such government actions. The lack of such a critical counterbalance can further embolden governments to engage in such tactics.

Corruption within the judicial system itself poses another significant threat to judicial independence. This corruption can take various forms, from bribery and extortion to favouritism and cronyism. Judges facing financial pressures or lacking sufficient protections may be susceptible to inducements from powerful individuals or entities seeking favourable rulings. Such corruption undermines the very foundation of impartiality, creating a system where justice is not only compromised but openly for sale. The consequences are far-reaching, eroding public trust in the judiciary, undermining the rule of law, and damaging the overall perception of fairness within society. Combating judicial corruption requires comprehensive reforms, encompassing stringent ethical guidelines, robust investigative mechanisms, and effective sanctions for those found guilty.

Case studies from around the world illuminate the devastating consequences of political interference and corruption in the judicial system. In some countries, systematic political manipulation of the judicial appointments process has created a judiciary overtly beholden to the ruling party. In other instances, budget cuts or resource limitations imposed by the executive branch have severely hampered the courts' ability to function effectively, contributing to extensive procedural delays and a decline in the quality of justice. Countries with weak institutional safeguards against political interference have often witnessed a chilling effect on judicial independence, leading to self-censorship among judges who fear retribution for unpopular rulings.

The erosion of judicial independence is not a sudden event but a gradual process that occurs over time. Early warning signs might include: a noticeable increase in public criticism of judges who render unpopular decisions, a pattern of delays in judicial appointments that favour government-aligned candidates, or a noticeable decrease in the resources allocated to the judiciary. Identifying these early signals is vital, as they can indicate the onset of a deeper and more systematic weakening of the judicial system. A proactive approach to safeguarding judicial independence necessitates strengthening institutional safeguards, promoting transparency and accountability, and fostering a culture of respect for the rule of law among all stakeholders.

The challenge of preserving judicial independence requires a multi-faceted approach. It requires not only strong institutional safeguards within the judiciary but also active vigilance from civil society organizations, the media, and the legal profession itself. Independent judicial oversight bodies, capable of investigating allegations of misconduct and corruption, are essential to maintaining accountability and deterring unethical behaviour. Transparency in judicial proceedings, particularly in the appointment process, also plays a crucial role in fostering public confidence and preventing political manipulation. A robust and independent media is also crucial in holding the judiciary and government accountable, shedding light on potential instances of political interference.

Furthermore, fostering a culture of judicial ethics is vital. Comprehensive judicial training programs that emphasize impartiality, integrity, and the importance of judicial independence can equip judges with the necessary tools to navigate complex political pressures. The establishment of clear ethical guidelines and enforcement mechanisms can help to deter corruption and maintain high standards of conduct within the judicial system. Finally, educating the public about the significance of judicial independence is critical. A well-informed citizenry is more likely to demand and defend the independence of the judiciary, creating a powerful counterbalance against political interference.

Safeguarding Judicial Independence

Potent ways of political influence can undermine the judiciary's impartiality. However, the fight to preserve this vital pillar of a just society isn't solely defensive; it necessitates proactive measures, structural safeguards, and procedural protections. These safeguards, built into legal systems worldwide, aim to insulate the judiciary from external pressures and ensure its continued ability to dispense justice fairly and without fear or favour.

One of the most fundamental safeguards lies in the constitutional framework itself. Many constitutions explicitly enshrine the principle of judicial independence, outlining the judiciary's powers and limitations, and often guaranteeing judges' security of tenure and immunity from political interference. These constitutional guarantees act as a bulwark against arbitrary actions by the executive or legislative branches.

Nations have incorporated similar provisions into their basic laws, emphasizing the importance of an independent judiciary for the protection of fundamental rights and the rule of law. However, the strength of such constitutional provisions hinges on their effective enforcement and the willingness of other branches of government to respect them. A constitution, no matter how well-drafted, is ultimately only as effective as the commitment to uphold its principles.

Beyond constitutional guarantees, the process of judicial selection is critical. A transparent and merit-based appointment process is key in preventing the infiltration of politically motivated or compromised individuals into judicial positions. Systems that prioritize qualifications, experience, and integrity over political affiliation are more likely to produce an independent judiciary. Some countries employ merit-based selection committees composed of legal experts, judges, and representatives from civil society to ensure a fair and impartial process. These committees meticulously vet candidates, assessing their qualifications and ensuring their adherence to the highest ethical standards. In contrast, systems where political appointments dominate risk undermining judicial independence, creating a judiciary susceptible to political influence. The balance between executive prerogative and the need for an independent judiciary frequently presents a challenge in many nations, leading to ongoing debate regarding the optimal selection process. The goal is to find a model that balances effective government oversight with the crucial need to prevent undue influence. Countries continuously refine their selection mechanisms, adapting them to the unique challenges of their political landscapes.

The concept of secure tenure plays a crucial role in safeguarding judicial independence. Judges must be free to make impartial decisions without fear of reprisal or losing their positions due to unpopular rulings. This security of tenure doesn't equate to immunity from accountability; rather, it ensures that judges can exercise their judicial functions without the constant threat of political interference. The mechanisms for removing judges from office should be robust, independent, and focused on serious misconduct, such as proven corruption or gross incompetence.

Impeachment procedures, for instance, are often employed in many legal systems, but they are usually subject to high thresholds and rigorous processes to prevent their misuse for political purposes. Impeachment should be a last resort, reserved for extreme cases of judicial wrongdoing, not utilized as a tool to silence dissenting voices or punish judges for unfavourable rulings. The balance between security of tenure and accountability is an essential one; the system must deter political interference while simultaneously maintaining mechanisms to address genuine misconduct.

Budgetary autonomy is another critical component of judicial independence. Judges should have control over their court's budget, free from political interference that might be used to influence their decisions. A judiciary that depends on the executive branch for funding may find its independence compromised. If the allocation of resources becomes a tool for political leverage, the judiciary's ability to function impartially and effectively will be undermined. A financially independent judiciary ensures that courts can function efficiently, hire competent staff, and provide necessary resources to effectively administer justice. This autonomy extends to the administrative aspects of the judiciary, including the appointment of court staff and the management of court resources. Independent oversight of the judiciary's budget can be provided by a specially constituted body, outside of the executive or legislative influence, ensuring accountability and transparency. This financial independence, coupled with transparent budgetary processes, fosters public trust in the judiciary's impartiality.

Moreover, the effective functioning of a transparent and accountable appeals process is vital. A robust appellate system allows for the review of lower court decisions, ensuring consistency in the application of the law and providing a mechanism to correct errors or address potential bias. The possibility of appeal acts as a check on the power of individual judges and helps to maintain the integrity of the judicial system. Access to appellate courts should be readily available and not unduly restricted, allowing for a fair and thorough review of judicial rulings. The availability of appellate review instils confidence in the fairness of the system and discourages potential abuse of power by judges at lower levels of the court system. This system of checks and balances helps to guarantee the integrity of the judicial process, further strengthening the principle of judicial independence.

In addition to these structural safeguards, procedural protections are essential for maintaining judicial independence. These measures focus on ensuring the fairness and impartiality of court proceedings. Rules of evidence, strict adherence to due process, and the requirement for reasoned judgments all contribute to creating a system where judicial decisions are based on law and evidence, not on political pressure or personal bias. The importance of reasoned judgments cannot be overstated; they offer transparency and accountability, allowing for scrutiny and appeal. These judgments also serve as precedents, shaping the evolution of the law in a predictable and consistent manner. The availability of transcripts and the obligation to provide reasons for judgments foster transparency, allowing for public oversight and accountability. These procedural protections, while seemingly technical, are fundamental to ensuring that the judiciary remains a trustworthy and impartial arbiter of justice. Any compromise in these procedural safeguards undermines the foundation of judicial independence.

Finally, the role of a well-trained and ethical judiciary itself is vital. Judicial education, ongoing training, and the establishment of ethical codes of conduct are fundamental in instilling a culture of integrity and impartiality within the judicial system. Judges must be equipped with the knowledge and skills necessary to navigate complex legal issues while maintaining their independence. Code of conduct, regularly updated to address emerging challenges, provide guidelines for judges to uphold ethical standards and to avoid conflicts of interest. Moreover, the establishment of independent judicial bodies that can investigate complaints of judicial misconduct and impose disciplinary measures is essential. Such bodies should be composed of individuals with impeccable integrity and experience, ensuring that investigations are impartial and fair.

A culture of self-regulation and accountability, within the judiciary itself, helps to ensure that judges maintain the highest ethical standards. This self-regulation complements the external checks and balances provided by constitutional provisions and other safeguards.

Judicial Independence

Judicial independence, a cornerstone of any just and functioning legal system, is a multifaceted concept with a rich history and diverse interpretations. Its essence lies in the judiciary's ability to adjudicate cases impartially, free from undue influence from other branches of government, political pressures, or private interests.

This freedom is not absolute, however, and must be balanced against the equally important need for judicial accountability. Historically, the concept of judicial independence evolved gradually, often in response to abuses of power by monarchs or other ruling elites. In early common law systems, judges were often appointed by the crown and subject to its direct influence, leading to biased decisions and a lack of impartiality. The rise of constitutionalism and the establishment of independent judiciaries marked a significant shift, aiming to protect the judiciary from political interference and ensure the fair and unbiased application of the law. The development of judicial review, the power of courts to declare laws unconstitutional, further solidified the concept of judicial independence by giving courts the authority to check the power of the legislature and the executive.

Philosophically, several perspectives underpin the concept of judicial independence. One dominant view emphasizes the separation of powers, arguing that an independent judiciary is essential for maintaining a balance of power among the different branches of government. This approach highlights the importance of checks and balances, where the judiciary acts as a safeguard against potential abuses of power by the legislature or executive. Another perspective focuses on the rule of law, asserting that judicial independence is crucial for ensuring that laws are applied fairly and consistently, regardless of the identity or influence of the parties involved. This perspective underscores the importance of impartiality and equal treatment under the law. A third, related perspective, emphasizes the protection of fundamental rights. An independent judiciary is seen as essential to safeguard individual liberties against potential government overreach. The ability of courts to protect individuals from unfair treatment and violations of their constitutional rights is a vital function of an independent judicial system.

The mechanisms for ensuring judicial independence vary significantly across different legal systems. The methods used for judicial selection and tenure play a critical role. In the United States, judges at the federal level are nominated by the President and confirmed by the Senate, serving life terms. This system, while aiming for independence, is also subject to political considerations, influencing judicial appointments and potentially affecting judicial impartiality. In contrast, the United Kingdom employs a different system where judges are appointed through a more meritocratic process, with a greater emphasis on legal expertise and experience, often based on recommendations from independent bodies. While this aims for independence, concerns remain about the potential for implicit biases influencing appointments. Germany, with its system of specialized judicial career paths and independent selection committees, seeks to ensure both expertise and insulation from political pressures in judicial appointments. These varied approaches demonstrate the complexities of establishing and maintaining an independent judiciary.

Moreover, the relationship between judicial independence and the protection of fundamental rights is a critical aspect of this discussion. An independent judiciary acts as the ultimate guarantor of individual rights and freedoms, ensuring that government actions comply with constitutional principles and international human rights standards. Courts play a crucial role in scrutinizing laws and government policies, ensuring they do not violate fundamental rights. In societies where fundamental rights are routinely violated, judicial independence serves as a bulwark against the abuse of state power. Without an independent judiciary, the protection of individual rights becomes precarious, at the mercy of the political whims of those in power. This protection, therefore, is fundamentally intertwined with the concept of judicial independence itself. The judiciary's ability to strike down unconstitutional legislation or to protect citizens from state-sponsored violations of their rights is crucial in upholding democracy and the rule of law.

The historical evolution of judicial independence, the philosophical underpinnings, and the varying approaches to securing it across diverse legal systems collectively illustrate the ongoing challenge of creating and maintaining a judiciary that is both independent and accountable. The next section will explore the crucial complementary element of judicial accountability, exploring why judges, while needing significant independence also must be answerable for their conduct and actions. The inherent tension between these two principles – independence and accountability –forms a critical challenge for any legal system striving for justice and fairness.

Independence and Accountability

The inherent tension between judicial independence and accountability forms the central paradox of a fair and effective justice system. While independence safeguards judges from undue political or external pressure, ensuring impartial decision-making, accountability is equally essential to maintain public trust and prevent abuses of power. This delicate balancing act requires careful consideration of the mechanisms employed to hold judges responsible for their actions, and a nuanced understanding of the potential pitfalls inherent in each approach. Striking the right balance is a continuous challenge, with varying degrees of success observed across diverse legal systems worldwide.

One of the most significant challenges lies in defining the scope of accountability. While gross misconduct, such as bribery or blatant bias, readily warrants disciplinary action, the line becomes blurred when considering less obvious infractions. For instance, the application of inconsistent legal interpretations, perceived leniency or harshness in sentencing, or even the simple matter of judicial demeanour can all become subjects of criticism and calls for accountability. Determining which actions constitute legitimate grounds for scrutiny and which fall within the realm of legitimate judicial discretion is a critical task, requiring clear guidelines and well-defined procedures to prevent arbitrary or politically motivated interventions.

The design and implementation of effective accountability mechanisms are essential. Appeals processes, while fundamental to ensuring judicial accuracy and fairness, often prove inadequate to address issues of judicial ethics or bias. Appeals typically focus on errors of law or procedure, not on a judge's overall conduct or potential biases. Furthermore, the appeal process itself can be lengthy, costly, and ultimately ineffective in correcting systemic issues or preventing future instances of misconduct. This highlights the need for supplementary mechanisms specifically designed to address ethical concerns.

Legislative oversight provides another avenue for accountability. Parliaments or legislatures may have the power to investigate judges, initiate impeachment proceedings, or even influence the appointment and confirmation processes. However, the potential for political manipulation is considerable. Legislative oversight can become a tool for silencing dissenting voices or punishing judges for unpopular rulings, thus undermining the very independence it aims to uphold. The effectiveness of legislative oversight hinges on its impartiality and adherence to due process, factors that are not always guaranteed, particularly in systems with weak checks and balances.

Judicial disciplinary bodies, including internal review mechanisms within the judiciary itself, provide a more targeted approach to accountability. These bodies often consist of senior judges or legal professionals tasked with investigating complaints of misconduct and imposing sanctions. However, the effectiveness of these mechanisms often depends on their independence and the transparency of their procedures. The risk of bias or collusion among judges remains a concern, particularly in jurisdictions lacking robust systems of checks and balances and where judicial independence is already compromised.

Public scrutiny, facilitated by a free press and access to information, plays a vital role in holding judges accountable. However, it requires a careful balance. While public awareness of judicial conduct is important in maintaining transparency and public trust, undue media pressure or public outrage can disrupt judicial impartiality and undermine the integrity of the legal process. A clear distinction must be made between constructive criticism and unwarranted attacks on judges and their decisions.

International comparisons highlight the varying approaches and challenges in balancing independence and accountability. Countries with strong traditions of judicial independence, such as the United States and Canada, often rely on a combination of appeals, impeachment processes, and internal disciplinary mechanisms. The effectiveness of these mechanisms varies, often depending on political and societal factors. Other countries, particularly those with weaker democratic traditions, may struggle to implement robust accountability systems due to political interference or a lack of resources.

The case of South Africa, which underwent a significant transition to democracy, provides a compelling illustration. Its constitution explicitly emphasizes both judicial independence and accountability. However, implementing effective mechanisms to balance these principles remains a complex challenge, often involving conflicts between different branches of government and ongoing debate over the optimal balance between these competing interests.

Similarly, the experience of many countries in Eastern Europe during and after the transition from communist rule demonstrates the difficulty in establishing independent and accountable judiciaries in the context of significant political and social upheaval.

The establishment of robust judicial systems requires not only constitutional guarantees but also the development of supporting institutional structures, a well-trained judiciary, and a strong civil society.

In contrast, countries with highly centralized legal systems may have more direct mechanisms for judicial accountability, but this can come at the cost of judicial independence. The delicate balance between the two is often shaped by the specific historical, political, and cultural context.

Finding solutions to this enduring tension demands a multi-pronged approach. Clear and comprehensive codes of judicial ethics are crucial, setting out explicit standards of conduct for judges and providing a framework for addressing deviations. Transparent and impartial disciplinary procedures are equally important, ensuring fair investigations and appropriate sanctions for misconduct.

Furthermore, robust systems of judicial training and continuing education can emphasize ethical considerations and best practices, enhancing the quality of judicial decision-making and reducing the incidence of misconduct.

The role of the legal profession and civil society is also significant. Bar associations and other professional organizations can play a key role in enforcing ethical standards, providing support and guidance to judges, and investigating allegations of misconduct. Civil society organizations can contribute by promoting transparency and public awareness of judicial conduct, advocating for judicial reform, and providing oversight of the judicial system.

Ultimately, the balance between judicial independence and accountability is not a static concept but a dynamic process requiring constant evaluation and adjustment. It necessitates a commitment to transparency, due process, and the ongoing pursuit of a just and fair legal system. The ideal is not to eliminate the tension but to manage it effectively, ensuring that both values are adequately safeguarded, thereby fostering a judiciary that commands public confidence and serves the interests of justice. The quest for this ideal remains a central challenge for legal systems around the world, demanding constant vigilance and ongoing reform.

The historical trajectory of judicial accountability reveals a complex interplay between societal expectations of judicial impartiality and the practical realities of holding judges responsible for their actions.

Early judicial systems, often lacking the formal structures we recognize today, relied heavily on informal mechanisms of accountability. Reputation and public opinion played a significant role in shaping judicial behaviour. Judges, particularly in smaller communities, were directly accountable to the local populace, whose views on their fairness and integrity directly influenced their standing within the community. The potential for social ostracism or economic hardship served as a powerful deterrent against judicial misconduct. This informal system, however, was inherently uneven, vulnerable to biases and lacking the consistent application of standards found in modern systems.

The development of formal legal structures, particularly the rise of codified laws and professionalized judiciaries, marked a significant shift in the landscape of judicial accountability. The emergence of appellate courts provided a crucial mechanism for review of lower court decisions, offering a degree of external control and promoting consistency in judicial interpretation. This hierarchical system of judicial review established a framework for correcting errors and addressing instances of judicial bias or incompetence. However, the effectiveness of appellate review depended heavily on the independence and impartiality of higher courts and the clarity of appeal procedures. Moreover, access to appellate review remained limited, particularly for those with fewer resources. This period also witnessed the early development of impeachment processes, though these were often politically charged and rarely employed.

The 18th and 19th centuries saw the rise of written constitutions in many nations, which often included provisions specifying the powers and responsibilities of the judiciary. These constitutional frameworks provided the legal basis for establishing more formalized mechanisms of judicial accountability. Constitutions generally sought to safeguard judicial independence from undue political influence while simultaneously outlining procedures for removing judges who engaged in serious misconduct. The balance between these competing goals became a central theme in constitutional debates across various jurisdictions. For example, the United States Constitution's impeachment process for federal judges, while designed to protect against judicial tyranny, also raised concerns about its potential for partisan exploitation. Similarly, the British system's reliance on parliamentary oversight, while offering a path to accountability, risked politicizing the process and potentially compromising judicial independence.

The 20th and 21st centuries witnessed a dramatic expansion of judicial accountability mechanisms, fueled by a growing emphasis on transparency and good governance. The establishment of independent judicial councils or commissions, tasked with investigating allegations of judicial misconduct and imposing sanctions, became increasingly common. These bodies, ideally composed of judges, legal experts, and representatives from the public, aimed to ensure a fair and impartial process for addressing complaints against judges. However, their effectiveness was heavily dependent on their independence from political pressures, the resources allocated to their operations, and the clarity of their mandates. Cases where these councils were effectively used to target politically inconvenient judges highlight the challenge of balancing accountability with independence.

The rise of international human rights law and standards also significantly impacted the development of judicial accountability mechanisms. International conventions and treaties emphasized the importance of an independent and impartial judiciary, while simultaneously demanding accountability for judicial misconduct. International monitoring bodies began to play an increasing role in scrutinizing judicial systems and assessing the adequacy of

mechanisms for addressing judicial misconduct. This international dimension further complicated the balance between accountability and independence, as states were now increasingly subject to external scrutiny in their treatment of judges. The interplay between domestic and international legal standards continues to shape discussions and reforms concerning judicial accountability around the globe.

Comparative analysis across various legal traditions reveals diverse approaches to judicial accountability. Common law systems, emphasizing precedent and adversarial procedures, often rely heavily on internal disciplinary mechanisms, such as peer review processes and judicial councils. Civil law systems, with their inquisitorial traditions, may place greater emphasis on external oversight mechanisms, such as parliamentary review or specialized judicial inspectorates. In some countries, particularly in those with weaker democratic institutions or a history of authoritarian rule, judicial accountability mechanisms may be underdeveloped or subject to political manipulation. In these contexts, the fear of retribution and the lack of robust protection for judges who make unpopular decisions can severely limit the effectiveness of accountability processes. The absence of a truly independent judiciary becomes a significant obstacle to upholding the rule of law.

The historical evolution of judicial accountability mechanisms is not simply a linear progression towards greater accountability; it's a dynamic process influenced by complex political, social, and cultural factors. Periods of political instability or authoritarian rule often witness the erosion of judicial independence and accountability, while periods of democratic consolidation tend to see the strengthening of these mechanisms. The role of civil society, including the media, non-governmental organizations, and legal professional organizations, also plays a significant role in shaping public perceptions of the judiciary and advocating for improvements in judicial accountability. A vibrant civil society can act as a critical check on judicial power, holding judges accountable through public pressure and advocacy. However, in the absence of an environment supportive of free expression and open public debate, the ability of civil society organizations to hold judges to account can be severely limited.

Throughout history, the tension between judicial independence and accountability has been a recurrent theme. The quest for a system that both protects judges from undue political interference and holds them responsible for their actions remains an ongoing challenge. Finding the right balance requires careful consideration of the specific context, including the strength of democratic institutions, the level of public trust in the judiciary, and the cultural norms governing judicial behaviour. The effectiveness of accountability mechanisms depends not only on their design but also on their implementation and enforcement. Even the well-designed system can fail if it lacks the political will to uphold its principles, or if it's undermined by corruption or political interference.

Moreover, the historical context provides insights into the potential pitfalls of specific approaches to judicial accountability. Overly aggressive external mechanisms can undermine judicial independence, leading to self-censorship and reluctance to render difficult or unpopular decisions. Conversely, a reliance on purely internal mechanisms may lack the transparency and impartiality necessary to address serious instances of misconduct effectively. An effective system of judicial accountability often requires a combination of internal and external mechanisms, meticulously designed and implemented to address the specific needs and challenges of a given legal system. The ultimate goal is to create a judiciary that is independent and accountable, capable of upholding the rule of law and serving the interests of justice. This continuous process of evolution requires constant reassessment of existing approaches and adaptation to the changing needs of society, ensuring that the judiciary maintains its legitimacy and remains a cornerstone of a just and equitable society. The ongoing challenge lies in ensuring that judicial accountability mechanisms are not merely formalistic, but truly effective in promoting judicial integrity and public trust in the rule of law.

Appeals and Judicial Review

Appeals and judicial review constitute a cornerstone of judicial accountability, offering a essential mechanism for correcting errors and ensuring consistency within the judicial system. The hierarchical structure of most judiciaries, with lower courts subject to review by higher courts, inherently provides a built-in accountability mechanism. This system allows for the scrutiny of lower court decisions, identifying instances of legal error, factual inaccuracies, or even potential bias. The ability to appeal a decision prevents the perpetuation of incorrect judgments and safeguards against the arbitrary exercise of judicial power. The effectiveness of this process, however, is intricately linked to several factors, including the accessibility of the appeals process, the independence and impartiality of the appellate courts, and the clarity and consistency of the legal rules governing appeals.

The process of appealing a judicial decision typically involves a formal application to a higher court, which assesses whether the lower court committed any errors of law or procedure. Errors of law encompass situations where the lower court misapplied or misinterpreted the relevant legal rules, leading to an incorrect outcome. Errors of fact involve situations where the lower court made factual findings that are not supported by the evidence presented or where the court failed to consider relevant evidence.

Appellate courts are not typically involved in re-examining the evidence de novo, meaning they rarely conduct a complete rehearing of the case. Instead, their focus lies on scrutinizing the lower court's application of the law to the established facts and the procedures followed.

Different jurisdictions employ varying appeals mechanisms. Some jurisdictions maintain a system of hierarchical appeals, allowing for multiple levels of review. The availability of multiple levels of appeal can enhance the likelihood of identifying errors, but it can also increase the time and cost associated with resolving a case, potentially impacting access to justice.

The effectiveness of appeals mechanisms is also significantly influenced by the independence and impartiality of appellate courts. If appellate courts lack independence from political or other external pressures, their ability to act as a check on lower courts is diminished.

Judges on appellate courts must be free to render decisions based on the law and evidence, without fear of retribution or favouritism. The composition of appellate courts, the selection process for judges, and the security of their tenure all play a crucial role in ensuring their independence and impartiality.

The clarity and consistency of the rules governing appeals are also vital. A complex or ambiguous appeals process can hinder the effective correction of judicial errors and lead to unpredictable outcomes. Uniform rules ensure that all litigants have a fair opportunity to challenge lower court decisions and that appellate courts apply the same standards consistently. This is particularly important in addressing concerns about inconsistency and disparity in judicial decision-making across different courts or judges.

Beyond the correction of legal errors, appeals and judicial review contribute to the development of jurisprudence. By examining lower court decisions, appellate courts clarify the meaning and application of legal rules, shaping the body of law within a jurisdiction. This ongoing process of refinement and interpretation enhances legal certainty and predictability. The decisions of appellate courts set precedents that serve as guides for lower courts, promoting consistency and uniformity in judicial application of the law.

The limitations of the appeals and judicial review process must also be acknowledged. Appeals are often time-consuming and expensive, creating a potential barrier to access to justice for individuals and entities with limited resources. The cost of legal representation, court fees, and the delay involved in the appeals process can discourage individuals from pursuing appeals, even if they believe their rights have been violated.

Further, the scope of appellate review is generally limited to questions of law and procedure, not the facts of the case. This limitation can frustrate individuals who believe that the lower court made incorrect factual findings, particularly if those findings are not clearly erroneous. The appellate court's deference to lower court findings of fact highlights the principle of judicial economy and the importance of fact-finding occurring at the trial level.

However, this limitation also raises questions about the ability of the appeals process to address all forms of judicial misconduct or error.

Furthermore, not all judicial decisions are subject to appeal. In some jurisdictions, there might be limited avenues for appeal from specific types of court decisions, such as those related to administrative law or family law. These limitations may restrict the scope of judicial review and its capacity to ensure accountability in these areas. The criteria determining whether a case is eligible for appeal are themselves often complex and subject to interpretation, potentially leading to further inequities.

Despite its inherent limitations, the appeals and judicial review system remains a fundamental mechanism of judicial accountability. It offers checks and balances within the judicial system, ensuring that decisions are grounded in law and fact, and promote consistency and fairness. However, the effectiveness of this system is contingent upon the independence and impartiality of appellate courts, clear and accessible procedures, and measures to address the cost and time-related barriers that can impede access to justice. Continuous improvements, including streamlining procedures, providing legal aid, and ensuring judicial independence, are vital for strengthening the role of appeals and judicial review in fostering a just and accountable judiciary.

The interaction between appeals and other mechanisms of judicial accountability is also crucial. For instance, appellate courts can play a role in investigating complaints of judicial misconduct. If a judge's conduct during a trial is challenged, the appellate court, during its review of the case, may assess whether the conduct fell short of ethical standards or impacted the fairness of the proceedings. Such assessments, while not explicitly designed to address misconduct, contribute to an overall picture of judicial behavior and can inform other accountability mechanisms. Similarly, findings by judicial conduct bodies, disciplinary committees, or other investigative bodies may be reviewed through appeals processes, further ensuring procedural fairness and transparency.

The role of judicial review extends beyond correcting errors made by lower courts; it also plays a vital role in safeguarding the constitutionality of laws and government actions. Judicial review involves the power of courts to determine whether a law or government action is consistent with the constitution. When a court strikes down a law as unconstitutional, it not only protects fundamental rights but also holds the legislature accountable for creating laws that violate those rights. This function acts as a powerful mechanism to ensure that the branches of government operate within their constitutional mandates. The very act of a court exercising judicial review can be subject to appeal and further review in higher courts, showcasing a complex interplay between different forms of judicial accountability.

However, the exercise of judicial review is not without its challenges and controversies. Concerns exist regarding the potential for judicial overreach and the politicization of judicial review. The appointment of judges themselves, the interpretation of constitutional provisions, and the balance of power between the judiciary and other branches of government remain areas of ongoing debate and scrutiny. These considerations highlight the importance of mechanisms that ensure the judiciary's own accountability in carrying out its constitutionally-mandated role of judicial review. A judicial system capable of holding itself accountable adds to the legitimacy and effectiveness of its power to review legislation. Transparency in the decision-making process, clear criteria for exercising judicial review, and mechanisms for addressing criticism of judicial decisions contribute to a more accountable system of judicial review.

Investigative journalism, in particular, has demonstrated its ability to uncover complex schemes of corruption and unethical behaviour, holding individuals accountable, including judges. Examples abound globally, demonstrating the power of investigative journalism to shed light on opaque systems and expose those who abuse their authority. For instance, investigative reports uncovering judicial bias in high-profile cases have resulted in public outcry and, in some cases, the subsequent removal or sanctioning of judges. The public pressure generated by such revelations can prompt internal investigations and disciplinary proceedings, thereby contributing to a more accountable judiciary.

The media's role in disseminating information regarding judicial proceedings and decisions also contributes significantly to public accountability. Transparency in the judicial process is a critical component of public trust. By providing coverage of trials, rulings, and judicial appointments, the media allows the public to assess the impartiality and fairness of the court system. This coverage serves as an indirect mechanism of accountability, as judges are aware that their actions are subject to public scrutiny. The potential for negative publicity can be a powerful deterrent against misconduct, encouraging judges to act in accordance with high ethical standards. However, this also requires a responsible media capable of avoiding sensationalism and focusing on factual reporting. The need for balance and accuracy in media reporting is crucial, as biased or inaccurate reporting can seriously undermine public trust in both the media and the judiciary.

However, the potential benefits of public scrutiny are tempered by significant risks. One major concern is the potential for biased or unfair criticism. Judges are often subject to intense public pressure, particularly when their decisions are unpopular or controversial.

This pressure can manifest as personal attacks, threats, and harassment, which undermine judicial independence and create an environment of fear. This is especially true in politically charged cases, where judicial rulings may provoke strong reactions from various segments of society. The media's role in amplifying public outrage must be approached with caution; responsible journalism demands a balanced presentation of facts, avoiding inflammatory language and protecting the reputation of judges who may be subject to unfair criticism.

Moreover, the potential for the media to be influenced by political agendas or vested interests poses a substantial threat to the integrity of public scrutiny. In some instances, media outlets may consciously or unconsciously adopt partisan positions, selectively highlighting criticisms of judges whose decisions run counter to their political leanings. This type of bias can distort public perception of the judiciary, leading to unfair judgments about the actions and decisions of judges. The need for media literacy among the public is therefore paramount; citizens need to develop critical thinking skills to analyze information objectively and differentiate between factual reporting and biased or misleading narratives. This ability to critically assess media coverage is crucial in ensuring that public scrutiny of the judiciary remains a constructive and fair mechanism of accountability.

Another significant challenge is the potential for public scrutiny to lead to undue influence on judicial decision-making. Judges, aware of public opinion, may be tempted to tailor their rulings to please the public or avoid attracting criticism, potentially compromising their impartiality and independence. This phenomenon of "judicial self-censorship" can be detrimental to the rule of law, undermining the capacity of the judiciary to make independent and impartial judgments. This pressure can be especially acute in cases concerning sensitive social or political issues, where strong public opinions are often present.

The balance between a free press holding the judiciary accountable and protecting judges from unfair criticism and undue pressure is a constant and delicate one. A robust legal framework that protects freedom of speech and expression is essential to allow for public scrutiny, but this framework must also include provisions to address defamation or other forms of malicious attacks on judges. The development of ethical guidelines for media coverage of judicial matters is crucial in promoting responsible journalism and preventing unfair or inaccurate reporting that might undermine public trust in the judiciary. Furthermore, the judiciary itself has a role to play in fostering a culture of transparency and accountability, making information more readily available to the public and engaging in constructive dialogue with the media about its role in judicial oversight.

Comparative analysis reveals significant variations in the effectiveness of public scrutiny across different legal systems. In countries with a strong tradition of freedom of the press and a high degree of media independence, public scrutiny can be a very effective mechanism for judicial accountability. In contrast, in countries with restricted press freedoms or where media outlets are controlled by the government or other powerful interests, public scrutiny is severely limited, creating a space for judicial misconduct to flourish. The level of public trust in the media also plays a significant role; high levels of public trust facilitate the effectiveness of media as a mechanism of accountability, while low levels of trust can weaken its impact.

Ultimately, public scrutiny and the role of the media are indispensable elements of judicial accountability. However, the potential benefits of a free and responsible press must be carefully balanced against the risks of bias, unfair criticism, and undue influence on judicial decision-making. A system of robust legal safeguards, coupled with responsible media practices and increased public media literacy, is essential to ensure that public scrutiny serves as a genuine mechanism for enhancing judicial integrity and maintaining public confidence in the judiciary's impartiality and independence. Striking the right balance is essential to upholding the rule of law and guaranteeing a just society. The ongoing discussion and refinement of mechanisms for public scrutiny, informed by comparative analysis and practical experience, are vital to achieving this crucial equilibrium.

Internal mechanisms of judicial accountability, residing within the judiciary itself, play a crucial role in maintaining ethical standards and addressing instances of judicial misconduct. These mechanisms, primarily codes of conduct and peer review processes, offer a framework for self-regulation and internal discipline, complementing external oversight mechanisms such as public scrutiny and legislative intervention. However, their effectiveness is contingent upon several factors, including the stringency of the codes, the independence and impartiality of the review processes, and the willingness of judges to engage in self-accountability.

Codes of conduct, formal written documents outlining expected ethical standards for judges, serve as foundational instruments for internal accountability. These codes typically address a broad range of issues, including impartiality, integrity, diligence, and the avoidance of conflicts of interest. The specifics of these codes vary significantly across jurisdictions, reflecting differing legal traditions and societal values. Some codes are highly detailed and prescriptive, providing explicit guidance on specific situations, while others are more general and principle-based, allowing for greater flexibility in application.

The effectiveness of codes of conduct depends heavily on their clarity, comprehensiveness, and enforceability. A well-drafted code should be easily understandable by all judges, leaving no room for ambiguity or misinterpretation. It should also encompass a wide range of potential ethical dilemmas that judges may face, providing clear guidance on appropriate conduct. Furthermore, the code must be backed by robust enforcement mechanisms, ensuring that violations are promptly investigated and appropriately sanctioned. Without effective enforcement, a code of conduct becomes merely a symbolic gesture, failing to meaningfully influence judicial behaviour.

Enforcement mechanisms for codes of conduct typically include internal disciplinary procedures, which can range from informal admonishments to formal investigations and sanctions. These procedures often involve a multi-stage process, beginning with an initial complaint or allegation, followed by an investigation to determine the facts of the case, and culminating in a decision on the appropriate sanction. The details of these procedures vary across jurisdictions, but generally aim to ensure fairness and due process for the judge under investigation. The sanctions that can be imposed range from reprimands and fines to suspension or removal from office, depending on the severity of the misconduct.

Peer review, another essential internal mechanism, involves the evaluation of a judge's performance and conduct by their fellow judges. This mechanism can take various forms, ranging from informal discussions and mentorship to formal evaluations conducted by a panel of judges. Peer review can be an effective means of identifying potential ethical concerns early on, providing an opportunity for corrective action before minor infractions escalate into more serious misconduct. It also allows for the sharing of best practices and the promotion of a culture of ethical behaviour within the judiciary.

The effectiveness of peer review is heavily dependent on the independence and impartiality of the review process. Reviewers must be free from external influence and must judge their colleagues based on objective criteria, ensuring fairness and avoiding biases based on personal relationships or political considerations. The confidentiality of the review process is also essential to protect the reputation of the judge under review and to encourage open and honest self-assessment. A transparent and well-defined process, with clear guidelines and standards of review, is crucial for ensuring the legitimacy and effectiveness of peer review.

However, peer review also faces inherent limitations. The very nature of peer review, where judges evaluate their colleagues, can create a potential for conflict of interest or reluctance to impose sanctions on fellow judges. A culture of collegiality, while valuable, can sometimes hinder the effective application of discipline. Judges may be hesitant to criticize or sanction their peers, particularly if it could damage their professional relationships or create friction within the judiciary. This can lead to a lack of accountability, allowing minor infractions to go unaddressed and potentially escalating into more serious problems.

Comparative analysis of judicial codes of conduct and peer review processes reveals significant variations across different legal systems. Some jurisdictions, such as the United States, have established comprehensive codes of conduct with detailed provisions and robust enforcement mechanisms. Other jurisdictions, particularly those with less developed legal systems, may have less developed codes or lack formal peer review processes altogether.

The differences reflect varying levels of institutional maturity, cultural norms, and political influences. Furthermore, the effectiveness of these mechanisms is often intertwined with the overall strength of the rule of law, judicial independence, and the level of public trust in the judiciary.

A culture of accountability, where judges actively engage in self-assessment and are willing to address shortcomings, is essential for the effectiveness of internal accountability mechanisms. Regular training on ethical standards, coupled with mentorship programs, can foster this culture and provide judges with the tools and resources to navigate complex ethical dilemmas.

Comparative analysis reveals considerable variations in the strength and effectiveness of these internal mechanisms across different legal systems, highlighting the need for ongoing refinement and adaptation to enhance their ability to promote ethical behaviour and address instances of misconduct within the judiciary. A balanced approach that effectively complements external accountability mechanisms is crucial to preserving judicial independence while maintaining a robust and accountable judiciary.

Defining Judicial Misconduct

Defining judicial misconduct presents a complex challenge, varying significantly across jurisdictions and legal traditions. There's no universally accepted definition, leading to inconsistencies in how judges are held accountable for their actions. The lack of a standardized definition often stems from the inherent difficulties in balancing the need for clear ethical guidelines with the equally important principle of judicial independence. Overly rigid definitions risk stifling judicial creativity and independent judgment, while overly vague definitions can lead to arbitrary and inconsistent application of accountability measures.

One approach to defining judicial misconduct focuses on a categorical listing of prohibited actions. These lists often include acts such as bribery, corruption, and perverting the course of justice–actions that clearly undermine the integrity of the judicial process. However, even within this approach, the specific details of what constitutes bribery or corruption can be debated, particularly in culturally nuanced contexts. What might be considered a straightforward bribe in one legal system might be interpreted differently under a different cultural lens, leading to potential disagreements on whether misconduct has occurred. This necessitates a nuanced understanding of cultural contexts when assessing alleged judicial misconduct.

Another approach employs a more principle-based definition, focusing on breaches of the judge's duty of impartiality, fairness, and integrity. This approach emphasizes the underlying ethical principles that govern judicial conduct, allowing for greater flexibility in dealing with novel or ambiguous situations. Instead of relying on a rigid list of prohibited acts, this approach assesses the judge's conduct in light of broader ethical norms and expectations. This flexible approach, however, presents its own challenges, as it relies on subjective interpretations of ethical principles, potentially leading to inconsistencies in the application of accountability measures. The lack of clearly defined standards can create uncertainty for judges, making it difficult to predict what actions might lead to disciplinary action.

Further complicating the matter is the distinction between minor infractions and serious breaches of ethical conduct. Minor infractions, such as procedural errors or breaches of courtroom etiquette, are often dealt with internally within the judiciary through informal reprimands or warnings. However, the line between a minor infraction and a serious breach can be blurry, making it challenging to determine the appropriate response. A procedural error, for instance, might be considered minor if it had no impact on the outcome of the case, but serious if it resulted in a miscarriage of justice. This requires a case-by-case evaluation, taking into account the context and consequences of the judge's actions.

The classification of judicial misconduct also differs across legal systems. Some jurisdictions have formal codes of judicial conduct, providing detailed guidelines for judges' behaviour. These codes often list specific prohibited acts and provide guidance on appropriate conduct in various situations. Other jurisdictions rely on more general principles of ethical conduct, leaving more room for interpretation and potentially leading to inconsistencies in application. The existence and nature of these codes significantly influence the definition of misconduct, with stricter codes potentially leading to a broader range of actions being considered misconduct. Moreover, the enforcement mechanisms vary drastically. Some systems rely heavily on internal mechanisms, while others incorporate external oversight and public scrutiny, creating different standards and levels of accountability.

The role of public perception is also essential. While objective standards are essential for defining judicial misconduct, public perception of a judge's actions also plays a significant role in shaping the outcome of accountability processes. Even if a judge's actions do not technically violate formal rules, public perception of a lack of impartiality or integrity can damage the judiciary's reputation and erode public trust. This highlights the need for judicial conduct to not only meet legal standards but also uphold the public's expectation of fairness and impartiality. Striking a balance between objective legal standards and subjective public perception poses a substantial challenge.

The use of comparative analysis helps illuminate the nuances in defining and addressing judicial misconduct. Civil law systems might emphasize different aspects, such as the role of the legislature or the public in overseeing judicial conduct. Comparative analysis can help identify best practices and pinpoint areas needing improvement in different legal frameworks.

Technological advancements also impact the definition of judicial misconduct. The increased use of technology in the judicial process opens up new avenues for misconduct, such as data breaches, inappropriate use of social media, or bias in algorithmic decision-making. The traditional definitions of misconduct may need to adapt to encompass these new forms of wrongdoing, requiring ongoing development and refinement of ethical guidelines to address the challenges posed by technological change. The evolving nature of technology necessitates continuous adaptation in defining and addressing judicial misconduct to ensure that accountability processes remain relevant and effective.

Furthermore, the increasing focus on diversity and inclusion within the judiciary has raised concerns about implicit bias and discrimination. While overt acts of discrimination are clearly forms of judicial misconduct, implicit biases – unconscious biases that affect decision-making – are more difficult to identify and address.

This requires a nuanced approach to defining misconduct, going beyond overt actions to encompass the potential for unintentional bias to impact judicial fairness and impartiality. Addressing implicit bias is a complex challenge, requiring training, awareness, and the development of mechanisms for identifying and mitigating the effects of unconscious biases on judicial decisions.

Finally, the issue of sanctions for judicial misconduct deserves further consideration. The appropriateness of sanctions should be proportional to the severity of the misconduct, ranging from warnings and reprimands for minor infractions to suspension or removal from office for serious breaches of ethical conduct.

Determining the appropriate sanction requires a careful evaluation of the circumstances of the misconduct, considering factors such as the judge's intent, the impact of their actions, and their prior record. The proportionality of sanctions is crucial for maintaining fairness and ensuring that accountability processes are neither overly lenient nor overly punitive.

Defining judicial misconduct is a multifaceted task that requires a nuanced understanding of legal principles, ethical norms, cultural contexts, and public expectations. While there's no single, universally applicable definition, a careful and thoughtful approach that balances the need for clear guidelines with the protection of judicial independence is essential. Comparative analysis and ongoing dialogue among legal professionals, policymakers, and the public are fundamental for refining definitions and ensuring that accountability processes remain fair, effective, and maintain public trust in the judiciary. The evolving nature of the judicial landscape, including technological advancements and increasing focus on diversity and inclusion, further underscores the need for ongoing adaptation and refinement of the definition and handling of judicial misconduct.

A critical and often overlooked aspect of judicial accountability lies in its profound connection to the prevention and eradication of corruption. A judiciary lacking adequate accountability mechanisms becomes fertile ground for corruption to flourish, undermining the very foundations of the rule of law and public trust. The absence of effective oversight creates opportunities for misconduct, allowing judges to operate with impunity and potentially engage in activities that benefit themselves or others at the expense of justice.

Identifying and Combating Judicial Corruption

The link between a lack of accountability and judicial corruption manifests in several ways. Firstly, without a credible threat of investigation and sanction, judges might be tempted to accept bribes, favouritism, or engage in other forms of unethical conduct.

Knowing that their actions are unlikely to face consequences diminishes the deterrent effect of ethical codes and legal norms. This lack of accountability emboldens corrupt actors, encouraging a culture of impunity where unethical behaviour becomes normalized and even expected. This can lead to a cascading effect, damaging the reputation of the entire judiciary and eroding public trust in the fairness and impartiality of the justice system.

Furthermore, the absence of accountability can lead to a culture of cronyism and nepotism within the judiciary. Judges might favour individuals connected to them through personal relationships or familial ties, bypassing established legal procedures and principles of meritocracy. This type of favouritism, often disguised as benign bias, gradually undermines the integrity of the judicial process, favouring certain interests over others and fostering inequality within the justice system. Such practices undermine the core tenets of a fair and just judicial process, rendering the legal system susceptible to manipulation and bias. This lack of transparency and impartiality directly contributes to public distrust in the courts, leading to a decline in respect for the law and its institutions.

The impact of judicial corruption is far-reaching, extending beyond individual cases to affect the broader societal fabric. When the judiciary is compromised, individuals and businesses lose confidence in the legal system, inhibiting investment, economic growth, and overall social stability. Corruption within the judiciary breeds cynicism and mistrust in government institutions, diminishing faith in the rule of law and potentially contributing to social unrest and political instability. This loss of faith in the justice system encourages individuals to seek alternative, often violent, means of resolving disputes, creating a fertile ground for criminal activities to flourish.

However, establishing a robust system of judicial accountability is not a simple task. It necessitates a delicate balancing act between ensuring judicial independence and holding judges accountable for their actions. Overly intrusive mechanisms for accountability can impinge upon judicial independence, potentially chilling judicial decision-making and encouraging self-censorship. Judges might hesitate to render unpopular decisions, fearing reprisal, thus undermining the principle of impartial justice. This dilemma underscores the need for carefully designed accountability mechanisms that strike a balance between these competing values.

Effective accountability systems typically involve multiple elements. Independent judicial disciplinary bodies, such as commissions or councils, play a critical role in investigating allegations of misconduct. These bodies should be composed of individuals with legal expertise and a strong commitment to ethical conduct, free from political interference. Their powers should extend to investigating complaints, gathering evidence, conducting hearings, and imposing sanctions such as reprimands, suspensions, or removal from office.

Transparency is vital in building public trust in the judicial accountability process. The procedures employed by disciplinary bodies should be open and transparent, ensuring public access to information while maintaining the confidentiality of sensitive material that might compromise the integrity of investigations or the privacy of individuals involved. The public needs to understand how complaints are investigated, how decisions are reached, and what sanctions are imposed. This transparency allows for public scrutiny, enhancing the legitimacy and accountability of the disciplinary process.

Furthermore, effective judicial accountability necessitates adequate resources and capacity. Disciplinary bodies must be properly funded and staffed with qualified individuals to ensure that investigations are thorough, efficient, and fair. This includes providing access to investigative tools, legal counsel, and support staff. Insufficient resources can significantly hamper the effectiveness of accountability mechanisms, allowing instances of misconduct to go unaddressed.

International standards and best practices provide valuable guidance in crafting effective accountability frameworks. Numerous international organizations, such as the United Nations and the

World Bank, have developed guidelines and principles on judicial independence and accountability. These resources offer valuable insights into the design and implementation of effective accountability systems, including best practices for investigation, hearing procedures, and sanctioning of judicial misconduct.

Adherence to these standards can enhance the credibility and effectiveness of national accountability mechanisms.

Comparative analysis of different judicial systems reveals a range of approaches to judicial accountability. Some jurisdictions rely heavily on internal mechanisms, such as peer review and self-regulation, while others prefer more external oversight, involving legislative or executive bodies. The optimal approach varies depending on the specific context and culture of a particular country, its legal tradition, and the existing level of public trust in the judicial system.

Ultimately, the link between judicial accountability and corruption is undeniable. A robust and effective system of accountability is not merely a matter of procedural fairness; it is a fundamental pillar of a just and stable society. It is a cornerstone of the rule of law, protecting the integrity of the judicial system and upholding the principles of fairness and impartiality. By strengthening accountability mechanisms, nations can significantly reduce the risk of judicial corruption, fostering public trust, promoting economic development, and strengthening the overall fabric of democratic governance. Continuous vigilance, adaptation, and investment in this critical area are essential for ensuring the integrity of the judiciary and the rule of law in any society. The ongoing development and refinement of accountability mechanisms must be a constant priority, a commitment to ensuring justice prevails and public trust is maintained. Only then can the judiciary truly fulfil its vital role as the guarantor of fairness and equality under the law.

One key element in identifying judicial corruption is the establishment of robust whistleblower protection programs. Judges, court staff, and even members of the public may possess vital information regarding corrupt activities within the judiciary.

However, they may be hesitant to come forward due to fear of retaliation, intimidation, or career damage. Effective whistleblower protection laws must guarantee anonymity, provide legal protection against reprisal, and ensure that whistleblowers are not subjected to harassment or discrimination. These protections are not simply a matter of ethical conduct; they are fundamental to uncovering instances of judicial corruption that might otherwise remain hidden.

International best practices emphasize the importance of independent bodies to receive and investigate whistleblower complaints, ensuring impartiality and protecting whistleblowers from any potential influence or pressure from the implicated judge or other actors within the system. The effectiveness of these programs hinges on the level of trust that can be engendered in the system and its guarantee of genuine protection. This includes adequate funding for investigation and protection, and clear, widely disseminated information about how to report suspected corruption, including the specific channels available and the expected processes.

Another vital preventative measure is the implementation of stringent financial disclosure requirements for judges and court personnel. Judges, by their very nature, hold positions of considerable influence and authority, which can be misused for personal gain. Mandatory financial disclosure regulations require judges to regularly disclose their assets, income, and liabilities. This transparency allows for scrutiny of their financial activities, making it more difficult to conceal illicit enrichment or unexplained wealth.

Effective financial disclosure systems require clear reporting standards, regular audits, and independent oversight bodies to analyze the disclosed information. Failure to meet these requirements should be subject to disciplinary action. The scope of disclosure must be comprehensive, encompassing not only the judge's personal finances but also those of their immediate family members. This is necessary to prevent the circumvention of disclosure rules through the use of family members as proxies for illicit activities. Furthermore, a robust system should include mechanisms for effective investigation into potential discrepancies identified through analysis of the disclosed financial information.

The analysis should compare declared income to known expenditures and investigate any assets that are disproportionate to the declared income. This process needs to be supported by sufficient resources and qualified personnel to carry out a thorough and timely review.

The prosecution of corrupt judges should be conducted by independent prosecutors who are free from any conflict of interest and operate outside the direct influence of the judiciary itself. This ensures the impartiality and effectiveness of the prosecution, safeguarding against potential interference or bias. The prosecutorial process should adhere to strict legal standards, ensuring that the rights of the accused are respected while upholding the integrity of the judicial system. Successful prosecution requires adequate legislative frameworks that clearly define corruption offenses within the judiciary, establish appropriate penalties for such crimes, and ensure that judges are subject to the same legal standards as other individuals. A system of appeal is vital, not only to ensure fairness in the process but also to build public confidence in the transparency and integrity of the judicial disciplinary procedures. These steps are critical in creating a credible deterrent to judicial corruption.

Investigating and prosecuting corrupt judges presents formidable challenges, often exceeding those encountered in prosecuting corruption within other branches of government. The very nature of a judge's position—their authority, their role in dispensing justice, and their often close ties within the legal community—creates a complex web of obstacles that hinder effective investigation and prosecution. One significant hurdle is the inherent difficulty in gathering sufficient evidence. Judges, by virtue of their position, often have access to sensitive information and resources that can be manipulated to conceal their corrupt activities. They may also be adept at manipulating legal procedures to delay or obstruct investigations. Furthermore, witnesses may be reluctant to come forward due to fear of retaliation or intimidation. The power imbalance between a judge and potential witnesses, coupled with the potential for repercussions within the judicial system, creates a climate of silence that shields corrupt judges from accountability.

The lack of resources dedicated to investigating judicial corruption further exacerbates the problem. Many jurisdictions allocate insufficient funding and personnel to specialized anti-corruption units focusing on the judiciary. This resource scarcity restricts the scope and depth of investigations, limiting the ability to uncover complex financial transactions or international networks involved in judicial bribery. The specialized skills required – forensic accounting, digital forensics, and international cooperation – are often lacking, particularly in developing countries. Consequently, investigations often remain superficial, failing to uncover the full extent of corrupt activities or identify all those involved.

Political interference poses a particularly insidious challenge. Judges may enjoy the protection of powerful political figures that benefit from their corrupt actions, making it extremely difficult to initiate or pursue investigations impartially. Political pressure may be exerted through various channels – influencing the appointment of prosecutors, delaying or obstructing investigations, or even interfering with court proceedings directly. This political shielding acts as a major deterrent to effective law enforcement, allowing corrupt judges to operate with a degree of impunity. The lack of political will to confront corruption within the judiciary is often a critical factor in the overall ineffectiveness of anti-corruption initiatives. Without strong political commitment, resources remain scarce, investigative bodies lack independence, and prosecutions are rarely pursued vigorously.

Another significant challenge is the inherent difficulty in proving corrupt intent. Judicial decisions, even those influenced by bribes or other forms of corruption, are often cloaked in the legitimacy of legal processes. Disentangling legitimate judicial actions from those motivated by corrupt intent requires meticulous investigation and irrefutable evidence. This evidentiary burden is often difficult to meet, resulting in many cases being dismissed or failing to secure convictions. Establishing a clear causal link between a bribe received and a specific judicial ruling requires demonstrating a direct connection, which is rarely straightforward and often necessitates access to confidential information and communication records. The use of sophisticated techniques to mask corrupt transactions further complicates the task of evidence gathering.

Furthermore, the legal frameworks designed to address judicial corruption often fall short. Many jurisdictions lack specific laws criminalizing various forms of judicial corruption, or the existing laws are poorly defined or inadequately enforced. Sentencing guidelines for judicial corruption may be lenient, failing to deter corrupt practices effectively. The lack of specialized training for law enforcement officers, prosecutors, and judges regarding investigations and prosecutions of judicial corruption also contributes to inadequate responses. The absence of clear protocols and coordination among different state institutions involved in anti-corruption efforts often results in fragmented and inefficient investigations.

Strategies to overcome these challenges necessitate a multi-pronged approach. Strengthening institutional frameworks is paramount, beginning with the establishment of independent oversight bodies with broad investigatory powers. These bodies must be shielded from political influence and well-resourced to investigate allegations of judicial corruption effectively. Investing in forensic accounting and digital forensics capabilities is essential to uncover sophisticated corruption schemes. Enhanced whistleblower protection programs are crucial, guaranteeing anonymity and ensuring that individuals who expose corruption within the judiciary are protected from retaliation. Furthermore, fostering a culture of transparency and accountability within the judiciary itself is vital. This includes implementing robust asset declaration requirements for judges, establishing clear ethical guidelines and codes of conduct, and enhancing judicial education and training on ethical standards and anti-corruption measures.

International cooperation also plays a crucial role, particularly in tackling transnational judicial corruption. Sharing information, best practices, and investigative techniques across jurisdictions is essential to track down corrupt judges and dismantle international criminal networks. The development of standardized legal frameworks for addressing judicial corruption, facilitating cross-border investigations, and ensuring the repatriation of stolen assets would considerably improve global efforts to combat this pervasive problem.

Ultimately, success in combating judicial corruption requires a concerted effort from multiple actors—legislatures, executive branches, law enforcement agencies, and the judiciary itself.

Political will and commitment are crucial, as is the establishment of strong, independent institutions capable of investigating and prosecuting corrupt judges effectively and impartially. The challenges are significant, but a comprehensive and sustained approach is vital for upholding the integrity of the judicial system and restoring public trust in the rule of law. This ongoing struggle necessitates a continuous assessment of the effectiveness of existing strategies, a willingness to adapt and evolve approaches, and an unwavering commitment to accountability and transparency within the judiciary. The ultimate goal is not merely the prosecution of individual corrupt judges, but the systemic reform of the judicial system to prevent future instances of corruption and ensure the administration of justice is free from undue influence and bias. This requires a long-term investment in institutional strengthening, ethical frameworks, and a commitment to transparent and accountable governance.

The Importance of an Accountable Judicial System for the Rule of Law

The very essence of the rule of law rests upon the bedrock of a fair, impartial, and efficient judicial system. This system, however, cannot function effectively, nor can it inspire public trust, without a robust mechanism for judicial accountability. Judicial independence, while crucial for ensuring impartial judgments free from political interference, is not an absolute value. It exists in dynamic tension with the need for accountability, the two principles mutually reinforcing rather than mutually exclusive. A judiciary shielded from any form of scrutiny, even for egregious misconduct, risks becoming a haven for corruption and tyranny, undermining the very foundations it is meant to uphold.

Accountability in this context doesn't imply subservience to the executive or legislature. Rather, it refers to a structured system of checks and balances ensuring that judges are held responsible for their actions, both professionally and ethically. This responsibility extends beyond mere adherence to legal statutes; it encompasses a commitment to upholding the highest standards of integrity, fairness, and impartiality. An accountable judiciary operates transparently, subject to scrutiny, and responsive to legitimate concerns about its performance. This accountability is crucial not only for individual cases but also for maintaining public confidence in the entire legal system. When citizens perceive the judiciary as untouchable and unaccountable, their faith in the rule of law erodes, creating a breeding ground for cynicism and potential unrest.

The lack of accountability manifests in numerous ways, each capable of severely damaging the rule of law. One clear indicator is the prevalence of judicial corruption. When judges are not subject to effective oversight, bribery and other forms of misconduct become more likely. This not only leads to unjust decisions but also creates a perception that the legal system itself is rigged, thereby undermining its legitimacy. This perception, in turn, encourages individuals to circumvent the legal system, resorting to extra-legal means to resolve disputes, fostering a climate of lawlessness.

Furthermore, a lack of accountability can lead to inefficiency and delays in the judicial process. When judges are not held responsible for their performance, they may become lax in their duties, leading to excessive delays in case resolution. This inefficiency discourages individuals from seeking legal redress, leaving them vulnerable to exploitation and injustice. The consequences extend beyond individual cases; protracted delays in the judicial system clog the courts, impacting the effectiveness of the entire system. Criminals might evade punishment due to slow processes, while legitimate claimants may see their rights unduly delayed or denied.

Another critical area affected by a lack of judicial accountability is the erosion of public trust. When judges are perceived as unaccountable, public confidence in the judicial system diminishes. This can manifest in various ways, including decreased willingness to engage with the legal system, reduced compliance with court orders, and a general sense of distrust in the institutions responsible for maintaining order and justice. Such mistrust fuels social instability, undermining the very foundations of a just and peaceful society. The inability of citizens to believe in the fairness and impartiality of the judiciary leads to a decline in social cohesion and a rise in vigilantism or other extra-legal means of conflict resolution.

The effects extend beyond the domestic sphere. International investors and businesses are often wary of investing in jurisdictions with weak judicial accountability. The uncertainty created by an unpredictable and potentially biased judicial system discourages foreign investment, hindering economic growth and development. A country's international standing is also impacted; a reputation for judicial corruption or inefficiency can damage a nation's credibility on the global stage, affecting its relationships with other countries and its ability to participate effectively in international forums.

The mechanisms of judicial accountability are diverse and vary across jurisdictions. Appeals processes, for instance, allow for review of judicial decisions by higher courts, ensuring consistency and correcting errors. However, appeals mechanisms alone are often insufficient, particularly in addressing issues of judicial misconduct that don't directly impact the outcome of a specific case. Similarly, legislative oversight, while important in setting standards and ensuring resource allocation, may be insufficient to address individual cases of misconduct, especially in the absence of effective investigative bodies.

External oversight bodies, including judicial councils or commissions, are becoming increasingly prevalent in many countries. These bodies typically have the power to investigate allegations of misconduct, impose disciplinary sanctions, and recommend removal from office. The effectiveness of such bodies, however, is contingent upon their independence from political influence and their access to sufficient resources and expertise. A truly effective oversight mechanism must be robust, impartial, and capable of effectively investigating and addressing allegations of misconduct, regardless of the judge's seniority or influence.

Public scrutiny also plays a vital role in judicial accountability. A free press and access to information are essential for enabling public debate and scrutiny of judicial decisions and conduct. While judges must be protected from undue pressure or harassment, a culture of transparency and accountability necessitates open discourse about the performance of the judiciary. This doesn't mean exposing judges to public vilification, but rather facilitating constructive criticism and public engagement with the judicial system.

Ultimately, the establishment and maintenance of a truly accountable judiciary requires a concerted effort from all stakeholders—the judiciary itself, the legislature, the executive, and civil society. This includes enacting and enforcing robust ethical codes, providing adequate resources for oversight bodies, protecting whistleblowers, and fostering a culture of transparency and accountability. It demands a commitment to upholding the rule of law, recognizing that an independent and accountable judiciary is not merely a desirable feature of a just society but its very cornerstone. The ongoing commitment to improvement, adaptation, and reform is crucial, recognizing that the pursuit of an accountable judiciary is a continuous process, demanding constant vigilance and unwavering dedication. Only through such sustained efforts can the vital balance between judicial independence and accountability be achieved, thereby securing the rule of law and safeguarding the fundamental rights and freedoms of all citizens.

Conceptual Frameworks for Judicial Accountability

Conceptual frameworks for analyzing judicial accountability are multifaceted, reflecting the inherent complexities of balancing judicial independence with the need for public trust and the prevention of misconduct. No single model perfectly captures the nuances of this relationship, and the optimal approach often varies depending on the specific context of a legal system, its history, its political culture, and its level of institutional development.

However, several key theoretical frameworks provide valuable lenses through which to examine different aspects of judicial accountability.

One prominent framework distinguishes between internal and external accountability mechanisms. Internal mechanisms, primarily focused on self-regulation within the judiciary, encompass codes of judicial conduct, peer review processes, and internal disciplinary bodies. Codes of conduct, often meticulously detailed documents outlining ethical standards and professional responsibilities, serve as the foundational guide for judicial behaviour. These codes typically address issues such as impartiality, fairness, diligence, and the avoidance of conflicts of interest. However, their effectiveness hinges on their clarity, comprehensiveness, and rigorous enforcement. Weakly enforced codes, or codes that lack specific guidelines, can become ineffective instruments of accountability.

Peer review, on the other hand, relies on the judgment of fellow judges to assess the conduct and performance of their colleagues. This approach leverages the collective expertise and experience of the judiciary, potentially fostering a culture of self-correction and mutual accountability. Yet, peer review mechanisms can face challenges related to potential bias, conflicts of interest, and the reluctance of judges to criticize their peers publicly, especially in hierarchical judicial systems. The effectiveness of peer review depends heavily on the culture of the judiciary, the level of trust among judges, and the existence of transparent and clearly defined procedures. The potential for self-preservation rather than genuine oversight is a significant limitation of this approach.

Internal disciplinary bodies, typically composed of senior judges or other legal professionals, are tasked with investigating allegations of judicial misconduct and imposing sanctions. These bodies' effectiveness hinges on their independence from political influence, their procedural fairness, and the transparency of their operations. The impartiality of these bodies is often crucial, as their decisions can have profound consequences on the careers and reputations of judges. Lack of transparency can fuel suspicions of bias or favouritism, eroding public trust. The challenge here is often to balance the need for decisive action against the need for due process and fair treatment of the accused judge.

External accountability mechanisms, in contrast, involve oversight and scrutiny from entities outside the judiciary. Legislative oversight, exercised through parliamentary committees or other legislative bodies, offers a means of investigating judges' conduct, although its effectiveness often depends heavily on the strength of democratic institutions and the political will to hold judges accountable. The potential for politically motivated actions presents a significant risk; legislatures may seek to influence the judiciary through intimidation or by using accountability mechanisms as tools to curtail judicial independence, particularly when judges issue decisions that are unfavourable to the ruling party or government. Impeachment procedures, although available in many jurisdictions, often involve a high bar for removal and can be protracted and politically charged processes.

Public scrutiny, facilitated by a free press and access to information, plays a vital role in holding judges accountable. A vibrant and independent media can act as a watchdog, scrutinizing judicial decisions and conduct and bringing to light potential instances of bias or misconduct. However, public pressure must be balanced with the protection of judicial independence from unwarranted attacks. The line between legitimate criticism and undue influence is a delicate one, and the potential for public opinion to sway judicial impartiality is a concern that needs careful management.

Comparative analysis reveals diverse approaches to judicial accountability across different jurisdictions. Common law systems, such as those in the United Kingdom and the United States, often rely heavily on internal disciplinary mechanisms, alongside external oversight through appellate processes and legislative review. Civil law systems, on the other hand, may emphasize different mechanisms, such as specialized judicial councils or high courts with oversight responsibilities. The effectiveness of these mechanisms varies widely, depending on factors such as the strength of democratic institutions, the rule of law, and the level of public trust in the judiciary.

Another conceptual framework for understanding judicial accountability emphasizes the role of norms and values. This framework suggests that judicial accountability is not simply a matter of formal mechanisms, but also of informal norms and expectations that shape judicial behaviour. A strong judicial culture, characterized by ethical standards, collegiality, and respect for the rule of law, can enhance accountability even in the absence of robust formal mechanisms. However, the effectiveness of this approach depends on the willingness of judges to uphold these norms, as well as the capacity of the judiciary to enforce them.

A further framework focuses on the concept of legitimacy. Judicial accountability, from this perspective, is not merely about holding judges responsible for misconduct, but also about maintaining the legitimacy of the judicial system in the eyes of the public. A legitimate judiciary is one that enjoys public trust and confidence, a vital prerequisite for effective judicial decision-making. Maintaining legitimacy requires transparency, fairness, and responsiveness to public concerns, thereby fostering a sense of trust and acceptance of judicial decisions. When a judiciary loses legitimacy, it risks undermining the rule of law and weakening the effectiveness of the justice system as a whole.

The choice of appropriate accountability mechanisms must consider the specific context and goals. A system overly reliant on external mechanisms may undermine judicial independence and create a climate of fear and self-censorship among judges. Conversely, a system that relies solely on internal mechanisms may lack the necessary transparency and impartiality to effectively address instances of misconduct. The optimal approach often involves a combination of internal and external mechanisms, tailored to the specific needs and circumstances of each legal system. This requires careful consideration of the potential trade-offs between independence and accountability and a continuing effort to find the best balance to ensure a just and efficient judicial system. The ongoing challenge lies in striking a balance that safeguards judicial independence, maintains public trust, and prevents abuses of power.

The Crisis of Confidence in the Judicial System

The erosion of public trust in the judiciary is not a subtle shift; it's a seismic event, threatening the very foundations of a just society. Decades of incremental disappointments, punctuated by shocking instances of corruption and perceived bias, have culminated in a widespread scepticism that extends far beyond isolated incidents. This crisis of confidence isn't merely a matter of public opinion; it has tangible and deeply troubling consequences for the rule of law. Numerous polls consistently reveal a significant decline in faith in the fairness and impartiality of courts across various jurisdictions. These aren't just abstract numbers; they represent the erosion of a social contract, the weakening of the bond between citizens and their institutions.

The implications are far-reaching. When citizens lose faith in the courts' ability to dispense justice equitably, their willingness to comply with laws diminishes. A sense of injustice breeds cynicism, fostering a climate where individuals feel less obligated to uphold the legal framework. This manifests in various ways, from increased disregard for traffic laws and minor regulations to a more profound distrust of the system's ability to address serious crimes and societal inequalities. The consequences extend beyond individual actions; a lack of trust in the judiciary undermines the legitimacy of the entire legal system, potentially fuelling social unrest and contributing to a breakdown in social order.

Consider, for instance, the protracted legal battles surrounding high-profile cases where perceived injustices have fuelled widespread protests and public outcry. These aren't isolated incidents; they are symptomatic of a larger problem. The lack of transparency in certain judicial proceedings, coupled with the perception of favouritism and influence-peddling, exacerbates public distrust. News reports detailing accusations of bribery, collusion, and unethical conduct by judges and lawyers further solidify this negative perception. The media plays a crucial role in shaping public opinion, and when the headlines consistently feature allegations of misconduct within the judiciary, the cumulative effect is a pervasive sense of disillusionment.

The societal ramifications of this decline in trust are profound. Without a strong, impartial judicial system, there's a greater risk of vigilantism and self-help justice, leading to increased violence and instability. The very fabric of a just society relies on the belief that the courts are fair and accessible to all, irrespective of social standing, wealth, or political affiliation. When this belief erodes, it creates a vacuum filled by suspicion, resentment, and ultimately, social division.

The lack of confidence in the judiciary also hampers the effectiveness of law enforcement. When citizens doubt the integrity of the justice system, they are less likely to cooperate with investigations or report crimes. This creates a climate of impunity, where criminals operate with less fear of apprehension and prosecution. The resulting decrease in crime reporting makes it more difficult for law enforcement agencies to address criminal activity effectively, leading to a vicious cycle of distrust and lawlessness. Furthermore, the legitimacy of the entire criminal justice system is jeopardized when individuals believe that justice is not being served fairly and impartially.

Specific examples from recent cases vividly illustrate the crisis of confidence. The protracted and highly publicized trials involving allegations of judicial bias, often fueled by media coverage highlighting perceived inconsistencies and questionable rulings, have left many questioning the impartiality of the court. Cases where wealthy individuals appear to receive preferential treatment, while the poor and marginalized are often disadvantaged, only further deepen this scepticism. Such perceptions, regardless of whether they are entirely accurate, significantly erode public trust.

The perceived lack of accountability for judicial misconduct also contributes to the problem. When judges and lawyers accused of unethical behaviour face minimal consequences, it sends a message that such actions are tolerated or even encouraged, fuelling further cynicism.

Beyond specific cases, systemic issues exacerbate the problem. The complexities of legal procedures, often perceived as opaque and inaccessible to the average citizen, contribute to a lack of understanding and a sense of alienation from the judicial process. This lack of understanding fuels suspicion and mistrust, particularly when legal outcomes seem arbitrary or unfair. Similarly, the inherent power imbalances within the legal system – the often-unequal access to legal representation and the complex interplay of legal jargon and procedural intricacies – can make it difficult for individuals to navigate the system effectively, leading to a sense of helplessness and distrust.

The appointment processes of judges also play a significant role. If the selection process appears to be influenced by political considerations rather than merit, this can undermine public confidence in the impartiality of the judiciary. Perceptions of political influence, even if unfounded, can be just as damaging to public trust as actual instances of bias. The seemingly arbitrary nature of some legal decisions, coupled with a lack of transparency in the reasoning behind those decisions, further fuels scepticism.

Addressing this crisis requires a multifaceted approach. Increased transparency in judicial proceedings, coupled with efforts to simplify legal processes and make them more accessible to the public, is essential. Improving the training and ethical standards of legal professionals, including robust mechanisms for accountability and disciplinary action, will also be vital. Independent oversight bodies, empowered to investigate allegations of misconduct and take appropriate action, are crucial in fostering trust and deterring corruption. Furthermore, promoting public education initiatives to increase understanding of the legal system and its workings can help to dispel misconceptions and build confidence in the fairness of the judicial process. The road to restoring faith in the judiciary is long and arduous, but it's a journey that must be undertaken if we are to preserve the foundations of a just and equitable society.

The Performance of Political Influence

The insidious influence of money on the judicial system is a pervasive problem, subtly yet powerfully corrupting the very principles of justice. While blatant bribery remains a concern, the more pervasive and difficult-to-detect forms of corruption stem from the financial incentives that shape the behaviour of legal professionals. These incentives, often deeply embedded within the system itself, create a fertile ground for unethical conduct, pushing individuals to prioritize personal gain over the pursuit of justice.

One of the most glaring examples of this systemic issue lies in the stark disparity between the financial realities faced by public defenders and their counterparts in private practice. Public defenders, tasked with representing indigent clients accused of crimes, often toil under crushing workloads, burdened by low salaries and inadequate resources. This financial hardship inevitably compromises their ability to provide effective legal representation.

Overworked and underpaid, these individuals often lack the time and resources necessary to thoroughly investigate cases, conduct proper discovery, or mount a robust defence. The result is a two-tiered system of justice, where the quality of legal representation directly correlates with the financial resources of the accused. This creates a profound injustice, where those who can afford top-tier legal counsel receive significantly better representation than those who cannot. This inherent inequality undermines the very foundation of a fair and equitable judicial system, leaving the poor and marginalized disproportionately vulnerable to wrongful convictions.

The financial pressures faced by public defenders are further exacerbated by the systemic issues plaguing public defender offices across the country. Many offices are chronically understaffed and underfunded, leading to overwhelming caseloads and a constant state of crisis. Attorneys often find themselves juggling dozens, if not hundreds, of cases simultaneously, leaving little time to dedicate the necessary attention to each individual client. This lack of resources extends beyond manpower, encompassing essential tools such as access to expert witnesses, investigative resources, and even adequate technology. The result is a system where public defenders are constantly fighting an uphill battle, striving to provide adequate representation under incredibly difficult circumstances. This perpetual struggle compromises their ability to uphold their professional obligations, creating a system where financial limitations directly impact the fairness of the judicial process.

In stark contrast to the challenges faced by public defenders, the high-stakes world of private legal practice often incentivizes a different set of ethical compromises. High-profile cases, particularly in corporate law and civil litigation, can generate immense financial rewards for successful lawyers. The pressure to win, coupled with the substantial financial incentives involved, can create a powerful temptation to prioritize victory over ethical conduct. This pressure can manifest in a variety of ways, from aggressive and ethically questionable legal tactics to the outright manipulation of the legal process. Lawyers may choose to bury evidence, distort facts, or engage in aggressive cross-examination tactics that cross the line into ethical misconduct. The pursuit of a lucrative outcome can often overshadow the fundamental duty to uphold the principles of justice and fairness. This imbalance creates a situation where the pursuit of financial gain can undermine the integrity of the legal process itself.

The problem is further amplified by the inherent power dynamics within the legal system. Wealthy clients, corporations, and powerful individuals often have access to resources and legal expertise that are simply unavailable to those with fewer financial means. This disparity in access to justice allows those with deep pockets to manipulate the system in ways that are unavailable to the average citizen. They can afford to hire the most skilled and aggressive lawyers, who are often willing to employ ethically questionable tactics to achieve victory. These lawyers, driven by the financial rewards associated with success, may be more willing to push the boundaries of ethical conduct, knowing that their wealthy clients can afford to absorb the potential costs of legal challenges or sanctions.

The financial incentives that drive unethical behaviour within the judiciary are not limited to lawyers. Judges, despite the safeguards in place to ensure impartiality, also face subtle pressures that can influence their decisions. While outright bribery remains a rare occurrence, the influence of campaign donations, lobbying efforts and the promise of future employment can subtly affect judicial impartiality. Judges, like all human beings, are susceptible to the allure of power and prestige, and these indirect forms of financial influence can create a subtle yet powerful bias. The potential for future employment within the private sector, for instance, can inadvertently influence judicial decisions, leading to a subconscious bias in favour of powerful interests. The lack of transparency surrounding judicial finances further exacerbates the problem, making it difficult to fully understand the extent of the influence of money on the judicial process. This lack of transparency creates an environment where the potential for corruption can thrive unchecked.

The problem extends beyond individual cases of misconduct. The systemic underfunding of the judicial system itself contributes to the problem. Courts across the country are often understaffed, under-resourced, and overwhelmed with an ever-increasing caseload. This chronic lack of resources creates a climate where ethical compromises are more likely to occur. Judges and court staff, overworked and underpaid, may be more susceptible to pressure from powerful interests, simply because they lack the resources to adequately resist such pressure. This underfunding creates a situation where the system itself is vulnerable to corruption.

Reforming this system requires a multi-pronged approach that addresses both the financial incentives and the systemic issues contributing to the problem. Raising salaries for public defenders, providing them with better resources and training, and reducing their caseloads are crucial steps. Increased transparency in judicial finances, stricter regulations on lobbying and campaign donations, and robust mechanisms for accountability are equally important. Comprehensive ethics reform within the legal profession, including stricter enforcement of ethical rules and harsher penalties for misconduct, is also crucial. Finally, improving public awareness of these issues and fostering greater public scrutiny of the judiciary are critical in ensuring accountability and upholding the integrity of the legal system. Only through a concerted effort to address these systemic problems can we hope to restore trust in the judicial system and ensure that justice is truly blind. The alternative is a continued erosion of the rule of law and a deepening crisis of confidence in the institutions that are supposed to uphold it.

The Performance of Political Influence

The insidious influence of money, discussed previously, is only one facet of the multifaceted corruption undermining the judiciary. Equally damaging, and often inextricably linked to financial pressures, is the pervasive impact of political influence. The erosion of trust in the judicial system isn't simply a matter of individual bad actors; it's a systemic failure stemming from the politicization of the very institutions meant to uphold the rule of law. This politicization manifests in various ways, from the appointment process itself to the subtle, yet powerful, pressures exerted by lobbying groups and campaign donations.

The appointment of judges, at all levels, is often a deeply political process. While the ideal is to select individuals based solely on their legal expertise, impartiality, and ethical conduct, the reality often falls far short. In many jurisdictions, judges are appointed by elected officials – governors, presidents, or even state legislatures – introducing a significant element of political calculation into the selection process. Candidates are often vetted not just for their legal qualifications but also for their political affiliations, ideological leanings, and perceived loyalty to the appointing authority. This inherently political process can lead to the selection of judges who prioritize political expediency over judicial integrity.

The consequences of this politicized appointment process are far-reaching. Judges selected for their political connections rather than their merits are more likely to rule in ways that favour the interests of the appointing party or its allies. This creates a perception, and often a reality, of bias and lack of impartiality within the judiciary. Public confidence erodes as citizens witness decisions that appear to be driven by political considerations rather than legal principles.

This perception alone can be as damaging as actual bias, creating cynicism and distrust in the fairness of the system.

Numerous examples illustrate this problematic dynamic. Consider the confirmation battles surrounding Supreme Court nominees in various countries. These battles often devolve into highly partisan affairs, with nominees subjected to intense scrutiny based on their past statements, judicial philosophies, and political associations.

The process often prioritizes ideological purity over judicial temperament and expertise, leading to the selection of judges who are more likely to act as political actors than impartial arbiters of justice. The resulting confirmation hearings become highly publicized spectacles, further eroding public trust in the judicial system's independence.

Beyond the appointment process, the ongoing influence of political pressure on judicial decisions is equally concerning. Lobbying efforts, often funded by powerful corporations and interest groups, exert a considerable influence on judicial outcomes. These lobbying efforts can take many forms, from direct attempts to influence individual judges to more subtle strategies aimed at shaping public opinion and influencing the political climate surrounding the courts. The lack of transparency surrounding these interactions makes it difficult to assess the full extent of their impact, but anecdotal evidence and documented cases suggest that lobbying activities can significantly impact judicial independence.

Documented cases clearly demonstrate the devastating consequences of political interference. In numerous instances, judges have been pressured, overtly or subtly, to rule in ways that favoured specific political interests. The pressure may come from within the judicial system itself – through hierarchical pressures, internal promotions, and career advancement strategies. It may also come from external sources, including powerful political figures, party leaders, and influential interest groups. These cases range from decisions overturned by higher courts based on political interference, to accusations of bribery and collusion.

The problem is further compounded by a lack of transparency and accountability. The inner workings of the judiciary are often shrouded in secrecy, making it difficult to track political influence and identify instances of improper conduct. The lack of comprehensive mechanisms for investigating and prosecuting judicial misconduct exacerbates the problem. Judges, who are meant to be independent and accountable only to the law, often operate with a degree of impunity that allows political pressure to exert its influence without fear of significant repercussions.

Addressing this systemic problem requires a multi-pronged approach. Reforming the judicial appointment process to prioritize merit and impartiality over political considerations is paramount. Increased transparency in judicial finances and campaign donations is essential, along with stricter regulations on lobbying activities that target judges. An establishing independent oversight body to investigate allegations of judicial misconduct, with sufficient authority to impose meaningful sanctions, is essential. Strengthening the mechanisms for public accountability, including increased media scrutiny and independent watchdog groups, is also essential.

Finally, fostering a culture of judicial independence and ethical conduct, starting with the education and training of judges, is critical to restoring public trust in the impartiality and fairness of the judicial system. Without addressing these systematic issues, the erosion of trust in the judiciary will continue, undermining the very foundations of a just and equitable society.

Further compounding the problem is the inherent power imbalance between lawyers and their clients. Clients often lack the legal expertise to assess the competence and ethical integrity of their lawyers, making them vulnerable to exploitation. This asymmetry of information puts clients at a distinct disadvantage, rendering them susceptible to malpractice and unethical behaviour. The lack of transparency in legal fees and billing practices further exacerbates this imbalance, leaving clients unaware of potential overcharges or unnecessary expenses. The lack of accessible and affordable legal representation for many individuals only intensifies this power imbalance, leaving vulnerable populations even more susceptible to exploitation by unscrupulous lawyers.

Moreover, the disciplinary processes within the legal profession themselves often fall short of their intended purpose. The systems for investigating and prosecuting lawyer misconduct are often overburdened, underfunded, and lacking in transparency. The resulting delays and lack of accountability effectively create a climate of impunity, allowing many instances of unethical behaviour to go unpunished. The leniency of some disciplinary actions – such as suspensions that are easily circumvented or minimal fines that don't deter future misconduct – sends a damaging message that ethical violations will not result in significant repercussions. This lack of serious consequences only further erodes the public's trust in the legal profession.

The lack of meaningful sanctions also disproportionately affects the most vulnerable clients. Individuals who lack the resources to pursue legal action against a negligent or unethical lawyer are left without recourse. This creates a system where those with the most resources have the greatest access to justice and the best chance of obtaining redress for legal malpractice, while the most vulnerable members of society are left without a pathway to accountability.

Reforming the legal profession requires a multi-pronged approach. Strengthening oversight mechanisms within state bar associations is paramount, including increased resources for investigations and a more robust enforcement of ethical standards. Implementing stricter penalties for ethical violations, including harsher sanctions for repeat offenders, is crucial in deterring future misconduct. This should include measures such as mandatory continuing legal education focusing on ethics and professional responsibility, designed to reinforce ethical standards and prevent malpractice. Moreover, increased transparency in legal fees and billing practices, combined with improved access to legal aid for low-income individuals, is essential in addressing the power imbalance between lawyers and their clients. Improving the accessibility and affordability of legal services will ensure that individuals are not forced to settle for less than competent representation due to financial constraints.

Furthermore, fostering a culture of ethical responsibility from law school onwards is critical in combating the erosion of trust. Legal education should place greater emphasis on professional ethics, providing future lawyers with a comprehensive understanding of their obligations and the potential consequences of unethical behaviour. A more rigorous approach to professional ethics during legal education, reinforced by mentorship programs and continuing legal education can help cultivate a culture of accountability and ethical practice within the legal profession. Ultimately, restoring faith in the integrity of the legal profession demands a fundamental shift in mindset, prioritizing ethical conduct above financial gain and ensuring that the system holds lawyers accountable for their actions, regardless of their status or influence. Only then can we begin to rebuild the trust that is so crucial to the proper functioning of the justice system.

The Systemic Nature of Judicial Corruption

The erosion of public trust extends beyond individual malfeasance within the legal profession; it reaches into the very foundations of the judicial system itself. The problem isn't just a few "bad apples," but a systemic rot, a network of interconnected weaknesses that allow corruption to fester and flourish. This systemic corruption manifests in various insidious ways, undermining the very principles of justice and fairness that the judiciary is sworn to uphold. To understand the depth of the crisis, we must examine the structural flaws and institutional failures that create a fertile ground for unethical behaviour.

One of the most significant contributors to judicial corruption is the lack of robust and independent oversight mechanisms. In many jurisdictions, the bodies responsible for investigating and addressing judicial misconduct are themselves under-resourced, understaffed, and lacking in the necessary authority to effectively hold judges accountable. This lack of sufficient resources often translates into lengthy delays in investigations, hindering timely resolutions and allowing potentially corrupt practices to continue unabated.

Moreover, the investigative processes frequently lack transparency, shielding the actions of judges from public scrutiny and reducing the pressure to maintain ethical standards. This opacity breeds a culture of impunity, where judges feel secure in the knowledge that their actions are unlikely to face significant consequences.

Inadequate accountability mechanisms are another critical factor contributing to the systemic nature of judicial corruption. Even when instances of misconduct are uncovered, the sanctions imposed are often insufficient to deter future wrongdoing. In many cases, judges facing serious accusations of ethical violations receive lenient punishments, such as temporary suspensions or minimal fines, which fail to reflect the gravity of their actions and send a damaging message that such behaviour will not be seriously addressed. The lack of consistently applied and appropriately severe sanctions undermines public confidence and emboldens unethical actors within the judiciary.

The insufficient resources allocated to the judicial system as a whole further exacerbate the problem. Underfunded courts often struggle to provide adequate support for judges, leading to increased workloads, pressure to expedite cases, and a general environment where ethical considerations can be easily overshadowed by the demands of efficiency. This resource scarcity can create a breeding ground for corruption, as judges under immense pressure may be more susceptible to bribery or other forms of influence peddling. The scarcity of funds also limits the ability to implement effective training programs for judges, hindering the development of crucial skills in ethical decision-making and conflict resolution.

Beyond resource constraints, legislative and regulatory failures contribute significantly to the systemic issue of judicial corruption. Ambiguous or outdated laws concerning judicial ethics can create loopholes that allow judges to engage in questionable practices without facing legal repercussions. The lack of clear guidelines and stringent regulations regarding conflicts of interest, financial disclosures, and interactions with external parties creates fertile ground for misconduct. The absence of effective mechanisms to prevent and detect corruption, such as robust auditing procedures and independent review boards, further compounds the problem.

The inadequate legislation can also create a culture of impunity where judges are hesitant to report misconduct among their peers due to fear of retaliation or a lack of support from higher authorities.

Furthermore, the political influence on the judiciary undermines its integrity and independence, creating another pathway for systemic corruption. In some instances, political pressure, either direct or indirect, can influence judicial decisions, leading to biased rulings and compromises in ethical conduct. Appointments to judicial positions based on political affiliations rather than merit, competence, and ethical standing further perpetuate the problem. These political appointments can lead to a situation where judges are beholden to political patrons, compromising their independence and impartiality, making them more susceptible to external influence and undermining public trust in the fairness and impartiality of judicial proceedings. This systemic weakness creates an environment in which judges may feel pressured to rule in favour of politically connected individuals or groups, irrespective of the merits of the case.

The systemic nature of judicial corruption also extends to the lack of protection for whistleblowers. Judges and court personnel who attempt to expose unethical practices within the system often face significant professional and personal repercussions, creating a climate of fear and silence. This lack of protection discourages individuals from reporting misconduct, allowing corruption to continue unchecked. The absence of effective whistleblower protection mechanisms prevents the exposure of wrongdoings and hinders investigations into potentially corrupt practices. The threat of retaliation—ranging from job loss to personal attacks—serves as a significant deterrent to those who might otherwise expose corruption within the judicial system.

The consequences of this systemic corruption are far-reaching. It undermines public trust in the legal system, erodes faith in the rule of law, and creates a climate of injustice where the powerful and well-connected can manipulate the system to their advantage. This, in turn, can lead to increased social unrest, reduced citizen participation in democratic processes, and a weakening of the foundations of a just and equitable society.

Addressing this systemic problem requires a comprehensive and multi-pronged approach. This includes increasing the resources allocated to judicial oversight bodies, strengthening accountability mechanisms, and implementing stricter penalties for judicial misconduct. It also demands improvements in legislative and regulatory frameworks to close loopholes, enhance transparency, and provide clear guidelines on ethical conduct. Moreover, the judiciary needs to foster a culture of ethics and integrity, encouraging the reporting of misconduct and protecting whistleblowers from retaliation. This includes implementing robust ethics training for judges and court personnel, as well as independent review mechanisms to ensure that investigations are thorough and impartial. Finally, promoting greater transparency and accountability within the judiciary, coupled with efforts to shield judicial appointments from undue political influence, will contribute significantly to restoring public trust and addressing the systemic corruption that plagues the system. The fight for a just and equitable judiciary demands a fundamental shift in approach—a move from reactive measures to proactive strategies aimed at preventing corruption before it takes root. Only through such a concerted and multifaceted effort can we hope to rebuild public trust and ensure the integrity of the judicial system for future generations.

Implicit Prejudice

Implicit bias, as defined by social psychologists, refers to the attitudes or stereotypes that affect our understanding, actions, and decisions in an unconscious manner. These biases are activated involuntarily and without an individual's awareness or intentional control. They are learned through societal conditioning, media portrayals, and personal experiences, often ingrained so deeply that they operate beneath the level of conscious thought. Unlike explicit biases, which are consciously held beliefs and prejudices, implicit biases are subtle and difficult to detect, even by the individuals harbouring them.

The implications of implicit bias in the judicial system are far-reaching. Judges, like all humans, are susceptible to these unconscious influences. While striving for objectivity, their decisions can be subtly shaped by implicit biases related to race, gender, socioeconomic status, and other demographic factors. This influence can manifest in various stages of the judicial process, from initial assessments of credibility to final sentencing decisions.

One area where implicit bias significantly impacts fairness is sentencing. Studies have consistently shown a disparity in sentencing outcomes based on the race and socioeconomic status of defendants. Even when controlling for factors like the severity of the crime and criminal history, research indicates that individuals from marginalized communities often receive harsher sentences than their counterparts from more privileged backgrounds. This disparity cannot be solely attributed to conscious prejudice. Implicit biases, operating at an unconscious level, can lead judges to perceive defendants from marginalized communities as more dangerous or less trustworthy, thereby influencing their sentencing decisions.

Implicit biases related to socioeconomic status can affect judicial decisions. Judges may unconsciously associate poverty with criminality or a lack of moral character. This can lead to harsher sentences for defendants from low-income backgrounds, even when their crimes are comparable to those committed by defendants from more affluent backgrounds. The presumption of guilt or lack of remorse, fueled by implicit bias, can undermine the presumption of innocence central to the American justice system.

Plea bargaining, a critical aspect of the criminal justice system, is also susceptible to implicit biases. Prosecutors, influenced by their own implicit biases, might be more likely to offer favourable plea deals to defendants from privileged backgrounds while pushing for harsher sentences against those from marginalized communities.

Defendants from marginalized communities, often facing inadequate legal representation and burdened by systemic disadvantage, might feel pressured to accept plea bargains even if they are innocent, simply to avoid the risks of a trial. This process, shaped by implicit biases at every stage, further perpetuates systemic inequities.

The impact of implicit bias extends beyond sentencing and plea bargaining. It can influence jury selection, witness credibility assessments, and even the interpretation of legal precedents. For instance, a judge might unconsciously give more weight to the testimony of a witness from a privileged background than a witness from a marginalized community, even if both testimonies are equally credible. The cumulative effect of these subtle biases can drastically alter the course of a trial and the ultimate outcome for the defendant.

Addressing the issue of implicit bias requires a multi-pronged approach. First, acknowledging its existence is crucial. Judges, lawyers, and all actors within the judicial system must recognize that they are not immune to the influence of implicit biases.

Second, education and training programs can help raise awareness of implicit bias and equip individuals with strategies to mitigate its impact. These programs should focus on promoting self-awareness, encouraging critical self-reflection, and developing strategies for making more objective decisions.

Furthermore, procedural reforms can be implemented to minimize the influence of implicit bias. For example, standardizing sentencing guidelines, increasing transparency in plea bargaining, and implementing blind procedures in certain stages of the judicial process (where identifying information about defendants is withheld) can help reduce the impact of unconscious biases. These measures can create a more level playing field, allowing judges to focus on the merits of the case rather than being swayed by extraneous factors.

Moreover, the collection and analysis of comprehensive data on sentencing disparities can highlight the extent of implicit bias within the judicial system. This data can provide evidence-based insights to inform policy changes and encourage accountability. The use of statistical analysis to identify patterns and trends can help expose hidden biases, leading to targeted interventions.

Finally, the culture of the legal profession needs to foster an environment of openness and critical self-reflection. Encouraging dialogue and discussion about implicit bias within the legal community can lead to greater awareness and a commitment to combating its insidious influence. This includes promoting diversity within the judiciary itself, as a more diverse bench is likely to be less susceptible to certain forms of implicit bias.

The challenge of addressing implicit bias in the judicial system is significant, but it is not insurmountable. By acknowledging its existence, implementing evidence-based strategies, and fostering a culture of accountability, we can work towards a more just and equitable legal system. The fight against implicit bias is a continuous process, requiring ongoing effort and commitment from all stakeholders within the judicial system. Only through sustained vigilance and a collective commitment to fairness can we hope to fully address the insidious erosion of impartiality caused by unconscious biases and truly uphold the principles of justice for all.

The alternative – a system riddled with unconscious prejudice –undermines the very foundation of a fair and equitable society, leaving vulnerable populations disproportionately exposed to the harsh realities of an unjust system. The pursuit of justice demands nothing less than a relentless effort to identify, understand, and mitigate the pervasive influence of implicit bias.

The insidious nature of implicit bias, represents only one facet of the problem of judicial impartiality. While unconscious prejudices subtly warp judgments, explicit bias—the overt expression of prejudice and discrimination—presents a more blatant, yet equally damaging, threat to justice. Explicit bias manifests as the conscious and intentional favouring or disfavouring of individuals or groups based on characteristics such as race, gender, religion, sexual orientation, or socioeconomic status. Unlike implicit bias, which operates beneath conscious awareness, explicit bias is a deliberate act of prejudice, often reflecting deeply ingrained societal biases and personal beliefs.

The consequences of explicit bias within the courtroom are profound and far-reaching. When judges openly demonstrate prejudice, they undermine the very foundation of a fair and equitable legal system. Their actions not only affect individual cases but also erode public trust in the judiciary as a whole. The perception—and often the reality—that justice is not blind, but rather coloured by the personal biases of those wielding its power, fosters cynicism and distrust, ultimately weakening the rule of law.

One prominent example of explicit bias involves cases where judges have made openly discriminatory remarks during trials or sentencing. Such statements, whether directed at defendants, witnesses, or even lawyers, directly demonstrate a lack of impartiality and constitute a serious breach of judicial ethics. The impact extends beyond the immediate parties involved; such pronouncements signal to the wider public that certain groups are viewed with inherent suspicion or hostility within the judicial system, further entrenching societal inequalities. The mere presence of such overtly biased judges sends a chilling message, dissuading victims from marginalized communities from reporting crimes or participating in legal proceedings, fearing that their claims will be dismissed or they will be unfairly treated.

Consider instances where judges have publicly expressed views that align with extremist ideologies or groups known for their discriminatory beliefs. Such expressions, even outside the context of a specific case, inevitably cast doubt on the judge's ability to maintain objectivity. The public's perception is that the judge's worldview significantly impacts their decision-making, undermining confidence in the impartiality of their rulings, regardless of whether this influence is directly evident in their judicial actions. Such blatant displays of prejudice undermine the integrity of the entire judicial process, casting a shadow of doubt on past, present, and future decisions issued by that judge. This can lead to widespread public calls for their removal, impeachment proceedings, or even reforms in judicial selection processes.

Another troubling manifestation of explicit bias is the disproportionate sentencing of individuals from marginalized communities. While implicit bias operates subtly, often without the judge's conscious awareness, explicit bias involves deliberate and intentional discrimination. This can involve handing down harsher sentences for defendants based on their race, gender, or socioeconomic status, even when the crimes committed are comparable to those of defendants from more privileged backgrounds. The overt nature of this type of discrimination readily displays the unequal application of justice.

Documentation and analysis of sentencing data often reveal stark disparities that highlight explicit bias. Studies consistently demonstrate that defendants from certain racial groups, for example, receive longer prison sentences than their counterparts from other groups, even after controlling for factors such as the severity of the offense and criminal history. This disparity cannot be solely attributed to chance or other extraneous variables; it points towards intentional, conscious bias influencing the decision-making process. The lack of transparency in some sentencing processes further compounds this issue, making it difficult to identify the root causes of these disparities and to hold judges accountable for their actions. The absence of readily available data and the lack of comprehensive records make the detection and exposure of explicit bias significantly more challenging.

The consequences of explicit bias extend beyond the immediate effects on individuals involved in individual cases. It contributes to a climate of distrust and cynicism, eroding the public's faith in the fairness and impartiality of the judicial system. When citizens perceive that the courts are not equally applying the law, they are less likely to trust the legal process and more likely to resort to extralegal means of resolving disputes. This undermines the very foundations of a stable and just society.

The challenge of combating explicit bias demands a multi-faceted approach. First and foremost, there is a need for robust mechanisms for reporting and investigating allegations of judicial bias.

Independent bodies, free from political influence, should be responsible for conducting thorough investigations into such claims, ensuring that appropriate disciplinary measures are taken against judges found to have engaged in explicit discrimination. This process requires clear and comprehensive guidelines defining what constitutes explicit bias, and transparent procedures for handling complaints.

Second, rigorous training programs for judges, lawyers, and other legal professionals are crucial. Such programs must go beyond mere awareness-raising; they should actively address the historical context of bias, encourage critical self-reflection, and equip participants with the skills to recognize and counteract their own prejudices. This training should also incorporate role-playing and simulations that help participants confront and challenge their preconceptions. The goal is not only to make participants aware of their biases but also to empower them to actively mitigate their influence in their professional lives.

Third, enhanced transparency in judicial decision-making is essential. Detailed explanations of sentencing decisions, along with readily available data on sentencing disparities, can aid in identifying patterns of potential bias and holding judges accountable. This transparency extends to making judicial deliberations more accessible, while also protecting the privacy and safety of individuals involved in cases. The goal is to strike a balance between accountability and preserving the integrity of the judicial process.

Finally, fostering diversity within the judiciary is critical. A more diverse bench, reflecting the population it serves, is less likely to exhibit explicit bias. Efforts to increase the representation of marginalized groups in the judiciary will create a more inclusive and equitable legal system, fostering greater trust and confidence in its fairness. This means promoting more inclusive selection processes, providing mentorship opportunities, and implementing targeted recruitment strategies to attract candidates from underrepresented groups.

Addressing explicit bias is not a simple task; it requires a long-term commitment from all stakeholders involved in the judicial system.

The fight against bias is an ongoing effort demanding continuous vigilance, self-reflection, and a collective resolve to ensure that everyone, regardless of their background, has equal access to justice. The alternative is to tolerate a system where bias undermines the very principles it strives to uphold, perpetuating inequalities and fostering a profound lack of faith in the rule of law. Only through sustained effort can we hope to build a truly just and equitable judicial system, one where the scales of justice are truly blind, and the pursuit of justice is not tainted by prejudice.

One of the most effective tools in combating judicial bias lies in comprehensive training programs designed for judges at all levels. Current judicial training often falls short, focusing primarily on legal procedure and case law rather than the critical examination of personal biases. A more robust approach necessitates a multi-faceted curriculum that directly addresses both implicit and explicit biases. This training must move beyond passive lectures and engage judges in active learning experiences that challenge their preconceptions and promote self-awareness.

Implicit bias, the unconscious and often unintentional biases that influence our perceptions and judgments, poses a significant challenge. Research in social psychology has demonstrated that even individuals committed to fairness can harbour implicit biases, impacting their decisions without their conscious awareness. To counteract this, training programs should incorporate techniques such as implicit association tests (IATs), which measure the strength of associations between concepts (e.g., race and positive/negative attributes) in an individual's mind. While IATs are not perfect measures, they provide valuable feedback and initiate a process of self-reflection. Furthermore, training should include discussions of relevant social science research on bias, helping judges understand the pervasive nature of these biases and their potential impact on judicial decision-making. Role-playing exercises simulating real-life courtroom scenarios can further enhance self-awareness by enabling judges to experience firsthand how biases might subtly influence their interactions with litigants and witnesses.

Explicit biases, on the other hand, are conscious and intentional prejudices. These are often more easily identified and addressed, but their impact can be equally devastating. Training should equip judges to recognize and challenge their own explicit biases, providing tools and strategies for mitigating their influence. This could involve exploring real-world examples of explicit bias in judicial decisions, discussing ethical dilemmas, and developing strategies for impartiality in challenging cases. Ethical decision-making frameworks, emphasizing principles of fairness, equity, and justice, can be valuable tools in this context. Moreover, training should explicitly address power dynamics within the courtroom, empowering judges to consciously resist biases that might favour individuals based on their social status, wealth, or other characteristics.

Beyond individual training, the structure of the judicial system itself needs revaluation. The lack of diversity within the judiciary often exacerbates bias. A judiciary that more accurately reflects the demographic makeup of the population it serves is less likely to harbour widespread implicit biases against certain groups. Therefore, promoting diversity in judicial appointments should be a central focus of judicial reform. This necessitates active recruitment strategies targeting underrepresented groups and creating pathways for individuals from diverse backgrounds to enter and succeed in the legal profession. Furthermore, mentoring programs specifically designed to support judges from marginalized communities can provide crucial guidance and support as they navigate the challenges of the judicial system.

Transparency in judicial decision-making is another critical component in mitigating bias. While confidentiality in certain cases is necessary to protect sensitive information, a lack of transparency can breed mistrust and suspicion. Making judicial opinions more accessible to the public, while protecting sensitive information, can foster accountability and allow for critical scrutiny of judicial decisions. Furthermore, publishing anonym data on sentencing trends, categorized by demographic factors, allows for the identification of potential biases in judicial decision-making. Data analysis can reveal patterns that might otherwise go unnoticed, providing valuable insights into the prevalence and nature of judicial bias. Such data, while not a perfect solution, allows for the detection of systemic issues, such as racial or gender disparities in sentencing, prompting a proactive response to address them.

However, increased transparency must be coupled with robust accountability mechanisms. Current mechanisms for addressing judicial misconduct are often slow, opaque, and inadequate. A more effective system should involve independent oversight bodies with the authority to investigate allegations of bias, conduct thorough inquiries, and impose meaningful sanctions. These bodies should be composed of individuals from diverse backgrounds and possess expertise in legal ethics, social science, and judicial procedure.

Strengthening internal mechanisms within the judiciary for addressing misconduct, such as peer review and mentorship programs focusing on ethical conduct, can complement external oversight. Furthermore, making the process of filing complaints accessible and straightforward, coupled with clear guidelines and timelines for investigation, is crucial in building confidence and ensuring accountability.

Finally, the fight against judicial bias is an ongoing process requiring constant vigilance and adaptive strategies. Regular review and evaluation of training programs, accountability mechanisms, and judicial practices are essential to ensure effectiveness and adapt to evolving challenges. The integration of technology and data analysis tools can aid in identifying biases, monitoring trends, and improving decision-making. For example, using predictive analytics to identify cases with a high risk of bias could allow for proactive intervention and reduce the likelihood of biased outcomes.

Statistical data paints a stark picture of this disparity. Studies consistently demonstrate significant racial and ethnic disparities in sentencing, bail decisions, and verdicts. This disparity isn't solely attributable to differences in criminal history; it persists even when controlling for factors like prior convictions and the severity of the offense. The data suggests that implicit and explicit biases play a significant role in shaping these outcomes, leading to a system that disproportionately punishes certain communities. Similarly, studies on bail decisions reveal that individuals from marginalized communities are more likely to be denied bail and held in pre-trial detention, despite similar risk assessments compared to more affluent defendants. This prolonged detention, even before conviction, can have devastating consequences, including job loss, family separation, and the erosion of personal stability.

The economic disadvantage faced by low-income individuals further compounds the impact of judicial bias. Limited access to legal representation is a significant barrier to justice for those who cannot afford competent attorneys. Public defenders, often overburdened and under-resourced, struggle to provide adequate representation to their clients, leading to compromised defence strategies and less favourable outcomes. The disparities are particularly stark in cases involving complex legal issues or lengthy trials, where the absence of robust legal representation can dramatically affect the final outcome. Moreover, low-income individuals are more likely to plead guilty, even if innocent, due to the pressure of facing lengthy pre-trial detention and the daunting prospect of navigating a complex legal system without adequate legal counsel. This plea-bargaining system often reinforces existing inequalities, punishing those who lack the resources to mount a robust defence.

The vulnerability of marginalized communities extends beyond race and socioeconomic status. Individuals with disabilities frequently face communication barriers and misunderstandings within the legal system. Their unique needs may not be adequately addressed, leading to misinterpretations of their actions and compromised legal representation. Similarly, members of the LGBTQ+ community can face prejudice based on their sexual orientation or gender identity, resulting in biased treatment and unfavourable outcomes in both criminal and civil cases. These biases can manifest in subtle ways, such as dismissive attitudes from judges or jurors, or in overt acts of discrimination that influence legal decisions.

The experiences of immigrants further illustrate the interconnectedness of bias and vulnerability. Language barriers, cultural differences, and fear of deportation can significantly impair their ability to navigate the legal system effectively. They may be less likely to understand their rights, less able to communicate their needs to their attorneys or the court, and more vulnerable to exploitation or unfair treatment. The fear of deportation can also lead to coerced pleas, even if the immigrant is innocent, simply to avoid removal proceedings. Moreover, the immigration court system itself often lacks the same procedural safeguards as criminal courts, creating a further vulnerability for immigrants facing deportation.

Case studies amplify these statistical trends, offering compelling illustrations of how judicial bias affects vulnerable populations. Consider the case of individuals from marginalized communities wrongly accused of crimes, often due to racial profiling or other forms of discriminatory policing. The absence of sufficient legal resources can lead to wrongful convictions, often based on flawed evidence or coerced confessions. Such cases represent a systemic failure to protect vulnerable populations from the harmful consequences of biased policing and judicial processes.

The cumulative effect of these biases can result in severely disproportionate outcomes, highlighting the complexity of addressing systemic inequality within the judiciary.

Targeted initiatives are essential to ensure that vulnerable populations have access to adequate legal representation, fair trials, and equitable outcomes. This involves significant investment in public defender programs, providing them with the resources and support needed to represent their clients effectively.

Simultaneously, efforts should focus on increasing diversity within the judiciary and legal profession, creating a system that better reflects the population it serves. Moreover, specialized training programs for judges and legal professionals should address the specific challenges faced by vulnerable populations, focusing on implicit bias, cultural competency, and effective communication strategies. Community-based legal aid organizations play a vital role in providing crucial support and advocating for the rights of marginalized individuals and their importance cannot be understated.

Finally, the collection and analysis of disaggregated data is crucial for tracking the impact of judicial bias on vulnerable populations.

This data can reveal patterns and trends that might otherwise remain hidden, allowing for targeted interventions and the assessment of the effectiveness of reforms. Transparency in the collection and dissemination of this data is essential to building trust and fostering accountability. Without comprehensive data on the lived experiences of vulnerable populations within the legal system, meaningful and sustainable reform will remain elusive. The fight against judicial bias is not simply about creating a fairer system; it's about ensuring that justice is equally accessible to everyone, regardless of their race, socioeconomic status, disability, sexual orientation, gender identity, or immigration status. The ultimate goal is to create a system that truly embodies the principles of equality and impartiality for all.

The Challenges Faced by Whistleblowers

The fight for justice within the judiciary is not solely a battle against biased rulings and discriminatory practices; it's also a struggle against a pervasive culture of silence that shields corruption and punishes those who dare to expose it.

Whistleblowers, the individuals who bravely risk their careers, reputations, and even their safety to reveal wrongdoing, face an uphill battle against a system often designed to protect the perpetrators, not the victims of their crimes. Their experiences highlight the chilling effect of retaliation and the desperate need for robust legal protections and a fundamental shift in the culture of the judicial system itself.

The challenges faced by whistleblowers are multifaceted and deeply ingrained in the structure of many judicial systems. Often, the first obstacle they encounter is a lack of clear and accessible reporting mechanisms. Many institutions lack formal channels for reporting misconduct, forcing whistleblowers to navigate complex bureaucratic procedures or risk retaliation by going outside established channels. Even when formal mechanisms exist, they can be cumbersome, ineffective, or even designed to discourage reporting. The fear of retribution is frequently a more potent deterrent than any hope of meaningful change.

Retaliation against whistleblowers can take many forms, ranging from subtle acts of intimidation to overt acts of violence. Subtle forms of retaliation can include ostracization, demotion, denial of promotions, unfair work assignments, or the withdrawal of support.

These actions, while less dramatic than overt threats or physical harm, can be equally damaging, eroding the whistleblower's morale, undermining their professional credibility, and ultimately forcing them out of their jobs. Such actions are frequently difficult to prove, allowing perpetrators to act with relative impunity.

More overtly hostile forms of retaliation include threats, harassment, and even physical violence. Whistleblowers have reported receiving anonymous threats, being subjected to smear campaigns designed to discredit their reputations, and even facing physical harm or violence. These threats are designed to instil fear and silence those who might consider reporting misconduct. The lack of sufficient protection for whistleblowers often leaves them vulnerable to these attacks, leaving them feeling isolated and exposed.

The legal repercussions faced by whistleblowers can be equally daunting. Many jurisdictions lack robust whistleblower protection laws, leaving whistleblowers vulnerable to lawsuits from those they accuse of wrongdoing. Strategic lawsuits against public participation (SLAPPs) are commonly used to intimidate and silence whistleblowers through costly and protracted legal battles, forcing them to bear the financial burden of defending themselves against baseless claims. Even when whistleblower protection laws exist, they are often poorly enforced, providing little practical protection to those who report misconduct.

The psychological toll on whistleblowers is often immense. The process of reporting corruption can be emotionally draining, requiring individuals to relive traumatic experiences, confront powerful figures, and face intense scrutiny. The isolation and lack of support from colleagues and superiors can further exacerbate the emotional burden, leading to feelings of anxiety, depression, and even post-traumatic stress disorder. The constant fear of retaliation and the uncertainty of the outcome can create a state of chronic stress, impacting their mental and physical health significantly.

Beyond the personal cost, the failure to protect whistleblowers has broader societal consequences. The culture of silence that protects corrupt practices undermines public trust in the judicial system, eroding its legitimacy and its ability to function effectively. When individuals fear retaliation for reporting wrongdoing, corruption goes unchecked, perpetuating a cycle of abuse and undermining the principles of justice and accountability. This ultimately harms the very individuals the judicial system is meant to protect.

Addressing this issue requires a multi-pronged approach. Stronger whistleblower protection laws are paramount, ensuring that those who report wrongdoing are shielded from retaliation. These laws must be comprehensive, covering a wide range of retaliatory actions and providing effective mechanisms for redress. Moreover, they must be accompanied by robust enforcement mechanisms, ensuring that perpetrators are held accountable for their actions.

Independent oversight bodies are crucial to investigate allegations of retaliation and ensure that whistleblowers receive fair and impartial treatment.

Beyond legislative reforms, a fundamental cultural shift is necessary within the judicial system. Creating a culture that values transparency and accountability, where whistle blowing is seen as a positive act rather than an act of disloyalty, is essential. This requires training programs for judges, lawyers, and other judicial personnel to foster an understanding of the importance of whistleblower protection and the ethical obligations to address reported misconduct. Moreover, creating a system where whistleblowers feel supported and empowered to come forward without fear of retaliation is crucial for fostering a more ethical and accountable judiciary.

Furthermore, increased public awareness of the challenges faced by whistleblowers is vital. Highlighting their bravery and the systemic obstacles they face can help create a climate of public support and encourage greater protection. Educating the public about their role in ensuring a fair and just judicial system can also foster greater accountability. Strengthening the role of independent media in investigating and reporting on allegations of corruption is equally important.

Ultimately, the protection of whistleblowers is not simply a matter of individual rights; it's a cornerstone of a just and accountable society. When individuals are empowered to expose wrongdoing without fear of retaliation, the very foundations of a functioning democracy are strengthened. The fight for a fairer, more transparent judicial system requires a concerted effort to protect those who bravely challenge the status quo and risk everything to expose the truth. The culture of silence must be shattered, replaced by a culture that values honesty, transparency, and the courageous voices of those who seek to uphold justice.

Case Studies Retaliation against Whistleblowers

Examining specific cases reveals the harsh realities faced by whistleblowers who dare to challenge the status quo within the judicial system. The following examples, drawn from real-world experiences, illustrate the various forms of retaliation employed and the devastating consequences for those who expose misconduct. These cases are not isolated incidents but rather symptomatic of a deeply ingrained problem requiring systemic reform.

Encouraging Reporting

Encouraging a robust system of whistleblower protection necessitates a multi-pronged approach that transcends mere legal frameworks. While strong laws are the cornerstone, their effectiveness hinges on the creation of a culture where reporting misconduct is not only permissible but actively encouraged. This requires a fundamental shift in mindset within judicial institutions, moving away from a culture of silence and towards one of transparency and accountability. The success of such a cultural transformation can be seen in the varying degrees of effectiveness witnessed in different countries' approaches to whistleblower protection.

One central element is the establishment of clear and easily accessible reporting channels. These channels must be designed to ensure confidentiality and protect whistleblowers' identities. A simple, anonymous online platform, for instance, can significantly lower the barrier to reporting. Furthermore, the reporting process must be streamlined, reducing bureaucratic hurdles and delays that can discourage individuals from coming forward. The experience should be designed to minimize the potential for intimidation or retaliation. Regular audits of these reporting systems are crucial to ensure they are functioning effectively and remain accessible.

Countries like the Netherlands, with their established and transparent reporting mechanisms, serve as a model for others to emulate. Their success stems not only from the ease of access but also from the swift and discreet handling of complaints.

Beyond readily available reporting channels, robust internal investigation mechanisms are paramount. These mechanisms must be independent, impartial, and adequately resourced to conduct thorough investigations. The investigators must be trained to handle sensitive information, maintain confidentiality, and deal with whistleblowers with empathy and respect. The independence of these internal bodies is crucial; they must be insulated from political influence and operates under strict ethical guidelines to ensure objectivity. Countries with successful internal investigation mechanisms often prioritize transparency in their processes, regularly publishing reports detailing the outcomes of investigations, thereby demonstrating their commitment to accountability. The contrast between countries with robust internal mechanisms and those with weak or non-existent ones highlights the significant difference in the success rate of whistleblower protection.

Providing comprehensive legal and psychological support to whistleblowers is another critical component. This support should be readily available from the moment a whistleblower comes forward. Access to experienced legal counsel is crucial to protect whistleblowers from potential retaliation and to guide them through the legal process. Legal aid should be readily available, especially for those from marginalized communities who may lack the financial resources to secure legal representation. Furthermore, access to mental health services is essential. The emotional toll on whistleblowers can be immense, and providing timely access to support can significantly mitigate the psychological impact of their actions. Many countries now incorporate mandatory psychological support into their whistleblower protection programs, recognizing the importance of this aspect of protection. A comparison of success rates in countries with and without such support clearly indicates the significant positive impact of such provisions.

The protection of whistleblower anonymity is fundamental. Robust legal frameworks should ensure that whistleblowers' identities are protected throughout the investigation and legal proceedings. This protection should extend to prohibiting the disclosure of their identity, even in court proceedings, unless absolutely necessary. The use of encrypted communication channels and secure platforms for reporting can enhance the protection of anonymity. Moreover, the legal frameworks should include provisions to penalize those who attempt to identify or retaliate against whistleblowers. The effectiveness of anonymity protection varies across jurisdictions, with some countries employing advanced technologies and stricter penalties, resulting in higher reporting rates. A comparative study of these differences would reveal the best practices in safeguarding anonymity.

Beyond legal frameworks and institutional mechanisms, cultivating a culture of ethical conduct is paramount. This requires a systemic shift in organizational culture, prioritizing ethical behaviour and fostering a climate of trust and accountability. Leadership must actively promote ethical conduct, setting the tone from the top and making it clear that reporting misconduct is valued and encouraged, rather than viewed as disloyalty. Regular ethics training for all employees is necessary, including education on whistleblower protection laws and procedures. Instilling a culture of ethical conduct is a long-term process, but the long-term benefits, including increased trust and reduced instances of corruption, far outweigh the initial investment. Examining the success rates of different cultural initiatives in fostering ethical behaviour across different countries can provide valuable insights into effective strategies.

The success of whistleblower protection initiatives is not solely measured by the existence of laws and mechanisms, but by their effective implementation and enforcement. This requires adequate resources allocated to investigative agencies and judicial bodies to ensure that complaints are thoroughly investigated, and that those found guilty of corruption or retaliation are appropriately sanctioned. Regular monitoring and evaluation of these systems are essential to identify areas for improvement and ensure their ongoing effectiveness. Countries with successful whistleblower protection systems typically have strong oversight mechanisms in place, ensuring accountability and transparency. Comparing the performance of these systems in different countries demonstrates the critical role of robust enforcement in encouraging reporting and achieving meaningful change.

Furthermore, the role of independent oversight bodies cannot be overstated. These bodies should be free from political influence and tasked with monitoring the implementation of whistleblower protection laws and investigating complaints of retaliation. Their independence and authority are critical to ensuring impartiality and fostering public confidence. The effectiveness of these bodies hinges on their resources, expertise, and authority to conduct thorough investigations and impose meaningful sanctions. A review of countries with well-functioning independent oversight bodies, contrasted with those lacking such institutions, clearly demonstrates the critical role they play in successful whistleblower protection programs.

International cooperation is also vital. Sharing best practices, providing technical assistance to developing countries, and working towards greater harmonization of whistleblower protection laws across jurisdictions are all essential components of a global strategy to combat corruption. International organizations can play a crucial role in facilitating this cooperation, fostering the exchange of information and expertise, and promoting the adoption of effective whistleblower protection measures worldwide. A comparative analysis of international cooperation initiatives, examining their successes and failures, would highlight best practices for global cooperation in this field.

Encouraging Reporting

The bedrock of any effective anti-corruption strategy, particularly within the often opaque world of the judiciary, lies in unwavering transparency and robust oversight. Without these essential components, whistleblowers remain vulnerable, corruption festers in the shadows, and public trust erodes further. The lack of transparency allows misconduct to proliferate, fostering a culture of impunity where wrongdoers believe they can operate with little fear of exposure. Conversely, a transparent and accountable system acts as a powerful deterrent, signalling that unethical actions will be investigated and punished.

Improving transparency within the judiciary requires a multi-faceted approach. One essential step is enhancing public access to judicial records. Many jurisdictions maintain antiquated systems where access to court documents is cumbersome, expensive, and often requires navigating bureaucratic mazes. This opacity shields judicial processes from public scrutiny, hindering effective oversight and allowing potential misconduct to remain hidden. Modernizing these systems through the implementation of user-friendly online portals, for instance, would significantly improve access, allowing citizens, journalists, and oversight bodies to readily examine court records and identify potential irregularities. Such digitalization efforts should be coupled with clear guidelines and policies that govern the release of information, ensuring that the balance between transparency and protecting sensitive information is carefully maintained. The experience of countries like Estonia, renowned for its digitally advanced public sector, demonstrates the feasibility and benefits of this approach. Their readily available online records provide a valuable example of how technology can be leveraged to enhance transparency and accountability in the judicial system.

Furthermore, the level of detail included in publicly accessible records is crucial. Simply making documents available is not enough; the information must be readily understandable and usable. This requires moving beyond cryptic legal jargon and structuring information in a clear and concise manner. Summary reports that highlight key aspects of cases, along with easily searchable databases, are vital for making judicial processes more accessible to the public. This requires investment in data analysis and information technology, but the payoff in increased transparency and public understanding is invaluable. Comparing the transparency levels in jurisdictions with similar legal systems but varying levels of public access can illuminate the impact of these measures on public perception and the level of corruption detected.

Beyond improving public access to records, strengthening oversight bodies is equally vital. These bodies, whether internal or external to the judiciary, play a critical role in scrutinizing judicial processes, investigating allegations of misconduct, and holding individuals accountable. To be effective, these bodies must be independent, adequately resourced, and empowered to act decisively. Their independence is paramount; they must be insulated from political influence and pressure to ensure impartial investigations and unbiased findings. This independence should be enshrined in law and reinforced through robust protection mechanisms that safeguard them from external interference. For instance, the structure and functioning of these bodies should be clearly defined by law and independent of the executive or legislative branches. Their budgetary autonomy is also critical, ensuring they have the resources necessary to conduct thorough and effective investigations. The contrast between the effectiveness of oversight bodies with strong independence and those lacking it is a stark reminder of their importance in combating judicial corruption.

The composition of these oversight bodies is also central. They should comprise individuals with diverse backgrounds and expertise, including legal professionals, academics, and representatives from civil society organizations. This diversity ensures a broad perspective and helps avoid groupthink or biases that might hinder effective scrutiny. The selection process for members of these bodies must be transparent and merit-based, fostering public confidence in their impartiality. Countries with well-established and diverse oversight bodies offer valuable lessons in the design and implementation of effective oversight mechanisms. Studying the structures and successes of these bodies can inform best practices and guide reforms in jurisdictions lacking similar effective oversight.

Transparency and oversight are not merely about preventing corruption; they are also vital for protecting whistleblowers. A transparent system makes it easier for whistleblowers to report misconduct without fear of retaliation, as their allegations are more likely to be investigated and taken seriously. Moreover, robust oversight mechanisms provide a safety net for whistleblowers, ensuring that their reports are handled confidentially and that they are protected from retribution. A culture of transparency and accountability empowers whistleblowers and strengthens their hand, making them less likely to be silenced or ignored. This is particularly crucial in the judiciary, where the potential for retaliation can be particularly severe. Analyzing the correlation between levels of transparency and the number of reported cases of judicial misconduct can illustrate the powerful protective effect of transparency.

The positive effects of transparency in other jurisdictions are demonstrably evident. Countries with robust transparency mechanisms, coupled with independent oversight bodies, often enjoy higher levels of public trust in their judicial systems and lower rates of perceived corruption. This improved public trust translates into greater compliance with the law and a stronger sense of social justice. Conversely, opaque judicial systems, lacking effective oversight, are often characterized by low public trust, high levels of perceived corruption, and a reluctance to report misconduct. By studying these contrasting examples, we can gain a clearer understanding of the crucial role that transparency and oversight play in building a just and accountable judicial system. Comparative studies analyzing the impact of transparency measures on judicial corruption across different jurisdictions could provide compelling evidence of their effectiveness.

Judicial Transparency

The lack of transparency and accountability manifests in various ways, hindering effective oversight and creating a culture of impunity. The opaque nature of certain judicial processes actively shields misconduct from public scrutiny, allowing corruption to fester in the shadows. One primary area where opacity fosters corruption is the limited public access to judicial records. While the ideal of open justice dictates that court proceedings should be accessible to the public, many jurisdictions fall far short of this ideal. Accessing court documents often requires navigating complex bureaucratic procedures, incurring significant expenses, or facing arbitrary denials based on vaguely defined exceptions. This creates an environment where vital information about cases, including evidence, judicial rulings, and the conduct of legal professionals, remains shrouded in secrecy. This lack of access significantly impedes effective oversight by journalists, civil society organizations, and even other judicial bodies tasked with monitoring ethical conduct.

Without the ability to scrutinize these records, identifying patterns of misconduct, biases, or systemic failures becomes exceedingly difficult. For example, a study of a particular jurisdiction might reveal that access to case files related to high-profile individuals or corporations is significantly more restricted than in cases involving ordinary citizens, highlighting a clear bias in the application of transparency rules. Such disparities underscore the need for systematic reform.

The use of complex and archaic legal jargon further contributes to the problem of limited transparency. Court documents are frequently written in highly technical language, impenetrable to the average citizen, even to many legal professionals outside the specific area of law. This intentional obfuscation serves to shield potentially corrupt practices from public view. The deliberate use of obscure terminology prevents meaningful public engagement and oversight, allowing instances of corruption to go unnoticed and unchallenged. This is not merely an issue of accessibility; it's a deliberate strategy of concealing unethical behaviour. A simple example might be the opaque language used in contracts or settlements involving government officials and private corporations, where hidden clauses or ambiguous wording can conceal conflicts of interest or payments disguised as legitimate fees. The lack of clear, concise summaries of judicial rulings exacerbates the problem. Even when documents are technically available, their complexity renders them practically useless for public scrutiny.

Furthermore, the lack of transparency extends beyond the simple accessibility of court records. It encompasses the entire process of judicial appointments, promotions, and disciplinary actions. In many jurisdictions, the selection of judges lacks transparency, leading to concerns about political influence and favouritism. The criteria used for appointments often remain unclear, making it difficult to assess the impartiality and qualifications of those appointed. The lack of publicly available information about the selection process creates an environment where unqualified or corrupt individuals can be appointed, eroding public trust in the judiciary. Similarly, the process of disciplining judges for misconduct often lacks transparency, leading to a sense of impunity among those who engage in unethical behaviour. Without clear and publicly available information about disciplinary actions taken against judges, it is impossible to assess the effectiveness of such measures in deterring misconduct. For instance, the absence of publicly accessible records concerning judicial complaints and investigations allows judges to escape accountability for their actions.

The absence of comprehensive and readily available statistics on judicial performance also undermines transparency. While some jurisdictions might publish aggregate data on caseloads or disposition rates, detailed information on individual judge performance or patterns of bias in sentencing remains largely unavailable. This lack of granular data makes it virtually impossible to identify systemic issues or individual misconduct that might be contributing to corruption. For example, the absence of data on the length of time it takes to resolve different types of cases can conceal delays strategically employed to favor certain parties. The inability to track the performance of individual judges in a transparent manner prevents effective monitoring and identification of potential bias or corruption. This absence of data serves as a significant obstacle to identifying and addressing systemic weaknesses within the judicial system.

Moreover, the lack of transparency extends beyond the judicial process itself. There is a significant need for greater transparency in the funding and budgetary allocations for judicial institutions. This often-overlooked aspect allows for potential misuse of funds and undue influence on judicial decisions. The opacity around judicial budgets creates an environment where corruption can flourish undetected. Detailed budget information should be readily available to the public, allowing for independent scrutiny of how funds are allocated and utilized. Without this level of transparency, it's impossible to ensure the effective and honest allocation of resources within the judicial system. For instance, the lack of scrutiny regarding expenditures on judicial travel, technology, and staffing can facilitate embezzlement or favouritism in procurement contracts.

These hidden financial dealings undermine the integrity of the entire system.

The lack of effective mechanisms for whistleblowers to report misconduct without fear of retribution further exacerbates the problem. In a climate of fear and intimidation, individuals who witness corruption are less likely to come forward, allowing unethical practices to continue unchecked. Strong legal protections for whistleblowers are crucial to encourage the reporting of misconduct and to ensure that those who report wrongdoing are not punished for doing so. A culture of fear silences potential witnesses and makes uncovering corruption far more difficult. Often, whistleblowers face significant professional and personal repercussions, including job loss, social ostracism, and even threats to their safety. The establishment of robust protection measures, including independent investigative bodies and confidential reporting mechanisms, is paramount in encouraging the reporting of misconduct and fostering a culture of accountability. The lack of such systems perpetuates a cycle of silence and impunity, hindering efforts to tackle corruption within the judicial system.

Inadequate Funding and Allocation Resources

Under-resourced courts, overworked judges, and understaffed support systems create an environment ripe for exploitation and bribery. This section will examine this critical systemic weakness, demonstrating its direct contribution to the pervasive corruption plaguing judiciaries worldwide.

The most immediate consequence of inadequate funding is the overwhelming workload faced by judicial personnel. Judges, already burdened with extensive caseloads, often lack the necessary support staff to effectively manage their duties. This leads to prolonged delays in case resolution, creating opportunities for bribery and influence-peddling. Parties involved in lengthy legal battles, facing mounting financial pressures and the uncertainty of prolonged proceedings, may be more susceptible to offers of expedited justice through illicit means. The sheer volume of cases coupled with insufficient administrative support often forces judges to rush through proceedings, potentially overlooking crucial details or evidence, leading to miscarriages of justice and eroding public confidence in the system's fairness. This pressure-cooker environment contributes directly to the vulnerability of the judiciary to corrupt practices.

Furthermore, understaffing extends beyond the judges themselves. Court clerks, bailiffs, and other support personnel are often overworked and underpaid, leaving them vulnerable to bribery and other forms of corruption. Individuals facing financial hardship are more likely to succumb to offers of illicit payments for expediting processes or altering documents. The lack of adequate training and professional development further exacerbates this vulnerability.

Without proper training, these essential personnel may lack the skills and awareness to identify and report corrupt practices effectively. This creates a system where corruption can flourish unnoticed, largely due to the lack of capacity within the court to effectively monitor and regulate itself.

The implications of inadequate funding extend beyond personnel issues. A lack of resources can compromise the quality of justice delivered. This includes inadequate access to technological advancements, vital for efficient case management and evidence processing. Many courts still rely on outdated systems, leading to inefficiencies, delays, and potential for manipulation of evidence.

The absence of modern technology increases the potential for corruption, as manual processes are inherently more susceptible to tampering and fraud. The absence of secure digital archives for court documents introduces risks of manipulation or loss of crucial evidence, which can be exploited for corrupt purposes. This technological deficit also impacts the ability of the courts to effectively communicate with the public, making access to information and oversight more difficult, and further compounding the transparency issues highlighted earlier.

Moreover, inadequate funding can lead to deterioration in court infrastructure. Poorly maintained buildings, inadequate security measures, and lack of appropriate facilities create an environment conducive to corruption. Unsuitable conditions can compromise the integrity of court proceedings, making them vulnerable to external influence. Insufficient security measures can allow for bribery and intimidation, compromising the impartiality of the judicial process.

Comparative studies reveal stark differences in funding levels across different jurisdictions. Developed nations often dedicate significantly more resources per capita to their judicial systems compared to developing countries. This disparity directly correlates with the prevalence of corruption. Countries with higher per capita judicial spending tend to exhibit lower rates of corruption, suggesting a strong link between resource allocation and the integrity of the judicial process. This discrepancy highlights the need for international cooperation and targeted financial assistance to help developing nations strengthen their judicial systems and combat corruption effectively. Such initiatives require a shift in global priorities, recognizing that the stability and fairness of the judicial system is fundamental to development and governance.

The lack of independent oversight and monitoring mechanisms related to judicial budgets further exacerbates the problem. Often, budgetary decisions for the judiciary lack sufficient transparency and independent scrutiny. Without adequate mechanisms to monitor how funds are allocated and spent, there is an increased risk of embezzlement and misuse of resources. This lack of transparency undermines public trust and fuels perceptions of corruption. The creation of independent budgetary oversight bodies, with authority to investigate potential financial irregularities and make recommendations for reform, is crucial to ensuring the integrity of judicial funding. This requires not just financial resources, but a political commitment to accountability and transparency in the management of public funds.

Furthermore, the inefficient allocation of existing resources contributes significantly to the problem. Even when adequate funding is available, its inefficient distribution can render it ineffective in combating corruption. Bureaucratic hurdles, a lack of planning, and ineffective prioritization of resources can lead to funds being wasted or misdirected. This requires a fundamental shift in how judicial budgets are managed, moving away from ad-hoc decision-making towards a more strategic and evidence-based approach. This would involve rigorous needs assessments, careful planning of resource allocation, and regular monitoring of the effectiveness of spending. The efficient use of funds should be seen as an equally vital element in addressing corruption as securing appropriate funding levels.

Reasoned Judgments

The principle that judicial decisions should not be arbitrary pronouncements but rather carefully considered and clearly articulated pronouncements is fundamental to the rule of law. This requirement serves multiple critical functions, enhancing both the internal consistency of the judicial system and its external accountability to the public.

The most immediate impact of reasoned judgments lies in their contribution to transparency. When judges are obligated to explain their decisions, the reasoning process becomes visible, allowing for scrutiny and understanding by all stakeholders. This transparency doesn't simply satisfy a formal requirement; it fosters trust and confidence in the judiciary. Citizens are more likely to accept judicial decisions, even if they disagree with the outcome, when they understand the rationale behind those decisions. Opaque judgments, on the other hand, breed suspicion and cynicism, undermining the legitimacy of the judicial system.

Furthermore, the requirement for reasoned judgments contributes significantly to the internal consistency and predictability of the law. When judges articulate the principles and precedents upon which their decisions are based, they create a body of jurisprudence that provides guidance for future cases. This consistency promotes fairness and reduces the potential for arbitrary or discriminatory application of the law. Judges, when confronted with similar cases, are guided by prior reasoned judgments, promoting predictability and limiting the scope for individual judicial discretion to unduly influence outcomes. This consistent application of legal principles strengthens the rule of law and ensures greater equality before the law.

The process of formulating a reasoned judgment also serves as an internal check on judicial impartiality. The very act of articulating a justification forces judges to rigorously examine the evidence, analyze legal arguments, and consider counter-arguments. This analytical process minimizes the risk of biased or hasty decisions. By compelling judges to articulate their reasoning, the system encourages careful deliberation and reduces the potential for unconscious biases to sway the judgment. The transparency inherent in this process further acts as a deterrent against potential abuses of power.

The specific requirements for reasoned judgments vary across jurisdictions, but several common elements are prevalent. Most legal systems mandate that judgments clearly identify the issues before the court, summarize the relevant facts, state the applicable law, analyze the arguments presented by the parties, and ultimately articulate the court's decision and the reasoning supporting it. Many jurisdictions also require a clear explanation of how the court resolved any conflicts between different legal authorities or precedents. This ensures that the judge's interpretation of the law is not arbitrary but rooted in legal principles and established jurisprudence.

The effectiveness of the requirement for reasoned judgments depends heavily on the quality of the judgments themselves. A well-reasoned judgment is more than a simple recitation of the facts and the applicable law; it requires a coherent and persuasive explanation of the judge's reasoning, addressing counter-arguments and demonstrating a careful consideration of the relevant factors. Poorly reasoned judgments, characterized by vagueness, inconsistencies, or lack of clarity, undermine the benefits of this crucial mechanism of accountability. Therefore, judicial training and continuing education programs play a vital role in equipping judges with the skills necessary to craft clear, concise, and persuasive judgments.

Beyond the content of the judgments themselves, the accessibility of those judgments is equally crucial for transparency and accountability. The publication of judicial opinions, often available online through court websites, allows for public scrutiny and contributes significantly to the transparency of the judicial process. Open courts, where the public can observe judicial proceedings, further enhance transparency, though practical limitations, including security concerns and logistical constraints, may necessitate exceptions. The balance between ensuring public access and protecting sensitive information often requires careful consideration and the implementation of appropriate mechanisms, such as redactions or protective orders.

However, the publication of judgments presents challenges. Concerns about protecting the privacy of individuals involved in legal proceedings, particularly in family law cases or cases involving vulnerable individuals, often necessitate redactions or limitations on access to specific parts of the judgment. Balancing the need for transparency with the protection of privacy is a crucial aspect of implementing effective transparency mechanisms. This requires a delicate balance, with clear guidelines to ensure consistency and fairness. Overly broad restrictions on access can undermine transparency, while inadequately safeguarding privacy can inflict undue harm on individuals.

Furthermore, the language and complexity of legal judgments often pose a barrier to public understanding.

While judges have a duty to provide clear and understandable justifications for their decisions, the inherent complexity of many legal issues can make it challenging to communicate the reasoning in a readily accessible manner. Initiatives aimed at simplifying legal language and utilizing plain English in judgments can significantly improve public understanding and trust in the judicial process. This includes providing summaries or explanations of complex judgments in more accessible language, utilizing visual aids where appropriate and considering the accessibility needs of diverse groups within the community.

The effectiveness of the requirement for reasoned judgments can also be enhanced through external mechanisms. Appeals processes provide an avenue for review of lower court decisions, ensuring that errors of law or fact are corrected. The appellate review process often scrutinizes the reasoning of lower court judges, contributing further to the accountability of the judiciary. Independent oversight bodies, such as judicial councils or commissions, can also play a role in monitoring the quality of judicial judgments and addressing concerns about inconsistencies or biases. These bodies can contribute to the development of best practices for judicial decision-making and can provide training and support to judges. They can also initiate investigations into complaints about judicial conduct if concerns about the quality or fairness of judgments are raised.

Addressing Partisanship and Ensuring Impartiality in Judicial Decision-Making

The pursuit of justice demands not only adherence to established legal procedures but also a profound commitment to impartiality. While the mechanisms discussed previously—reasoned judgments, robust appeals processes, and external oversight—address aspects of judicial accountability, the insidious threat of bias remains a significant challenge. Bias, whether conscious or unconscious, can subtly or overtly distort the application of the law, leading to unfair and inequitable outcomes.

Addressing this challenge requires a multi-faceted approach, encompassing preventative measures, proactive strategies, and robust mechanisms for redress.

One of the most effective preventative measures is comprehensive judicial training. This training should extend beyond the technicalities of legal doctrine to include critical self-reflection on potential sources of bias. Implicit bias—the unconscious attitudes or stereotypes that affect our perceptions and decisions—are particularly insidious, as it operates below the level of conscious awareness. Training programs designed to raise judges' awareness of their own biases and to equip them with strategies for mitigating their influence are crucial. These programs should incorporate interactive exercises, case studies, and discussions, fostering a culture of self-reflection and continuous learning within the judiciary. The effectiveness of such training is demonstrably linked to its comprehensiveness and the ongoing commitment to reinforcement and updating. A one-off training session is unlikely to have a lasting impact; rather, ongoing professional development, incorporating feedback mechanisms and incorporating evolving research on implicit bias, is essential.

Beyond individual training, institutional strategies play a critical role in ensuring impartiality. Promoting diversity within the judiciary is paramount. A diverse bench, reflecting the demographic realities of the society it serves, can help to mitigate the risk of biased decision-making.

Diversity, however, extends beyond simple numerical representation; it encompasses a diversity of experiences, perspectives, and backgrounds. Judges from diverse backgrounds bring a richer understanding of the complexities of society and are more likely to identify and address issues of bias that might otherwise be overlooked. The appointment process itself needs to be transparent and merit-based, ensuring that qualified candidates from all backgrounds have an equal opportunity to serve. This requires active efforts to identify and encourage talented individuals from underrepresented groups to pursue careers in law and the judiciary. Blind review processes for judicial appointments, shielding the candidate's identity from the selection committee until after initial evaluation, can also help mitigate bias in the selection process itself.

Recusal procedures provide a mechanism for addressing potential conflicts of interest or biases that might compromise a judge's impartiality. These procedures, which require judges to withdraw from cases where their impartiality might reasonably be questioned, are critical in safeguarding the integrity of the judicial process. However, the effectiveness of recusal procedures depends on their clarity, transparency, and the willingness of judges to utilize them. Ambiguous or overly permissive standards for recusal can undermine their efficacy, while judges' reluctance to refuse themselves, even in the face of potential bias, can erode public confidence in the judiciary. The establishment of clear, objective criteria for recusal, alongside independent mechanisms for reviewing recusal decisions, can enhance the integrity and effectiveness of this crucial safeguard.

Another vital component of ensuring impartial judicial decision-making is the development of clear and transparent guidelines for judicial conduct. Codes of judicial ethics, coupled with robust mechanisms for investigating allegations of misconduct, are essential for maintaining the highest standards of professionalism and impartiality. These codes should not only prohibit overt bias but also address the subtle forms of bias that can affect decision-making. They should also clearly outline the procedures for handling complaints of bias, ensuring fairness and transparency in the investigation and resolution of such complaints. Public access to information about judicial misconduct investigations, subject to appropriate limitations to protect privacy and ongoing proceedings, enhances accountability and fosters public trust. Furthermore, the establishment of independent bodies tasked with investigating complaints of judicial misconduct is essential for ensuring objectivity and impartiality in the process. Such bodies should be comprised of individuals with relevant expertise and experience, free from political influence or potential bias.

Beyond these institutional mechanisms, the role of public scrutiny and accountability cannot be overstated. A robust and informed citizenry, capable of critically evaluating judicial decisions, plays a crucial role in ensuring the impartiality of the judiciary. Free and independent media, investigative journalism, and access to judicial decisions are all essential for holding the judiciary accountable.

Transparency in judicial proceedings, subject to appropriate limitations regarding the protection of sensitive information, allows for public observation and scrutiny, thereby discouraging biased actions. Furthermore, academic research and public discourse on judicial bias can help identify systemic issues and inform policy changes. By examining case law, analyzing patterns in judicial decisions and conducting empirical studies, researchers can provide valuable insights into the nature and extent of bias within the judiciary. This research can then inform the development of more effective training programs, institutional strategies, and accountability mechanisms.

The fight against bias in judicial decision-making is an ongoing process, demanding constant vigilance and adaptive strategies. The effectiveness of any single approach is limited; a comprehensive and integrated strategy, encompassing preventative measures, proactive initiatives, and robust mechanisms for redress, is required. The commitment to impartiality must be not merely a stated ideal but a lived reality, reflected in every aspect of the judicial system, from the training of judges to the appointment processes, recusal procedures, and the overall culture of the institution. The ultimate goal is a judiciary that truly reflects the principles of fairness, equality, and justice for all, regardless of background, circumstance, or identity. This demands not only individual accountability but also a systemic commitment to addressing the root causes of bias, fostering a culture of constant learning and improvement within the judicial system. Only then can we hope to achieve a just and equitable legal system worthy of the ideals it purports to uphold. The ongoing evolution and refinement of these mechanisms, informed by comparative analysis, best practices, and a dedication to accessibility for diverse populations, will be crucial for building a stronger, fairer, and more trustworthy judicial system that serves the needs of all citizens. This is not simply a matter of technical legal compliance; it is a fundamental requirement for maintaining public trust and confidence in the rule of law itself.

The Performance of Prosecutors in Ensuring Justice

The public prosecutor occupies a pivotal position within the criminal justice system, serving as a crucial linchpin in upholding the rule of law and ensuring justice is served. Their role transcends mere prosecution; it involves a complex interplay of investigative responsibilities, legal judgment, and ethical considerations that directly impact the fairness and efficiency of the entire process. Understanding this multifaceted role is paramount to appreciating the significance of prosecutorial independence and accountability in a functioning democracy.

The primary function of a public prosecutor is to represent the interests of the state in criminal proceedings. This differs significantly from the role of a private attorney, who advocates solely for their client. The prosecutor's duty is to pursue justice, a concept broader than simply securing convictions. While obtaining convictions for guilty parties is a key aspect of their work, it must be balanced with a commitment to fairness, the protection of the innocent, and the overall pursuit of justice for all involved. This necessitates a nuanced approach, demanding careful consideration of evidence, rigorous investigation, and a dispassionate assessment of the merits of each case.

The prosecutorial process begins long before a case reaches the courtroom. It often involves extensive investigation, gathering evidence, interviewing witnesses, and collaborating with law enforcement agencies. This investigative phase is critical, as it forms the foundation upon which the entire prosecution will be built. A thorough and impartial investigation is crucial to ensuring that only valid and reliable evidence is presented in court, protecting against wrongful convictions. The prosecutor's role in this initial stage demands not only competence but also a profound understanding of ethical considerations, ensuring all evidence is gathered fairly and legally. Failure to uphold these standards can lead to the dismissal of cases and undermine public trust in the justice system.

Following the investigation, the prosecutor must make the fundamental decision of whether to charge a suspect with a crime.

This is not a decision taken lightly; it requires a careful evaluation of the evidence gathered, a thorough understanding of applicable laws, and an assessment of the likelihood of securing a conviction. The prosecutor must weigh the strengths and weaknesses of the case, considering the potential impact on the accused, the victims, and the overall interests of society. Overcharging, or filing charges that are not adequately supported by the evidence, not only wastes valuable resources but also undermines the integrity of the system. Conversely, failing to bring appropriate charges against individuals who have committed serious crimes undermines public safety and jeopardizes the credibility of the judicial system.

Once charges are filed, the prosecutor's role shifts to the courtroom. Here, they are responsible for presenting the state's case to the court, presenting evidence, examining witnesses, and countering the arguments presented by the defence. This requires a high level of legal expertise, strategic thinking, and courtroom advocacy skills.

Prosecutors must effectively communicate complex legal concepts to judges and juries, ensuring they fully understand the evidence and its implications. Their conduct in the courtroom must be professional and ethical, adhering to strict rules of evidence and procedure. Manipulative tactics or attempts to mislead the court not only violate professional ethics but also cast doubt on the fairness of the proceedings.

The concept of impartiality and objectivity is absolutely central to the role of the public prosecutor. They are not advocates for a particular outcome but rather impartial arbiters of justice, seeking to ensure that the truth is revealed and that justice is served, regardless of personal biases or external pressures. This impartial stance is essential to safeguarding the integrity of the justice system and maintaining public trust. Any deviation from this principle, whether intentional or unintentional, can severely damage the reputation of the prosecutor's office and undermine the fairness of the criminal justice process. This demands a rigorous adherence to ethical standards, coupled with a commitment to continuous professional development to hone their abilities in impartial evidence evaluation and presentation.

However, the prosecutor's role does not exist in a vacuum; it is influenced by a range of factors that can challenge their ability to remain impartial and objective. Political influence, societal biases, and even personal beliefs can all unconsciously or consciously impact prosecutorial decision-making. For instance, political pressure to secure a conviction in a high-profile case, particularly one with significant political implications, can compromise the impartiality of the prosecutor. Similarly, unconscious biases based on race, gender, or socioeconomic status can inadvertently lead to disparate treatment of defendants, resulting in injustices within the system.

To mitigate these risks, various accountability mechanisms are implemented to ensure that prosecutors remain accountable for their actions. Internal review processes within prosecutor's offices provide a level of oversight, allowing for the review of charging decisions, evidence gathering techniques, and courtroom conduct. External bodies, such as judicial oversight committees or investigative agencies, may also play a role in scrutinizing prosecutorial decisions, investigating alleged misconduct, and taking disciplinary action if necessary. These oversight measures are vital in addressing potential abuses of power and ensuring that prosecutors act in accordance with the law and ethical standards. Transparent processes and robust investigation protocols are critical elements in maintaining public trust in the efficacy and impartiality of these oversight mechanisms.

Moreover, effective training programs designed to inculcate ethical considerations and impartiality are critical components in building a strong and ethical prosecutorial system. Such training should emphasize the importance of objective decision-making, unbiased case evaluation, and responsible courtroom conduct. It should also include modules on recognizing and mitigating unconscious biases, ensuring that prosecutors are equipped to approach every case with fairness and equity. Regular review and updating of these training programs is crucial to account for evolving societal norms, legal precedents, and best practices in prosecutorial ethics.

The duty of a public prosecutor to seek justice, not just convictions, is vital. This ethical imperative transcends the pursuit of winning cases; it compels prosecutors to actively consider the broader impact of their decisions on individuals, communities, and the integrity of the justice system. Prosecutors have a responsibility to ensure that only those truly guilty are convicted, to protect the rights of the accused, and to ensure that the criminal justice process itself is fair and equitable. A dedication to this ethical principle is essential not just for individual cases but also for the overall health and reputation of the legal system itself. This commitment must permeate every stage of their work, from initial investigations to courtroom proceedings and beyond.

A system that incentivizes convictions over justice is a system fundamentally flawed and destined to erode public trust.

Ultimately, the role of the public prosecutor is a complex and demanding one. It requires a blend of legal expertise, investigative skills, ethical judgment, and unwavering commitment to justice. By fostering prosecutorial independence, implementing effective accountability mechanisms, and prioritizing ethical considerations, societies can work towards creating a criminal justice system that is both efficient and truly just, ensuring that the pursuit of justice remains paramount in all aspects of the prosecutorial function. The commitment to ongoing reform, training, and oversight is a continuous process that demands constant attention and improvement to ensure the integrity and fairness of the system. Only through such vigilance can we maintain public trust in the administration of criminal justice and foster a society governed by the rule of law.

Mechanisms for Holding Prosecutors Accountable

The integrity of the justice system rests heavily on the independence of its key actors, and none is more crucial in this regard than the public prosecutor. While the previous section established the fundamental role of the prosecutor, this section delves into the critical challenge of shielding them from the insidious influence of political power.

Politically motivated prosecutions, driven by partisan interests rather than the impartial application of the law, represent a profound threat to the very foundations of a fair and equitable legal system. Such actions erode public trust, undermine the rule of law, and can lead to serious injustices.

The threat of political interference manifests in various forms. Direct pressure from government officials, subtle suggestions to prioritize certain cases or individuals, or even the manipulation of resource allocation to influence prosecutorial decisions are all potential avenues for undermining independence. The temptation to utilize the prosecutorial office as a tool for political expediency can be particularly strong during periods of heightened political tension or when an administration seeks to consolidate its power. This is not simply a theoretical concern; history offers numerous examples of prosecutors succumbing to political pressure, leading to wrongful convictions, the suppression of legitimate investigations, and the fostering of a climate of fear and self-censorship within the legal community.

Different countries have adopted various models to safeguard prosecutorial independence. Some jurisdictions opt for a system where prosecutors are appointed for fixed terms, insulated from the whims of the current administration. This approach seeks to provide a degree of security from political retribution, allowing prosecutors to make independent decisions without fear of losing their positions. However, even with fixed terms, the threat of political influence cannot be entirely eliminated. The subtle pressures of political expectation, the desire for career advancement, and the inherent power dynamics within the governmental structure can still impact prosecutorial decision-making.

Other nations have embraced the model of a fully independent prosecutorial agency, operating autonomously from other branches of government. This model often includes mechanisms for financial independence, ensuring that the prosecutor's office is not subject to budgetary control that could be used as a lever for political influence. Such independence allows prosecutors to prioritize cases based on merit rather than political considerations. Moreover, it empowers them to investigate and prosecute even high-ranking officials, a crucial aspect of accountability in a democratic society. Yet, even within this seemingly robust structure, vulnerabilities can exist. For instance, the appointment process of the head of the agency itself could be subject to political manoeuvring, influencing the overall direction and priorities of the agency.

Furthermore, the effectiveness of any model for ensuring prosecutorial independence hinges on other supporting mechanisms. Robust legal frameworks are necessary to delineate the powers and responsibilities of prosecutors, clearly outlining their autonomy while also establishing mechanisms for accountability. This includes establishing clear guidelines regarding conflicts of interest and ensuring that prosecutors are subject to disciplinary procedures in case of misconduct or breach of ethical standards. Without these safeguards, even the most well-intentioned independence model can falter.

A critical component of maintaining prosecutorial independence lies in establishing and nurturing a strong culture of ethics and professionalism within the prosecutor's office. Comprehensive training programs that emphasize ethical decision-making and the importance of impartiality are essential. Prosecutors must be equipped to navigate the complex ethical dilemmas inherent in their role, and this requires ongoing education and support. The promotion of a culture of integrity, where ethical considerations are paramount, is crucial to mitigating the risk of political influence. Furthermore, the creation of internal mechanisms for oversight and accountability, such as ethical review boards or internal disciplinary processes, can help to deter any attempts to compromise the independence of the office.

Transparency also plays a vital role in safeguarding prosecutorial independence. Public access to information about prosecutorial decisions, subject to appropriate privacy considerations, can deter political interference and enhance public trust. When the reasoning behind prosecutorial decisions is open to public scrutiny, it becomes harder for political actors to manipulate the process without facing public accountability. The availability of information on case statistics, resource allocation, and the overall performance of the prosecutor's office can help to identify any patterns of potential political influence.

International cooperation and the sharing of best practices among countries also contribute significantly to strengthening prosecutorial independence. Learning from the experiences of other jurisdictions, identifying effective mechanisms for ensuring independence, and working collaboratively to develop stronger legal frameworks and professional standards can bolster efforts to safeguard the independence of prosecutors globally. The exchange of information, expertise, and best practices can provide valuable insights and lessons learned to adapt and improve existing models, leading to a more effective and just system.

Moreover, the judiciary's role in safeguarding prosecutorial independence should not be underestimated. Judges who are themselves independent and act impartially play a crucial role in preventing politically motivated prosecutions from succeeding. By carefully scrutinizing the evidence presented by the prosecution, ensuring the application of fair procedural rules, and delivering independent judgments, the judiciary provides a critical check on any attempts to misuse the prosecutorial power for political gain. A strong and independent judiciary, committed to the rule of law, is a critical partner in safeguarding prosecutorial independence.

Accountability Mechanisms for Public Prosecutors

One fundamental aspect of accountability lies in internal oversight. Many jurisdictions have established internal disciplinary systems within the prosecutor's office itself.

These systems typically involve hierarchical review processes, where supervisors monitor the work of their subordinates, checking for adherence to legal standards, ethical guidelines, and office policies. This can range from informal mentoring and feedback to formal reviews of case files, decisions, and charging practices. The effectiveness of such internal mechanisms, however, hinges critically on the independence and integrity of the supervising officials. If supervisors themselves are susceptible to political pressure or lack the courage to challenge questionable actions, the internal oversight system becomes inherently weak.

Furthermore, a culture of collegiality, where criticism is discouraged or perceived as disloyalty, can stifle meaningful internal accountability. Therefore, internal oversight must be supported by a strong organizational culture that values ethical conduct and encourages open communication and scrutiny.

Beyond internal reviews, more formal disciplinary procedures exist in many jurisdictions. These procedures typically involve investigations into allegations of prosecutorial misconduct, which may range from minor infractions of office policy to serious breaches of ethical rules or criminal offenses. These investigations can be initiated by complaints from the public, defence attorneys, or even internal whistleblowers. The investigative process may involve internal review boards, independent disciplinary panels, or even external audits. The penalties for proven misconduct can vary significantly depending on the severity of the infraction, and may include reprimands, suspensions, demotions, or even dismissal from office. The effectiveness of disciplinary procedures is often hampered by several factors. Lengthy and cumbersome procedures can create delays and frustrate complainants, while the fear of retribution can deter individuals from coming forward with complaints. Furthermore, the standards of proof required for disciplinary action may be higher than in criminal proceedings, making it difficult to secure sanctions even in cases of clear misconduct. The composition of disciplinary panels is also crucial; ensuring their independence from political influence and their expertise in prosecutorial ethics is paramount to their effectiveness.

External review processes represent another critical aspect of accountability. These mechanisms involve external bodies, independent of the prosecutor's office, that scrutinize prosecutorial conduct. These bodies may include legislative oversight committees, judicial review processes, independent commissions on prosecutorial conduct, or even specialized investigative agencies. Legislative oversight committees can summon prosecutors to testify, review their budgetary allocations, and investigate allegations of misconduct.

Judicial review, through appeals and habeas corpus petitions, provides a crucial check on prosecutorial decisions relating to charging, plea bargaining, and sentencing. Independent commissions, often composed of legal experts, representatives of the public, and perhaps even former prosecutors, can provide valuable insights and recommendations for improvement. Specialized investigative agencies, similar to those found in some countries, can focus solely on prosecutorial conduct, allowing for dedicated and thorough investigations. The effectiveness of external review hinges on the independence and authority of the reviewing bodies. Without robust powers of investigation and sanction, external review remains largely symbolic. Furthermore, the transparency of these processes is critical. Public access to reports and findings can deter misconduct and enhance public confidence in the justice system.

Another important dimension of accountability is the requirement for transparency in prosecutorial decision-making. Prosecutors should be able to justify their actions and decisions, providing clear and concise reasons for charging, dismissing charges, or accepting plea bargains. This requirement is often underpinned by the need for reasoned judgments, a fundamental principle of judicial decision-making. While prosecutors are not formally required to produce reasoned judgments in the same way as judges, the increasing emphasis on transparency and accountability is leading to greater documentation of prosecutorial actions and rationale. This increased transparency aids in identifying potential bias or misconduct, as well as facilitating external review and oversight. Moreover, it contributes to public understanding and acceptance of the prosecutorial process, fostering public trust in the fairness and impartiality of the justice system.

However, the practical implementation of this principle can be challenging. The sheer volume of cases handled by prosecutors, coupled with the complexities of the legal processes involved, can make the thorough documentation of every decision a significant undertaking. Finding a balance between the need for thorough documentation and the practical limitations of the prosecutorial workload remains a crucial challenge.

Furthermore, the issue of prosecutorial discretion warrants careful consideration. Prosecutors possess significant discretion in deciding whether to initiate prosecutions, what charges to file, and how to negotiate plea bargains. This discretion is essential for the effective functioning of the justice system, allowing prosecutors to prioritize cases, consider the evidence, and exercise judgment in the best interests of justice. However, this power also carries with it the potential for abuse and bias, necessitating robust accountability mechanisms to ensure that this discretion is exercised fairly and impartially. The lack of sufficient transparency or external checks on prosecutorial discretion can lead to arbitrary and discriminatory outcomes, undermining public trust and eroding the integrity of the justice system. Therefore, clear guidelines and regulations are necessary to guide prosecutorial discretion, coupled with robust oversight mechanisms to monitor its exercise.

The effectiveness of all accountability mechanisms hinges on several factors, including the political will to enforce them, the availability of resources to support them, and the willingness of individuals to utilize them. Insufficient resources, both financial and human, can hinder the effectiveness of internal oversight, disciplinary procedures, and external reviews. A lack of political will can lead to ineffective enforcement of rules and regulations, even when clear mechanisms exist. Finally, even with effective mechanisms in place, they will be useless if individuals are unwilling or afraid to utilize them due to fear of retaliation or lack of trust in the system. Therefore, fostering a culture of accountability and transparency within the prosecutorial branch and the broader justice system is crucial.

The pursuit of justice demands not only the prevention of external manipulation of the prosecutorial function but also the unwavering commitment to internal impartiality. A prosecutor, entrusted with immense power to initiate criminal proceedings, wields a significant influence on the lives of individuals and the course of justice. Any bias, conscious or unconscious, introduced into their decision-making process can irrevocably distort the fairness and equity of the system. This section will delve into the critical importance of impartiality and the avoidance of bias in prosecutorial decisions, exploring the insidious ways in which bias can creep into the process and outlining strategies for mitigation.

One of the most significant challenges lies in the inherent human tendency toward bias. Cognitive biases, deeply ingrained patterns of thought and perception, can affect even the most well-intentioned individuals. Confirmation bias, for instance, is the tendency to seek out and interpret information that confirms pre-existing beliefs, while neglecting contradictory evidence. In a prosecutorial context, this can manifest as selectively pursuing charges against individuals who fit a preconceived stereotype, overlooking exculpatory evidence, or framing evidence to fit a narrative already established in the prosecutor's mind. Similarly, anchoring bias, the tendency to overemphasize the first piece of information received, can lead to a prosecutor fixating on an initial hypothesis, even in the face of mounting contradictory evidence. This can lead to unjust prosecutions based on flawed initial assumptions.

Another decisive aspect is the impact of implicit biases. These are unconscious associations and stereotypes that influence our judgments and decisions without our conscious awareness. Implicit biases related to race, ethnicity, gender, socioeconomic status, and other demographic factors can significantly influence prosecutorial decisions, leading to disparate treatment of individuals based on factors irrelevant to their guilt or innocence. Studies have consistently shown that implicit biases can manifest in various ways, from charging decisions to sentencing recommendations, creating systemic inequalities within the justice system. Recognizing the existence and potential influence of implicit biases is crucial, as they operate below the level of conscious awareness and are therefore difficult to detect and mitigate.

The pressure to secure convictions, often stemming from political pressures or the desire to maintain a high conviction rate, can also introduce bias into prosecutorial decision-making. This pressure can lead to overcharging, selectively pursuing cases that are easily winnable, or overlooking cases with complex factual scenarios, even if those cases merit prosecution. The ambition to achieve a high conviction rate, while appearing to signify efficiency, can actually compromise the pursuit of justice by incentivizing shortcuts, overlooking procedural safeguards, and sacrificing accuracy for expediency. This pressure to "win" can lead to a neglect of the prosecutor's fundamental role: not simply to convict, but to seek justice.

Furthermore, the influence of personal beliefs and values cannot be underestimated. Prosecutors, being human, are not immune to their own personal biases and beliefs. While their personal viewpoints should not dictate their professional decisions, the subtle influence of personal convictions can inadvertently affect the prioritization of cases, the nature of the charges pursued, and even the sentencing recommendations made. This requires a consistent effort towards self-reflection and a commitment to adhering strictly to legal principles, devoid of personal biases.

Mitigating these risks requires a multi-pronged approach.

Firstly, robust training programs designed to enhance awareness of cognitive and implicit biases are crucial. This training should go beyond simple awareness raising, incorporating practical exercises and strategies to help prosecutors identify and mitigate their biases in their daily work. Structured decision-making frameworks can also prove beneficial, ensuring that prosecutorial decisions are guided by clear criteria and consistent application of legal principles, rather than subjective judgment. Such frameworks should prioritize the evaluation of evidence objectively and independently, reducing the potential for bias to influence the decision-making process.

Secondly, establishing transparent and accountable internal review mechanisms is essential. This includes internal audits of prosecutorial decisions, allowing for the identification of patterns of potential bias and providing opportunities for corrective measures. Independent oversight bodies, external to the prosecutorial office, can play a valuable role in scrutinizing prosecutorial practices and ensuring adherence to ethical standards and legal principles. This external oversight can provide an independent perspective, identifying instances of bias that might otherwise go unnoticed.

Thirdly, enhancing data collection and analysis can provide invaluable insights into potential bias within the prosecutorial system. Tracking prosecutorial decisions, including charging decisions, plea bargains, and sentencing recommendations, and analyzing them for any disparities based on demographic factors, can reveal systemic bias and inform targeted interventions. Transparency in data collection and sharing is paramount, allowing for public scrutiny and accountability.

Finally, fostering a culture of ethical conduct and continuous professional development within prosecutorial offices is crucial. This includes establishing clear ethical guidelines and codes of conduct, providing ongoing training on ethics and bias mitigation, and creating an environment where reporting of potential misconduct is encouraged and protected from retaliation. Such a culture, focused on ethical conduct and professional excellence, can promote responsible and impartial prosecutorial decision-making.

The consequences of prosecutorial bias are far-reaching. Unjust prosecutions, driven by bias, undermine public trust in the legal system. They lead to wrongful convictions, the deprivation of individual liberty, and the erosion of confidence in the impartiality of justice. Moreover, biased prosecutorial decisions perpetuate existing social inequalities, disproportionately affecting marginalized groups and undermining the principle of equal justice under the law. Case studies demonstrating the devastating effects of prosecutorial bias abound, highlighting the crucial need for ongoing efforts to mitigate this pervasive threat to the integrity of the legal system. The ultimate aim must be to foster a system where prosecutorial decisions are consistently fair, equitable, and devoid of the influence of bias, thereby strengthening the very foundation of justice. This continuous striving for impartial justice is not simply a matter of legal procedure; it is a moral imperative, a testament to the foundational principles of a just and equitable society.

The Prosecutor's Duty to Seek Justice, Not Just Convictions

The prosecutor's unwavering duty to seek justice, a concept that transcends the mere pursuit of convictions. This fundamental principle demands a profound shift in perspective, away from a win-at-all-costs mentality towards a commitment to fairness and equity, even when it means forgoing a potential conviction.

The pursuit of justice, as opposed to the relentless pursuit of convictions, requires a nuanced understanding of the prosecutorial role. It necessitates a rigorous examination of the evidence, an objective assessment of the merits of the case, and a willingness to dismiss charges or recommend leniency when warranted, even if it means facing criticism or perceived weakness. This commitment demands courage, intellectual honesty, and a deep-seated understanding of the potential consequences of their actions on individuals' lives and the integrity of the legal system. It is a responsibility that cannot be divorced from the broader context of societal values and the pursuit of a just and equitable society.

The implications of this duty extend far beyond individual cases. A prosecutor who prioritizes convictions above justice risks creating a system where the scales of justice are tipped unfairly, where the powerful are protected and the vulnerable are disproportionately punished. This not only undermines the public's faith in the legal system but also fosters cynicism and distrust, eroding the very foundation of societal order. A justice system predicated on the mere accumulation of convictions is inherently flawed and ultimately unsustainable.

Ethical dilemmas are an inevitable part of a prosecutor's work. They are constantly confronted with decisions that require careful weighing of competing values and interests. For example, a prosecutor might possess sufficient evidence to secure a conviction on a lesser charge but might believe that a more thorough investigation could reveal evidence of a more serious crime. The decision to proceed with the lesser charge immediately or to delay proceedings to pursue the potentially more serious, but less certain, charge represents a classic ethical dilemma. The choice must be guided by a commitment to justice, balancing the interests of the victim, the accused, and the public's interest in the pursuit of truth and fairness.

The role of ethics training and professional standards in upholding the prosecutor's duty to seek justice cannot be overstated. Continuous professional development, encompassing ethical decision-making frameworks, case studies of ethical dilemmas, and opportunities for reflection and critical self-evaluation are vital. These training initiatives should go beyond simple legal instruction, delving into the philosophical underpinnings of justice and fairness, encouraging a holistic and nuanced understanding of the prosecutor's role in society. The establishment and enforcement of robust professional codes of conduct, incorporating specific provisions regarding the pursuit of justice, are equally crucial. These codes must be accompanied by effective mechanisms for accountability, ensuring that breaches of ethical standards result in appropriate sanctions, preventing any erosion of public trust.

The enforcement of these ethical standards is not solely the responsibility of professional bodies. Independent oversight mechanisms, such as judicial review of prosecutorial decisions, can play a critical role in ensuring that prosecutorial conduct aligns with the duty to seek justice.

This oversight should not be viewed as an attack on prosecutorial independence but rather as a safeguard against potential abuses of power, ensuring that the pursuit of justice is not compromised by biases, pressures, or self-interest.

The concept of "justice" itself is not static or monolithic. It evolves over time, influenced by societal shifts in values and understandings of fairness. This necessitates continuous critical reflection on the meaning of justice within the specific context of the legal system. Prosecutors must engage with these evolving understandings, constantly questioning their own practices and assumptions, striving to adapt their approach to reflect the evolving demands of a just and equitable society. This ongoing engagement is not merely a professional obligation; it is a moral imperative. The pursuit of justice requires constant vigilance, a continuous striving for improvement, and a commitment to ethical conduct that transcends the mere pursuit of convictions.

Furthermore, the prosecutor's duty to seek justice extends beyond the courtroom. They play a crucial role in shaping public perceptions of the legal system. Their conduct, both in and out of the courtroom, influences the public's trust in the system's integrity.

Therefore, prosecutors have a responsibility to communicate effectively with the public, explaining their decisions and the rationale behind them in a transparent and accessible manner. This transparency fosters public understanding and strengthens public confidence in the legal system, reinforcing the vital link between the administration of justice and the health of a democratic society.

The impact of a prosecutor's actions reverberates far beyond the immediate parties involved in a case. Decisions made in the pursuit of justice, or the absence thereof, influence legislative reform, shape societal attitudes towards crime and punishment, and ultimately affect the overall well-being of the community. Therefore, a prosecutor's ethical obligations must be seen as a social responsibility, a commitment to safeguarding the fairness and equity of the entire system. It is not merely a matter of upholding legal principles but of ensuring that the justice system serves as a vital instrument in creating a just and equitable society.

The Problem of Delays in Criminal Proceedings

Procedural delays in criminal proceedings represent a significant challenge to the effective functioning of justice systems worldwide. The consequences extend far beyond mere inconvenience; they inflict profound harm on victims, compromise the rights of the accused, and undermine public confidence in the fairness and efficiency of the legal process.

The sheer scale of the problem is staggering. Studies across numerous jurisdictions consistently reveal alarming statistics on the length of time it takes to bring criminal cases to trial.

In some countries, cases languish for years, even decades, before reaching a conclusion. This protracted process has devastating consequences for victims, who are forced to relive traumatic experiences during lengthy court proceedings, often facing continuous uncertainty and delayed access to justice and redress. The emotional toll is immense, potentially exacerbating the psychological trauma associated with the initial crime. Furthermore, the passage of time can significantly impair the ability of witnesses to recall events accurately, weakening the prosecution's case and potentially leading to wrongful acquittals.

For the accused, lengthy delays also present significant hardships. The presumption of innocence, a cornerstone of many legal systems, is significantly eroded when an individual faces prolonged uncertainty regarding their fate. The stress and anxiety associated with pending charges can impact their mental and physical health, as well as their employment and family relationships. Furthermore, the very length of the process can be seen as a form of punishment in itself, even if the accused is ultimately acquitted. The societal cost of these delays should not be underestimated.

Keeping individuals under suspicion for extended periods imposes a considerable burden on society's resources, tying up law enforcement, prosecutorial, and judicial personnel who could be working on other, more urgent cases.

Moreover, prolonged delays erode public confidence in the criminal justice system. When citizens witness the slow pace of justice, it fuels cynicism and mistrust, making it harder to maintain the legitimacy and authority of the legal framework.

Understanding the causes of these delays is crucial in developing effective solutions. One major contributing factor is inadequate caseload management. Many courts, particularly in resource-constrained jurisdictions, are overwhelmed by excessive numbers of cases, leading to significant backlogs and prolonged waiting times. This is compounded by a shortage of judicial personnel, court staff, and other essential resources, such as interpreters, expert witnesses, and investigators. The complexity of legal procedures also plays a significant role. Overly intricate rules of evidence, cumbersome procedural requirements, and frequent appeals can significantly prolong the length of trials.

Furthermore, the lack of effective communication and coordination between different actors within the justice system contributes to delays. For instance, inefficiencies in the exchange of information between law enforcement agencies, prosecutors, and the courts can create bottlenecks and unnecessary delays. A lack of technological infrastructure also plays a role. Without appropriate training, judicial officers and lawyers may be unaware of efficient methods for managing cases, leading to unnecessary delays and increased costs.

Addressing these challenges requires a multi-pronged approach. Improved caseload management is vital.

Streamlining legal procedures by eliminating unnecessary complexities and promoting alternative dispute resolution mechanisms can also shorten processing times. Increased inter-agency collaboration and coordination can ensure smooth information flow and minimize bottlenecks. It is also imperative to invest in appropriate training for all legal professionals involved in criminal proceedings to improve their understanding and application of efficient case management techniques.

The implementation of effective monitoring and evaluation mechanisms is essential to track progress and identify areas for improvement. This requires the establishment of performance indicators to measure the efficiency of the justice system and to assess the effectiveness of various interventions. Regular data collection and analysis can provide valuable insights into the causes of delays and inform policy adjustments. International best practices and comparative studies can also offer valuable lessons and models for reform. By examining successful strategies employed in other jurisdictions, countries can identify approaches best suited to their own context and legal systems.

However, simply implementing technological solutions or streamlining procedures is insufficient without addressing deeper systemic issues. Addressing resource constraints, improving infrastructure, and fostering a culture of efficiency and accountability are vital components of effective reform. Furthermore, any reform efforts must consider the impact of such changes on the rights and interests of all stakeholders. A balance must be struck between ensuring the efficiency of the justice system and protecting the fundamental rights of both victims and the accused. It requires a holistic and comprehensive approach involving all stakeholders, including judges, prosecutors, defense lawyers, law enforcement agencies, and policymakers, working together towards a shared goal of a more just and efficient criminal justice system. Without this collaborative approach, even the most well-intentioned reforms are likely to fall short of their objectives.

The ultimate aim of any reform is to restore public trust and confidence in the fairness and efficiency of the criminal justice system. Delayed justice is not only inefficient but also undermines the very principles of justice it purports to uphold. By addressing the systemic challenges that contribute to these delays, jurisdictions can work towards a more equitable and timely resolutions of criminal cases, ensuring that victims receive prompt justice and that the rights of the accused are fully protected. This requires a sustained commitment to reform, a willingness to embrace innovation, and a clear understanding of the multifaceted nature of the problem. The path toward a more just and efficient system is complex, requiring continuous evaluation and adaptation, but the long-term benefits for society are well worth the effort.

The efficient administration of justice is fundamentally hampered by procedural delays, a problem exacerbated by a confluence of factors. Analyzing these root causes is essential to developing effective solutions. Caseload management, or the effective handling of the sheer volume of cases a court system faces, is a critical element.

Many jurisdictions struggle with overwhelming caseloads, leading to significant backlogs. This isn't simply a matter of too many cases; it's about the management of those cases. Inefficient scheduling, inadequate prioritization systems, and a lack of sufficient judicial personnel contribute to escalating delays. Consider, for example, a jurisdiction with a limited number of judges handling a rapidly increasing population.

Even with dedicated judges working diligently, the sheer volume of cases inevitably leads to extended waiting periods for hearings, trials, and ultimately, judgments. The lack of sufficient support staff, including court clerks, bailiffs, and administrative personnel, further exacerbates this problem.

Without adequate support, judges are forced to spend valuable time on administrative tasks, detracting from their ability to focus on the core function of adjudicating cases.

This administrative burden directly contributes to delays. Furthermore, the prioritization of cases can be a significant source of delays. The lack of a clear and efficient system for prioritizing cases based on urgency and severity can lead to less serious cases being unnecessarily delayed while more pressing matters are addressed. This can be particularly problematic in criminal cases where the timely resolution of cases is crucial for both victims and defendants. The development and implementation of sophisticated case management systems, employing technology such as case management software and electronic filing, can assist in tracking cases, streamlining processes, and ensuring that urgent matters are given appropriate precedence. However, the successful implementation of such systems requires investment in training, technological infrastructure and ongoing maintenance. The absence of such resources can negate the potential benefits of such technology, potentially leading to further delays and inefficiencies.

Resource constraints represent another critical contributing factor to procedural delays. This goes beyond just caseloads; it encompasses the broader availability of resources within the judicial system. Funding limitations often translate into insufficient courtrooms, outdated technology, and a shortage of trained personnel. Understaffed courts struggle to manage even moderate caseloads, let alone cope with surges in filings or complex litigation. For instance, a court lacking sufficient court reporters may experience significant delays in transcribing proceedings, leading to postponements and extending the overall timeline of a case. Similarly, a lack of adequate technology, such as electronic filing systems, can create significant bottlenecks in the processing of documents and evidence.

The problem extends beyond the courtroom itself. Public defenders' offices, often underfunded and overworked, struggle to provide adequate representation to indigent defendants. This can lead to delays as public defenders grapple with overwhelming caseloads and limited resources to effectively investigate and prepare cases. These delays, often unintended, nevertheless contribute to the overall inefficiency of the system and can disproportionately impact defendants who rely on publicly funded legal assistance. Similarly, understaffed prosecutors' offices can face similar challenges, impacting the speed at which cases are brought to trial. The need for adequate funding for all aspects of the judicial system is paramount; without it, even the most well-intentioned efforts at case management are ultimately undermined.

The complexity of legal procedures is an often-overlooked contributor to delays. Modern legal systems are intricate, incorporating numerous rules, regulations, and procedures and navigating this labyrinthine system, especially for those unfamiliar with legal processes, can lead to significant delays.

The complexity is not limited to civil cases. Criminal proceedings, with their emphasis on due process and the protection of defendants' rights, can also be highly complex and time-consuming. Pre-trial motions, evidentiary hearings, and jury selection can all contribute to substantial delays, especially in cases involving multiple defendants or complex factual issues. The requirement for detailed legal argumentation and adherence to established procedures adds to the overall time involved in bringing a case to trial.

Furthermore, the complexities of modern evidentiary rules, particularly concerning the admissibility of scientific or technical evidence, can lead to lengthy pre-trial battles over the admissibility of such evidence, further adding to procedural delays.

The increasing sophistication of legal arguments, particularly in areas like intellectual property or antitrust law, also contributes to the complexity. These cases often require specialized expertise and extensive investigation, stretching the resources of both courts and the parties involved. The necessity for expert testimony further adds to the delays as experts need to be located, interviewed, and prepared for trial, a process that can take considerable time. These specialized cases frequently involve complex factual scenarios and extensive documentation, requiring thorough examination and analysis by the court.

The lack of standardized procedures across different jurisdictions further contributes to delays, particularly in cases involving interstate or international elements.

Differences in rules of evidence, procedural requirements, and court practices can lead to confusion and delays as the court attempts to navigate the complexities of applying the appropriate jurisdictional rules. The lack of interoperability between different court systems' technology further complicates this issue, hindering the efficient exchange of information and documents.

Addressing these multifaceted challenges requires a comprehensive and multi-pronged approach. Solutions involve enhancing caseload management through improved technology, better prioritization strategies, and increased judicial personnel. Addressing resource constraints requires increased funding for the judicial system as a whole, including support staff, public defenders' offices, and prosecutors' offices. Finally, simplifying legal procedures, perhaps through streamlining rules and implementing standardized processes, can help reduce unnecessary complexity. The implementation of these solutions will require a commitment to both short-term and long-term reforms, as well as a clear understanding of the interplay between these contributing factors. Only through a comprehensive and sustained effort can we hope to mitigate the pervasive problem of procedural delays and restore public confidence in the timely and efficient administration of justice. The ultimate goal remains a justice system that is not only fair and just but also efficient and accessible to all.

The corrosive effect of delay in the judicial process extends far beyond mere inconvenience. It casts a long shadow over victims, accused individuals, and the very fabric of the justice system itself, undermining its credibility and effectiveness. For victims of crime, the protracted wait for justice can be a profoundly agonizing experience, compounding the trauma they have already endured. The delay acts as a constant, painful reminder of the violation they suffered, hindering their ability to heal and move forward with their lives. The drawn-out proceedings can reopen old wounds, reigniting feelings of fear, anger, and vulnerability.

This psychological toll can manifest in various ways, including anxiety, depression, post-traumatic stress disorder (PTSD), and difficulties in maintaining healthy relationships. The constant postponement of hearings, the uncertainty surrounding the outcome and the feeling of being forgotten by the system can lead to a sense of helplessness and disillusionment. Victims may find themselves re-traumatized by the need to repeatedly recount their experiences in court, reliving the painful details of the crime. This repeated reliving of trauma can exacerbate their suffering and potentially hinder their recovery. The lack of timely resolution can also have devastating financial consequences, particularly if victims are unable to work due to the emotional distress caused by the delay or if they incur significant expenses related to legal representation and travel to court proceedings.

The impact on the accused is equally profound, albeit different in nature. The presumption of innocence, a cornerstone of any fair legal system, is significantly eroded by lengthy pre-trial delays. The longer an individual remains under a cloud of suspicion, the greater the pressure to plead guilty, even if innocent, simply to avoid the prolonged uncertainty and potential financial ruin. The stress and anxiety associated with the pending charges can have a devastating impact on the accused's mental health, their relationships, and their employment prospects. The inability to move on with their lives, to secure employment, or to maintain stable relationships, creates a sense of limbo that can be deeply damaging. The costs of legal representation can be exorbitant, placing an undue burden on individuals, particularly those from disadvantaged socioeconomic backgrounds. This inequality of access to effective legal counsel further exacerbates the impact of delays, as individuals without sufficient financial resources may be forced to represent themselves, placing them at a significant disadvantage in the legal process. Moreover, the extended period of uncertainty can impact the accused's ability to prepare their defence effectively, potentially leading to an unfair trial. Witnesses may relocate, memories may fade, and crucial evidence may be lost or become unavailable over time. The delay itself can, therefore, compromise the fairness of the trial and the integrity of the justice system.

Beyond the individual consequences for victims and the accused, the cumulative effect of procedural delays undermines public confidence in the justice system as a whole. When cases drag on for years, without any apparent resolution, it breeds cynicism and distrust. The perception of inefficiency and lack of accountability erodes public faith in the courts' ability to deliver fair and timely justice. This erosion of public trust can have far-reaching consequences, affecting public participation in the legal process, reducing willingness to report crimes, and hindering the system's effectiveness in upholding the rule of law. The delays lead to perceptions of injustice and inequality, particularly when disparities in the length of proceedings are observed between different cases or between different socioeconomic groups.

This perception fuels social unrest and undermines the legitimacy of the judicial branch. The cumulative cost of these delays to the state is also significant, encompassing increased expenditure on legal aid, court administration, and prison populations while productive members of society remain stalled in protracted legal processes.

Addressing these systemic issues necessitates a comprehensive approach, moving beyond reactive measures and embracing proactive reforms. Firstly, improved case management techniques are crucial. This includes implementing stricter deadlines at each stage of the process, streamlining administrative procedures, and promoting more effective communication between the various stakeholders involved. The use of technology can play a vital role in improving efficiency. Online case management systems can streamline communication, track progress, and facilitate the timely exchange of documents. Video conferencing can reduce the need for in-person appearances, saving time and resources. Furthermore, investing in adequate training and development for judicial personnel and legal professionals is crucial. Well-trained personnel are better equipped to manage cases effectively, utilize available technologies, and adhere to strict timelines.

Judicial reforms aimed at reducing case backlogs and improving court efficiency is also essential. This may involve increasing the number of judges and court staff, creating specialized courts for certain types of cases, and implementing alternative dispute resolution mechanisms.

Greater accountability for all parties involved, including judges, lawyers, and prosecutors, is crucial. Mechanisms for monitoring and evaluating the performance of individual judges and the efficiency of the court system are necessary.

Transparent performance metrics and regular audits can help identify bottlenecks and areas for improvement. The adoption of standardized procedures, clear guidelines for case management, and prompt sanctions for unnecessary delays can ensure greater accountability and encourage timely resolutions. Furthermore, improvements in the infrastructure of the courts themselves can significantly contribute to efficiency. This includes investing in modern technology, improving physical facilities, and ensuring access to adequate resources for all court personnel.

Collaboration between all stakeholders is essential for success. Judges, lawyers, prosecutors, court staff, and policymakers must work together to implement and support effective reforms. Regular meetings, collaborative planning sessions, and shared goals are vital for creating a culture of efficiency and accountability. The establishment of dedicated committees or working groups focused on reducing delays can help facilitate this collaboration. Finally, educating the public about the importance of timely justice and their role in the process is critical. Increased public awareness can promote greater understanding, encourage patience and cooperation, and help ensure that the public understands the complexity of the justice system.

Ultimately, the goal is not simply to expedite the process but to ensure that justice is served fairly and efficiently. This requires a nuanced approach that balances the needs of victims, the rights of the accused, and the overall integrity of the justice system. The efficient administration of justice is not merely a matter of administrative convenience; it is fundamental to the principles of fairness, equality, and the rule of law. It is an ongoing commitment to improvement, requiring continuous monitoring, evaluation, and adjustment to ensure that the system remains responsive to the evolving needs of society and delivers justice promptly and effectively. The pursuit of justice should not be a marathon of delays but a race towards a fair and timely resolution for all involved. This requires a fundamental shift in mindset, prioritizing efficiency without compromising fairness, and ensuring that justice is not only served but served swiftly, preserving both the dignity of the individuals involved and the integrity of the legal process. Only then can the judicial system truly fulfil its fundamental purpose of upholding the rule of law and securing justice for all.

The Importance of Timely Execution of Court Orders

The timely execution of court orders is not merely a procedural matter; it is a cornerstone of a functioning legal system and a critical component of upholding the rule of law. A court order, whether it mandates the payment of damages, the transfer of property, the enforcement of a contract, or the incarceration of a convicted criminal, represents the culmination of a judicial process. Its timely execution ensures the legitimacy and effectiveness of the entire system.

Delays undermine public trust, erode confidence in the judiciary, and diminish the perceived efficacy of legal recourse. When individuals and entities are compelled to wait extended periods for court orders to be implemented, the perceived justice is diluted, fostering cynicism and potentially encouraging disregard for the law itself. This is particularly true in cases involving criminal justice, where delays can compromise the rehabilitation process for offenders, impede victim recovery, and compromise the integrity of the justice system.

The impact of delayed execution extends far beyond individual cases. Consider, for example, the consequences of protracted delays in enforcing environmental protection orders. The longer pollution is allowed to continue due to the slow execution of a court order, the more severe the environmental damage becomes, leading to irreversible harm and increased costs for remediation. Similarly, in commercial disputes, delays in enforcing contractual obligations can cripple businesses, lead to financial instability, and even result in bankruptcies. These economic repercussions extend to the broader economy, creating a ripple effect that impacts employment, investment, and overall economic growth.

The effective execution of court orders requires a coordinated effort involving multiple actors within the justice system and beyond. This includes, but is not limited to, the judiciary, enforcement agencies (such as the police, bailiffs, and other specialized bodies), and the relevant government ministries or departments. A breakdown in any part of this chain can result in delays. For instance, insufficient resources allocated to enforcement agencies can hamper their capacity to execute court orders effectively. A lack of clear communication and coordination between the judiciary and enforcement agencies can also lead to delays and confusion. Moreover, bureaucratic red tape and cumbersome administrative procedures frequently contribute to substantial delays in the implementation process. This can manifest in a multitude of ways, from the slow processing of paperwork to the lack of clear guidelines for handling different types of orders.

Furthermore, the effectiveness of enforcement mechanisms is directly related to accountability. When there are no clear mechanisms for tracking the execution of court orders, monitoring progress, and identifying bottlenecks, the risk of delays increases significantly. Without accountability, enforcement agencies may lack the incentive to prioritize the timely execution of orders, leading to a backlog of unfulfilled mandates.

This highlights the necessity of robust monitoring and evaluation systems designed to track the efficiency of the enforcement process. Regular audits and performance reviews of enforcement agencies can help identify areas of improvement and address systemic issues that contribute to delays. Such evaluations should include not only quantitative data, such as the average time taken to execute different types of orders, but also qualitative assessments of the efficiency and effectiveness of the enforcement processes.

Improvements to judicial processes themselves can reduce delays in enforcement. This includes clear guidelines and standardized procedures for handling different types of court orders, training for judicial personnel on effective order drafting and enforcement, and the development of a more efficient case management system within the courts. Equally important is ensuring adequate resources are allocated to the judiciary and enforcement agencies to support their roles in this process. This includes not only financial resources but also adequate staffing levels, training opportunities, and access to necessary technology. Without sufficient resources, even the well-designed system can be overwhelmed, leading to delays and inefficiencies.

A truly independent judiciary can issue orders free from political influence or pressure, ensuring that the orders reflect the rule of law. Furthermore, accountability mechanisms within the judiciary are essential to address any instances of judicial delay or inefficiency. Judges should be held responsible for the timely issuance of orders, and mechanisms for addressing complaints related to delayed execution should be readily available and transparent. This includes mechanisms for reviewing the actions of enforcement agencies and providing recourse to those impacted by delays.

The implementation of effective monitoring and evaluation systems is vital to understanding the extent and causes of delays in executing court orders. Data collection should track various aspects of the process, including the time it takes to issue an order, the time it takes for the order to be received by the enforcement agency, the time it takes for the agency to initiate enforcement action, and the final time until the order is fully executed. This data, analyzed regularly, can identify systemic bottlenecks and inform the development of targeted strategies for improvement. Transparency in this data is critical to fostering public trust and accountability within the system. The data should be accessible to stakeholders, including the public, to allow for scrutiny of the enforcement process.

Furthermore, a comparative analysis of enforcement mechanisms in different legal systems can provide valuable insights. Learning from best practices in other jurisdictions can help identify effective strategies for improving timely execution of court orders. This includes examining the organizational structures of enforcement agencies, the processes used for coordinating enforcement efforts, and the mechanisms used for accountability and monitoring.

Adopting successful models from other countries can provide a framework for developing and implementing improvements in the domestic legal system.

The ideal of swift and certain justice, so eloquently enshrined in legal principles, often clashes with the realities of implementation. While courts may issue timely and well-reasoned orders, the journey from judgment to execution is frequently fraught with obstacles that significantly impede the timely enforcement of these directives.

These obstacles are multifaceted, stemming from bureaucratic inertia, resource limitations, and a pervasive lack of coordination among the various arms of government involved in the enforcement process.

Bureaucracy, with its inherent complexities and procedural requirements, often acts as a significant impediment. The sheer volume of cases handled by various government agencies responsible for executing court orders—from bailiffs and sheriffs to tax collectors and prison authorities—can lead to substantial delays. The intricate web of rules, regulations, and internal procedures often necessitates multiple layers of approval and processing, creating bottlenecks and extending the time it takes for an order to be acted upon. A simple court order to seize assets, for instance, might require going through multiple departments within a government agency, each with its own internal processes and timelines. This procedural labyrinth, often lacking transparency, can lead to significant delays, frustrating both parties involved and undermining the authority of the court.

Furthermore, inadequate staffing within these agencies exacerbates the problem, resulting in a backlog of cases and prolonged waiting periods. This is particularly acute in jurisdictions with limited resources and understaffed enforcement arms.

The effective execution of court orders requires financial resources, personnel, and technology. Many jurisdictions, particularly those with limited budgets, struggle to allocate sufficient resources to enforcement agencies. This scarcity of resources can translate directly into delays. Consider the enforcement of judgments involving the transfer of property.

A shortage of qualified assessors to determine property values, a lack of sufficient personnel to conduct necessary inspections, or the absence of reliable systems for recording property transfers can all delay the execution of the court's order. Similarly, in criminal justice cases, resource constraints can manifest in delays in transferring prisoners, implementing community service programs, or providing adequate supervision for probationers. These delays not only hinder the timely implementation of court orders but can also compromise the efficacy of the overall justice system, impacting public confidence and the perceived legitimacy of the judicial process.

The lack of coordination between different branches of government further complicates the timely execution of court orders. Court orders often require the cooperation of multiple agencies, such as the judiciary, the executive branch, and sometimes even legislative bodies, depending on the nature of the order. When these branches fail to communicate effectively or collaborate seamlessly, delays are almost inevitable. Similarly, orders involving international cooperation, such as extradition requests or the enforcement of foreign judgments, require intricate coordination across national borders, where jurisdictional differences and communication gaps can lead to prolonged delays. This inter-agency dysfunction necessitates a significant overhaul of inter-governmental communication and cooperation protocols to ensure efficiency and timeliness.

The impact of these obstacles extends beyond simple inconvenience. Delays in the execution of court orders can have far-reaching consequences. In civil cases, prolonged delays can cause significant financial hardship for the winning party, as they may be deprived of the benefits of the judgment for extended periods. This can lead to economic instability and even bankruptcy. For example, a creditor winning a judgment for debt repayment might face significant financial difficulties if the debtor successfully delays enforcement through bureaucratic manoeuvrings or by exploiting resource limitations within the enforcement system. In criminal cases, delays can compromise the integrity of the justice system.

Lengthy delays between conviction and sentencing can undermine the deterrent effect of punishment, while delays in the implementation of correctional programs can impede rehabilitation efforts and increase the risk of recidivism. Furthermore, delays in enforcing orders related to child custody or domestic violence can have devastating consequences for victims. The longer the court order remains unenforced, the more vulnerable victims may become, further eroding public trust in the judicial system's ability to protect vulnerable individuals.

Addressing these obstacles requires a multifaceted approach. Judicial reform is crucial, including streamlining internal court processes, improving case management systems, and enhancing the training of court personnel in efficient case handling. Fostering greater inter-agency coordination through the development of clear protocols, improved communication channels, and joint training programs is essential to breaking down bureaucratic silos and promoting more effective collaboration. These systemic changes are not merely administrative improvements; they are vital steps in ensuring that the promise of swift and certain justice is more than just an aspiration. They represent a fundamental commitment to upholding the rule of law and reinforcing public faith in the judiciary.

Furthermore, the role of accountability mechanisms cannot be overstated. Regular audits of enforcement agencies, coupled with transparent reporting of performance metrics, can help to identify bottlenecks and areas requiring improvement. Establishing clear performance indicators, including targets for processing times and case completion rates, can incentivize efficiency and improve accountability.

This could include publishing regular reports detailing the timelines for executing different types of court orders, allowing for public scrutiny and encouraging transparency. Additionally, mechanisms for redress should be in place for individuals experiencing undue delays in the execution of court orders, enabling them to seek recourse and hold responsible parties accountable for their inaction. This could involve establishing independent oversight bodies to review complaints and investigate cases of excessive delays, ensuring that those responsible are held to account.

The effective execution of court orders hinges not only on the judiciary's pronouncements but also, and critically, on the actions of enforcement agencies. These agencies, ranging from the police force to specialized regulatory bodies depending on the nature of the order, are the crucial link between judicial pronouncements and tangible real-world consequences. Their role is not merely ministerial; it is a vital component in ensuring the rule of law and upholding the integrity of the justice system. A court order, however meticulously crafted and legally sound, remains a symbolic gesture without the muscle of effective enforcement. This section will analyze the critical role of these agencies, highlighting the necessary elements for their optimal functioning.

A primary consideration is adequate training. Enforcement officers, tasked with executing a diverse range of orders—from eviction notices to injunctions against pollution, from child custody arrangements to asset freezes—require specialized training tailored to the specific types of orders they may encounter. Generic training is insufficient; officers need to understand the nuances of legal documents, the procedures for execution, and the potential legal ramifications of non-compliance or inappropriate actions.

This training should encompass not only the technical aspects of order execution but also crucial elements of de-escalation, conflict resolution, and sensitivity to the individuals involved. Officers executing orders related to child custody must understand the delicate emotional dynamics involved and act with sensitivity and professionalism. A well-trained officer is not just an instrument of the court; they are a guardian of due process, ensuring that the execution of orders is conducted fairly and lawfully.

Resource allocation is equally crucial. Enforcement agencies often face significant resource constraints, including insufficient personnel, inadequate equipment, and limited financial resources. These limitations directly impact their ability to effectively execute court orders. A shortage of personnel can lead to delays in responding to orders, while inadequate equipment can hinder the efficient and safe execution of orders, particularly in complex or dangerous situations.

Adequate resource allocation is not merely a matter of budgetary decisions; it reflects a societal commitment to upholding the rule of law. It's a fundamental investment in the efficient functioning of the justice system and in ensuring public trust in its ability to deliver justice. The allocation of resources should be directly correlated with the volume and complexity of court orders, with adjustments made to account for fluctuations in caseloads or emerging enforcement challenges.

Accountability mechanisms are vital for maintaining the integrity and effectiveness of enforcement agencies. These mechanisms must ensure that officers adhere to legal protocols, respect individual rights, and execute orders efficiently and fairly. This necessitates robust internal review processes, independent oversight bodies, and clear channels for public complaints. Internal review should not be a mere formality but a rigorous examination of officers' actions, identifying any instances of misconduct or procedural irregularities. Independent oversight bodies, such as ombudsman offices or specialized investigative units, provide an external check on the agency's operations, ensuring transparency and accountability.

Clear and accessible mechanisms for the public to lodge complaints are essential, providing avenues for redress when individuals believe their rights have been violated during the execution of a court order. Furthermore, a culture of accountability within the agency itself is crucial. This involves clear guidelines, regular training on ethical conduct, and a commitment to transparency and responsiveness to public concerns. The establishment and maintenance of these accountability mechanisms are not merely administrative requirements; they are fundamental components of a just and equitable society, safeguarding against potential abuses of power and maintaining public confidence in the integrity of the enforcement process.

The interaction between enforcement agencies and other parts of the justice system is equally important. Seamless communication and collaboration between the judiciary, prosecutors, and enforcement agencies are essential to guarantee the swift and efficient execution of court orders.

Delays often stem from a lack of coordination, with information gaps and miscommunication hindering timely action. Improving communication channels, such as dedicated liaison officers or centralized information platforms, can greatly streamline the process. For example, the court could provide enforcement agencies with electronic copies of orders, allowing for immediate access and faster response times.

Regular meetings and joint training sessions between judges, prosecutors, and enforcement officers can foster a better understanding of each other's roles and responsibilities, promoting collaboration and improving the overall efficiency of the system. Furthermore, feedback mechanisms are crucial. Enforcement agencies should provide feedback to the judiciary on the challenges they face in executing orders, allowing for adjustments to court orders or procedures to enhance their feasibility and effectiveness.

This cyclical process of communication and adaptation is crucial for the continuous improvement of the system. The effectiveness of enforcement agencies is further enhanced by the strategic use of technology. This includes the use of electronic case management systems, which provide immediate access to court orders and relevant information, reducing the likelihood of delays caused by paperwork or logistical issues. The use of GPS tracking technology can facilitate the efficient monitoring of assets subject to court orders, ensuring compliance and preventing tampering or concealment. Digital communication platforms can streamline communication between enforcement officers and the court, facilitating rapid responses to urgent matters.

Finally, the timely execution of court orders is not just a matter of efficiency; it is a cornerstone of a just and equitable society. Delays in enforcement undermine public confidence in the justice system, causing disillusionment and eroding faith in the rule of law. Conversely, swift and decisive enforcement fosters a sense of justice and strengthens the legitimacy of the judicial process. It demonstrates the capacity of the system to deliver on its promises and uphold the rights of individuals and society as a whole. The commitment to timely enforcement must extend beyond the judicial system itself, involving all stakeholders in the process.

This includes legislative action to address resource allocation, public awareness campaigns to highlight the importance of compliance with court orders, and robust mechanisms for addressing non-compliance. The effective execution of court orders is a shared responsibility, demanding collaboration and a collective commitment to upholding the rule of law. The timely execution of court orders is not merely a procedural matter; it is a fundamental pillar of a functioning democracy. It represents the tangible manifestation of justice and serves as a vital indicator of a society's commitment to fairness and equity.

The effectiveness of a judicial system is not solely measured by the quality of its judgments but also, and perhaps more significantly, by the prompt and faithful execution of those judgments. A meticulously crafted court order, however legally sound, remains a hollow promise without robust mechanisms for its enforcement and a system for rigorously monitoring and evaluating the success of those mechanisms.

This is where the critical function of monitoring and evaluation comes into play. It's not enough to simply issue orders; we must ensure those orders translate into tangible results. This requires a multifaceted approach, encompassing technological advancements, refined data analysis, and a renewed commitment to accountability at every level.

One of the most fundamental aspects of monitoring enforcement is the establishment of a comprehensive tracking system. This system should ideally be electronic, allowing for real-time monitoring of the progress of each court order. This technological solution offers several key advantages. Firstly, it provides a centralized repository of data, eliminating the potential for lost files or conflicting information. Secondly, it allows for the efficient identification of bottlenecks and delays.

A well-designed tracking system can pinpoint specific stages of the enforcement process where delays are most prevalent, providing crucial information for targeted improvements. Furthermore, such a system can flag potential issues, such as missing documentation or lack of communication between different agencies involved in the enforcement process, alerting relevant authorities to intervene proactively. The implementation of such a system requires careful planning and coordination among various stakeholders, including the judiciary, law enforcement agencies, and potentially even the legislative branch for the necessary legal frameworks and resource allocation.

The development of robust performance indicators is another crucial element of effective monitoring. These indicators should be carefully designed to accurately reflect the efficiency and effectiveness of the enforcement process. While simple metrics like the average time taken to execute a court order can be informative, a more nuanced approach is needed to capture the complexities of the enforcement process. For instance, indicators should account for the different types of court orders, as some, such as those involving complex financial transactions or international cooperation, are inherently more time-consuming than others.

Furthermore, indicators must differentiate between delays attributable to genuine logistical challenges and those resulting from negligence or deliberate obstruction. The creation of a comprehensive set of performance indicators requires careful consideration of the specific context and challenges within a given jurisdiction, ensuring that the indicators are both meaningful and measurable. Regular review and adjustment of these indicators are essential to reflect evolving realities and priorities. For example, new technology or legislative changes could affect the time needed for enforcement, therefore necessitating a modification of the performance indicators.

Data analysis plays a key role in interpreting the information gathered through tracking and performance indicators. A purely quantitative approach, however, is insufficient. Qualitative analysis, involving detailed case studies and interviews with stakeholders, provides critical context and insight into the underlying reasons for delays or failures in enforcement. For example, the analysis might reveal systemic issues, such as a lack of resources, inadequate training, or insufficient inter-agency coordination, that contribute to ineffective enforcement. It may also highlight instances of corruption or wilful obstruction of justice. The results of this comprehensive data analysis should inform the development of targeted interventions, addressing the specific challenges identified.

This could range from providing additional resources to enforcement agencies to implementing new training programs or revising legal frameworks to streamline the enforcement process.

Accountability is an indispensable aspect of any effective monitoring system. There needs to be a clear process for identifying and addressing instances of delay or failure in the execution of court orders. This requires establishing clear lines of responsibility, ensuring that individuals and agencies are held accountable for their actions or inaction. A robust system for investigating complaints and addressing grievances should be in place, providing avenues for recourse to those affected by delays or failures in enforcement. This accountability mechanism should encompass a range of sanctions, tailored to the severity of the infraction. These might include reprimands, fines, suspensions, or, in cases of serious misconduct, criminal prosecution. It is crucial that this accountability system is transparent and impartial, ensuring that all stakeholders are subject to the same standards of scrutiny.

Furthermore, public transparency regarding the enforcement of court orders should be promoted. Regularly publishing aggregate data on the performance of enforcement agencies can foster public trust and accountability. This data could include the average time taken to execute various types of orders, the percentage of orders executed successfully, and the number of complaints received concerning delays or failures in enforcement. Transparency also requires clear communication to the public regarding the reasons for any delays or failures', ensuring the public understands the challenges involved in the enforcement process and appreciates the efforts made to address them. By promoting open communication and sharing information, trust in the judicial system and its ability to deliver justice is strengthened.

The monitoring and evaluation process should not be a static endeavour; it requires continuous refinement and improvement.

Regular reviews of the system should be conducted to identify areas for enhancement, incorporate lessons learned, and adapt to evolving circumstances. This iterative process involves engaging with all relevant stakeholders, including judges, enforcement agencies, legal professionals, and members of the public, to ensure that the monitoring and evaluation mechanisms remain effective and responsive to the needs of the justice system. Feedback gathered through surveys, focus groups, and other methods can provide valuable insights into the effectiveness of the system and areas needing improvement.

Finally, the successful monitoring and evaluation of enforcement mechanisms is not merely a technical exercise but a fundamental component of a just and equitable society.

By ensuring that court orders are promptly and effectively executed, the judicial system demonstrates its capacity to deliver justice, fostering public trust and strengthening the rule of law. This, in turn, contributes to a more stable, secure, and just society for all. The commitment to robust monitoring and evaluation is a testament to the enduring commitment to the principles of justice and fairness. The timely execution of court orders, enabled and enhanced by careful monitoring and evaluation, is not simply a procedural matter; it is the very heartbeat of a functioning and credible legal system. It is the difference between a system that upholds its promises and one that fails to deliver on its core function: the administration of justice. Without constant vigilance and a commitment to improvement, even the most well-intentioned legal frameworks will ultimately fall short.

Case Study

This Case Study centres on a courageous lawyer who, driven by a sense of justice and spurred by firsthand observation of unethical practices, initiates a campaign to expose corruption within the OAP. Ironically, this virtuous act quickly leads to disciplinary action for allegedly violating professional secrecy, a charge that throws the lawyer into a precarious legal battle.

The ensuing events reveal a startling web of deceit, collusion, and intimidation. The pressure exerted on the lawyer to participate in a dubious deal, designed to suppress a high-profile case against a powerful lawyer connected to the former District Bar's president, exposes the extent of the rot within the organization. The legal manoeuvrings, the clandestine meetings, the court proceedings—all lay bare—reveal a system seemingly impervious to accountability.

This intricate legal struggle is further complicated by the lawyer's past, bringing to light a history of questionable actions dating back to the Estado Novo dictatorship, further revealing a system where abuse of power and impunity are deeply ingrained.

The culminating act of violence against the lawyer—a brutal aggression orchestrated by the very former president he sought to expose— underscores the perilous lengths to which those in power will go to protect their interests.

This gripping narrative is not simply a recounting of events; it is a critical examination of the Portuguese legal system and professional national Association Ordem dos Advogados Portugal, exploring the historical context of such abuses, the deep-rooted societal factors that contribute to them, and the vital need for significant and lasting reform. This case study intends to dissect the legal, political, and social ramifications of this case, providing insightful analyses of professional ethics, the dynamics of power within legal institutions, and the enduring legacy of authoritarianism in shaping the contemporary Portuguese landscape.

The ultimate aim is to spark a crucial conversation about justice, accountability, and the crucial role of a robust and transparent legal system in a democratic society.

It started by an agreement between a person representative of Transparency International that was and the Minister of Finances and the Public General Attorney establishing a day every year to make a general appeal to public with the slogan" Say No to Corruption – Denounce".

The Portuguese Bar Association following the news of this initiative wrote to the Lawyer responsible for the national agreement with Minister of Finances and the Public General Attorney notified him with the following letter: "Say No to Corruption Hotline/ Portuguese Culture Federation - Taking into account considering the news published in the newspaper "Publico" on 24/4/97 and information complementary information received by this District Council, notably the content of the statement disclosed to the media on 4/23/97, it is decided to immediately institute of an inquiry process, within the scope of which Mr. ... must be notified from now on, to express their views on their participation in the event mentioned service, since the facts indicate that the rules of art. 76 n° 1, 78, f9 and g), 80 and 81 of the E.O.A. (DI. 84/84 of 16/ 3) respecting professional secrecy violation. The notification to be forwarded to the Lawyers in cause must contain a copy of the deliberation, transcribed, giving them a period of 5 (five) days to state. Notification to be sent by registered mail.

He presented its written defence alleging that he was acting not as a lawyer but as President of an Institution devoted to prevent corruption.

The investigation into the Ordem dos Advogados Portugueses (OAP) unearthed far more than just isolated incidents of corruption; it exposed a deeply entrenched culture of impunity, stretching back decades and intertwined with the legacy of Portugal's authoritarian and corporative past.

Disciplinary decision – case 1/22/97 – Decision: Due to the importance and complexity of the situation, particularly with regard to the intention to institutionalize the anonymous complaint, disciplinary proceedings were ordered against the lawyer. It seems clear to us that the lawyer's conduct is reprehensible from a disciplinary standpoint, as his behaviour does not properly honour the profession. Despite having served as president of a civil institution, he forwarded a complaint to the Attorney General of the Republic. Now, the denunciation made is not compatible with the duty to fight for the defence of Justice and Law. He is subject to the professional secrecy that he violated and therefore the sanction of censure applies.

Member of the Superior Council of OAP Professor Germano Marques da Silva voted against as he understands that the lawyer acted in an annual initiative and outside his profession as a lawyer.

After some time another the defendant was approached by a member of the Supreme Council of Justice saying that the President of the BAR delegated on him to clear out the sanction, archiving the disciplinary case if he agreed to sign a document to give up some cases of a client against its protégée a lawyer that was also a owner of night clubs and condemned by aggression – He said that this lawyer was its protégée had should be cleared out of court by debts to a client of him. He said that if the condemn layer would sign a document compromising to give up the debt case the President of the BAR would just clear out the sanction.

So that happened. That member of the Supreme Council of Justice in the name of the President of the National BAR of Portugal signed a document with this agreement.

The lawyer was suspicious of the legal validity of this action and after signing put a court case about the validity of this agreement.

The **Administrative Court – 1º Juizo Liquidatario in case 349/ 01** decided as follows: "that the member of Supreme Council of Justice also a lawyer, could never sign in the name of the President of the BAR of Portugal such a document and that the content of the document was illegal because could not make a deal that would be against the BAR bylaws. He just dismissed from the Supreme Council of Justice.

More, the decision says that "It turns out that the "conciliation term" whose declaration of nullity comes claimed in the proceedings, in view of the terms in which it was concluded, nor does it aim to achievement of any public interest, nor is it part of the person's duties collective Order of Lawyers, as the Author himself claims. In fact, the Portuguese Bar Association is a public association whose statute was approved by DL No. 84/84, of 16.03, using legislative authorization granted by Law No. 1/84, of 15.02, which was subject to successive amendments, last of which, considering the date of the celebration of the so-called "term of conciliation" in question in the proceedings, operated by Law No. 33/94, of 6.09.

The duties of the Bar Association must be continued through their own bodies, in the exercise of their respective powers statutorily provided for, the question immediately arises as to whether it is possible consider that in the "conciliation term" in question in the proceedings, the following party appears as Portuguese Bar Association, since it does not result from the terms in which it was celebrated that the respective intervening holders of bodies of the BAR act in the exercise of their powers statutorily provided for pursuit of the Order's duties. Indeed, despite the "conciliation term" in question being act in exercise of his powers statutorily provided for pursuit of the Order's duties.

Indeed, despite the "conciliation term" in question being granted in the presence of the President of the Porto Sectional Council of the Ordem dos Advogados, and another distinguished lawyer "intervening on behalf of the delegation of His Excellency President of the Portuguese Bar Association", is not visible under which the statistical powers made such intervention take place, provided that it is the advice district, constituted under the terms of art. 46° (today, to the ethics councils, operating within the jurisdiction of each district council - cf. art. 48° -C, al.a) of the EOA, as amended by Law No. 80/2001, of 20.07), and not to the president of the district council or any other body, which is responsible for striving to compose granted in the presence of the President of the Porto Council of the Order of Lawyers, and another distinguished lawyer "intervening by delegation of the His Excellency President of the Portuguese Bar Association", is not visible under what statutory powers did such intervention take place, since it is the council district, constituted under the terms of art. 46° (today, to the ethics councils, that operate within the jurisdiction of each district council - cfr. art. 48° -C, al. a) of the EOA, as amended by Law No. 80/ 2001, of 20.07), and not to the president of the district council or any other body, which is responsible for striving to compose. In any case, it is true that the so-called "conciliation term" in the cause in the proceedings has the sole objective of obtaining the extinction of certain legal and criminal actions instituted against two of the illustrious lawyers signing the said agreement, identified in the two lists attached to the event, to which the Bar Association is completely unrelated, and in which patrimonial interests protected by civil law are necessarily at stake or, in the case of criminal proceedings.

The next day The President of The BAR Association came to newspaper Independente declare that he did not knew at all what was going on.

After sometime he found the lawyer seated in a coffee and pushed him to the street and beat him. Was judged by aggression and condemned in **Porto Criminal Court - case 5681/06.9TDPRT** in the following terms: ... in view of the proven facts, it is unequivocal that the defendant constituted as the material author of a crime of simple offenses against physical integrity. In fact there is a worthless result, translated into the injury suffered by the offended, this result is attributable, by an inexorable causal link, to a specific "facere" by part of the defendant lawyer Mr...., having caused injury to the physical integrity of the offender who suffered pain and trauma to both ears, which caused him to be out for 5 days illness, without affecting the ability to work.

In addition to the objective elements mentioned, it is necessary to mention, at the same time, a specific intentionality in the action of the defendant, translated into the representation of conscious will and free from causing harm to the physical integrity or health of the assistant, thus equally filling the subjective element of the type.

In fact, the defendant Lawyer Mr..... acted with intent that, freely, deliberately and consciously, as well knows that his conduct was prohibited and punishable by law wanting to reach the person of offended Lawyer Mr ..., in his physical integrity as a result of his conduct in a direct manner.

In view of the factual matter given as proven, there can be no doubt that the conduct of the Defendant Lawyer Mr ... fulfilled the type of offense of simple offense to physical integrity, on the other hand, given the explicit intention of publicly harassing the assistant by attacking an adult, we believe that this does not comply with the requirement to remove censorship ethical-social and legal-criminal.

Furthermore, regardless of whether pain or after-effect is not an element required by the type, this result of the conduct cannot be ignored in this analysis plan, due to the additional distance in relation to the duty to be collectively required that it adds to the conduct.

In fact, and since pain is a complex phenomenon and can have multiple origins, it is certain that its origin in the case in question is clearly associated with the bio physiological reaction caused by an aggression, which is at the same time harmful to physical integrity - since the tissues in the area where the force was exerted were mechanically affected - and to health - since it triggered a penalizing bio psychological reaction in the organism, i.e. a functional alteration of the organism and also of the psychological well-being of the victim.

The lawyer victim of the aggression complained to the BAR and after examining the complaint the BAR Superior Council decided that the aggressor lawyer just did the aggression in its private life and was nothing to do with its lawyer profession.

Consequently I decide to convict the Defendant Lawyer Mr ... , for the material authorship of the crime of bodily harm, p. ep. by art. 143°, n01 of the Penal Code, with a penalty of 120 (one hundred and twenty) days-fine, at a daily rate of €15 (fifteen) euros, by application of n°4, of art. 2 of the Penal Code, which amounts to a total value of 1,8000 (one thousand and eight hundred Euros).

About the personal profile of the lawyer attacker: He was along the dictatorial period in Portugal, a Political Prosecutor against defendants that were against the dictatorial regime. After the coup d'état that restored the democracy in 25 April 1975 was dismissed by the government from Prosecutor alleging its low morality. He pleaded against that decision and got rehabilitation and was nominated Judge. After some years he left this profession to become lawyer. Got President of the BAR in Portugal and together with its layer profession got a job teaching in courses to prepare to public examination to magistrates in a University and at the same time he was part of jury in those public examinations. Finally he got a society of lawyers witch main client was a football club witch president he was a defendant lawyer in court in corruption cases.

Bibliography

Abel, R.L., 1988. The Politics of Informal Justice. New York: Academic Press

Acker, J., 2006. Class Questions: Feminist Answers. Lanham, MD: Rowman & Littlefield.

Alexander, M., 2010. *The New Jim Crow: Mass Incarceration in the Age of Colorblindness*. New York: The New Press.

Alford, C.F., 2001. *Whistleblowers: Broken Lives and Organizational Power*. Ithaca, NY: Cornell University Press

Alston, P. and Goodman, R., 2013. *International Human Rights*. 3rd ed. Oxford: Oxford University Press.

Burbank, S.B. and Friedman, B., 2002. Judicial Independence at the Crossroads: An Interdisciplinary Approach. Thousand Oaks, CA: SAGE Publications

Buscaglia, E. and Dakolias, M., 1999. Comparative International Study of Court Performance Indicators. Washington, DC: World Bank Technical Paper No. 430

Carothers, T., 2006. *Promoting the Rule of Law Abroad: In Search of Knowledge*. Washington, DC: Carnegie Endowment for International Peace.

Coates, T.-N., 2015. Between the World and Me. New York: Spiegel & Grau.

Craig, P., 2012. Administrative Law. 7th ed. London: Sweet & Maxwell.

Daniels, N., 2008. Just Health: Meeting Health Needs Fairly. Cambridge: Cambridge University Press.

Davis, A.Y., 2003. Are Prisons Obsolete? New York: Seven Stories Press

Donnelly, J., 2013. *Universal Human Rights in Theory and Practice*. 3rd ed. Ithaca, NY: Cornell University Press.

Dobbin, F. and Kalev, A., 2022. Getting to Diversity: What Works and What Doesn't. Cambridge, MA: Harvard University Press.

Dorling, D., 2015. Injustice: Why Social Inequality Still Persists. Bristol: Policy Press.

Farmer, P., 2005. Pathologies of Power: Health, Human Rights, and the New War on the Poor. Berkeley: University of California Press

Fraser, N., 2009. Scales of Justice: Reimagining Political Space in a Globalizing World. New York: Columbia University Press

Fraser, N., 1997. Justice Interruptus: Critical Reflections on the "Postsocialist" Condition. New York: Routledge

Freire, P., 1970. Pedagogy of the Oppressed. New York: Herder and Herder

Ganz, M., 2010. Why David Sometimes Wins: Leadership, Organization, and Strategy in the California Farm Worker Movement. Oxford: Oxford University Press.

Gloppen, S., 2004. How to Assess the Political Role of the Judiciary: The Case of South Africa. Critique of Anthropology, 24(2)

Geyh, C.G., 2016. Courting Peril: The Political Transformation of the American Judiciary. Oxford: Oxford University Press

Hacker, J.S. and Pierson, P., 2010. *Winner-Take-All Politics: How Washington Made the Rich Richer—and Turned Its Back on the Middle Class. New York: Simon & Schuster

Hammergren, L., 2002. Do Judicial Councils Further Judicial Reform? The Experience of Latin America. Carnegie Endowment Working Papers, No. 28

Honneth, A., 2007. Disrespect: The Normative Foundations of Critical Theory. Cambridge: Polity Press.

Hooks, b., 2000. Where We Stand: Class Matters. New York: Routledge

Hooks, b., 1994. *Teaching to Transgress: Education as the Practice of Freedom*. New York: Routledge

Kang, J. et al., 2012. Implicit Bias in the Courtroom. UCLA Law Review, 59(5)

Johnston, M., 2014. Corruption, Contention and Reform: The Power of Deep Democratization. Cambridge: Cambridge University Press.

Nussbaum, M.C., 2010. Not for Profit: Why Democracy Needs the Humanities. Princeton, NJ: Princeton University Press

MacCormick, N., 2005. Rhetoric and the Rule of Law: A Theory of Legal Reasoning. Oxford: Oxford University Press.

Miceli, M.P., Near, J.P. and Dworkin, T.M., 2008. Whistle-Blowing in Organizations. New York: Routledge.

Mills, C.W., 1997. The Racial Contract. Ithaca, NY: Cornell University Press

Moyn, S., 2010. The Last Utopia: Human Rights in History. Cambridge, MA: Harvard University Press.

Okin, S.M., 1989. Justice, Gender, and the Family. New York: Basic Books.

Piketty, T., 2014. Capital in the Twenty-First Century. Cambridge, MA: Harvard University Press

Piven, F.F. and Cloward, R.A., 1979. Poor People's Movements: Why They Succeed, How They Fail. New York: Vintage

Pogge, T., 2002. World Poverty and Human Rights. Cambridge: Polity Press

Rhode, D.L., 2004. Access to Justice. New York: Oxford University Press.

Rose-Ackerman, S. and Palifka, B.J., 2016. Corruption and Government: Causes, Consequences, and Reform. 2nd ed. Cambridge: Cambridge University Press.

Rawls, J., 1971. A Theory of Justice. Cambridge, MA: Harvard University Press.

Russell, P.H. and O'Brien, D.M., 2001. Judicial Independence in the Age of Democracy: Critical Perspectives from Around the World. Charlottesville: University of Virginia Press.

Sandefur, R.L., 2008. Access to Civil Justice and Race, Class, and Gender Inequality. *Annual Review of Sociology*, 34, pp.339–358.

Sandel, M.J., 2009. Justice: What's the Right Thing to Do? New York: Farrar, Straus and Giroux.

Sen, A., 2009. The Idea of Justice. Cambridge, MA: Harvard University Press

Shetreet, S. and Turenne, S., 2013. Judges on Trial: The Independence and Accountability of the English Judiciary*. 2nd ed. Cambridge: Cambridge University Press

Shiva, V., 2005. Earth Democracy: Justice, Sustainability, and Peace. Cambridge, MA: South End Press.

Stiglitz, J.E., 2012. The Price of Inequality. New York: W.W. Norton & Company

Young, I.M., 1990. *Justice and the Politics of Difference*. Princeton, NJ: Princeton University Press.

Tate, C.N. and Vallinder, T., 1995. *The Global Expansion of Judicial Power*. New York: New York University Press

Tilly, C., 2004. *Social Movements, 1768–2004*. Boulder, CO: Paradigm Publishers

Uelmen, G.F., 1993. *Judicial Misconduct: A Cross-National Comparison*. In: S. Shetreet, ed. *The Role of the Judiciary in the Protection of Human Rights*. Dordrecht: Martinus Nijhoff, pp.365–380

West, C., 1993. Race Matters. Boston, MA: Beacon Press

Williams, J.C., 2021. Bias Interrupted: Creating Inclusion for Real and for Good. Boston, MA: Harvard Business Review Press.

Wilkinson, R. and Pickett, K., 2009. The Spirit Level: Why More Equal Societies Almost Always Do Better. London: Allen Lane.

About the Author

Trained lawyer, President of an Educational Foundation, Representative of Brazilian institutions in Europe involved in military affairs (ADESG) or commercial and industrial affairs - (the Federation of South American Chambers of Commerce and Industry).

Researcher in geopolitics and national defense.

Currently involved in various professional activities in various areas such as international partnerships with development and cooperation in common.

Author of books, essays and articles on my current activity and past professional experience.

Professionally, I give university lectures, conferences and skills assessments.

* Skills and expertise: Strategic studies and advice, leadership of organizations and management of organizations, international business ventures and contacts, investigation into crimes linked to National Defence and president of various non-profit institutions.

* Past experience focused on fundraising, National Defense institutions, social and economic development in new democracies and E-Learning methods for African countries.

Read more at https://observare.autonoma.pt/investigador/artur-victoria/.

www.ingramcontent.com/pod-product-compliance
Lightning Source LLC
LaVergne TN
LVHW090309210926
848480LV00001B/182
* 9 7 9 8 2 3 1 6 5 0 2 5 5 *